# Phonology

# Cognitive Linguistics in Practice (CLiP)

A text book series which aims at introducing students of language and linguistics, and scholars from neighboring disciplines, to established and new fields in language research from a cognitive perspective. The books in the series are written in an attractive, reader-friendly and self-explanatory style. They include assignments and have been tested for classroom use at university level.

## Executive Editor

Günter Radden
University of Hamburg

## Editorial Board

René Dirven
University of Duisburg-Essen

Suzanne Kemmer
Rice University

Kee Dong Lee
Yonsei University

Klaus-Uwe Panther
University of Hamburg

Johanna Rubba
California Polytechnic State University

Ted J.M. Sanders
University of Utrecht

Soteria Svorou
San Jose State University

Elżbieta Tabakowska
Cracow University

Marjolijn H. Verspoor
University of Groningen

## Volume 3

Phonology. A cognitive grammar introduction
by Geoffrey S. Nathan

# Phonology

A cognitive grammar introduction

Geoffrey S. Nathan
Wayne State University

John Benjamins Publishing Company
Amsterdam / Philadelphia

 TM  The paper used in this publication meets the minimum requirements of the American National Standard for Information Sciences — Permanence of Paper for Printed Library Materials, ANSI Z39.48-1984.

**Library of Congress Cataloging-in-Publication Data**

Nathan, Geoffrey S.
    Phonology : a cognitive grammar introduction / by Geoffrey S. Nathan.
    p.   cm. -- (Cognitive Linguistics in Practice, ISSN 1388-6231 ; v. 3)
    Includes bibliographical references and index.
    1. Grammar, Comparative and general--Phonology. 2. Cognitive grammar. I. Title.
P217.N38      2008
414--dc22                                                                                                      2008030015
ISBN 978 90 272 1907 7 (Hb; alk. paper)
ISBN 978 90 272 1908 4 (Pb; alk. paper)
ISBN 978 90 272 9088 5 (Eb)

© 2008 – John Benjamins B.V.
No part of this book may be reproduced in any form, by print, photoprint, microfilm, or any other means, without written permission from the publisher.

John Benjamins Publishing Company • P.O. Box 36224 • 1020 ME Amsterdam • The Netherlands
John Benjamins North America • P.O. Box 27519 • Philadelphia PA 19118-0519 • USA

# Table of contents

**Preface** ................................................................................................... IX

CHAPTER 1
**Introduction to phonology** ........................................................... 1
1.1   Preamble   1
1.2   A short history of phonology   2
1.3   The basic building blocks of phonology   6

CHAPTER 2
**A brief overview of phonetics** .................................................... 11
2.1   Basic classes   11
2.2   Manner of articulation   14
2.3   Points of articulation   14
2.4   Laryngeal and other features   17
2.5   Vowels   18
2.6   Suprasegmentals   21
2.7   Exercises   25

CHAPTER 3
**Phonemes: The fundamental category** .................................... 27
3.1   Phonemes, allophones and other basic bits   28
3.2   How to find phonemes   30
3.3   Phoneme inventories   33
3.4   Phoneme discovery exercises   40

CHAPTER 4
**Syllables, feet, words: Phonological constructions** ............... 43
4.1   Groups of sounds   43
4.2   The internal structure of the syllable   47
4.3   The sonority hierarchy   47
4.4   Between syllables   53
4.5   Feet   54
4.6   The word as a unit   56
4.7   Exercises   58

CHAPTER 5
**Processes – The forces shaping phonology**    59
5.1   Introduction to processes and features   59
5.2   Major class features   60
       5.2.1   Sonorant   60
       5.2.2   Consonantal   61
             5.2.2.1   Approximant   61
5.3   Manner features   61
       5.3.1   Continuant   62
       5.3.2   Nasal   62
       5.3.3   Strident   62
       5.3.4   Lateral   62
5.4   Point of articulation features   63
       5.4.1   Labial   63
       5.4.2   Coronal   63
             5.4.2.1   Distributed   63
             5.4.2.2   Anterior   63
             5.4.2.3   Strident   64
       5.4.3   Dorsal   64
       5.4.4   Guttural   64
5.5   Basic vowel features   64
5.6   Translation equivalents   67
       5.6.1   Laryngeal features   67
             5.6.1.1   Spread glottis   67
             5.6.1.2   Constricted glottis   67
5.7   Stress patterns   68
5.8   Processes   72
       5.8.1   Fortitions: The selection of basic sounds   75
       5.8.2   Lenitions: The implementation of speech   77
             5.8.2.1   Assimilations   77
             5.8.2.2   Nasal assimilation   77
             5.8.2.3   Voicing assimilation   78
             5.8.2.4   Nasalization   78
             5.8.2.5   Palatalization and other assimilations   79
       5.8.3   Deletions   80
       5.8.4   Insertion   81
5.9   Writing 'Rules'   83
5.10   Exercises   85

## CHAPTER 6
## Alternations 87
6.1  Introduction  87
6.2  An extended example  88
6.3  Exercises on alternations  93
    6.3.1  English past tense  93

## CHAPTER 7
## Fluent speech 95
7.1  Introduction  95
7.2  English  96
7.3  German casual speech processes  100
7.4  French reductions  100
7.5  Exercises  101

## CHAPTER 8
## Historical phonology – Processes frozen in time 103
8.1  Introduction  103
8.2  Simple phonetic changes  105
8.3  Phonologization  106
    8.3.1  Merger  106
    8.3.2  Split  107
    8.3.3  Alternations  108
    8.3.4  Chain shifts  110
8.4  Exercises  113
    8.4.1  Phonetic changes  113
    8.4.2  Phonetic changes  114

## CHAPTER 9
## First and second language acquisition 117
9.1  First language acquisition  117
    9.1.1  Introduction  117
    9.1.2  What are the basic facts?  118
9.2  Second language acquisition  119
    9.2.1  Introductory comments  119
    9.2.2  Conflicting categories  119
9.3  Exercises  122
    9.3.1  First language phonology  122
    9.3.2  Socond language phonology  123

CHAPTER 10

## Theoretical apparatus and formalisms    125

10.1  Introduction to theoretical issues    125
10.2  European structuralism and the Prague School    125
10.3  American structuralism    127
    10.3.1  The Trager-Smith analysis of English    128
10.4  Generative phonology    130
    10.4.1  Classic generative phonology    130
    10.4.2  The abstractness question    133
    10.4.3  Rule ordering    137
    10.4.4  Autosegmental phonology – innovations in representation    139
    10.4.5  Optimality theory    144
10.5  Usage-based and Exemplar Theories    152
10.6  Some concluding thoughts on OT and cognitive phonology    154

## Glossary    157

## References    161

## Index of languages    165

## Index of names    167

## Index of subjects    169

# Preface

This book is an introduction to most aspects of contemporary twenty-first century phonology, but makes the assumption that much of what is valid in the first decade of that century is not brand new, but rather is built on a foundation that is, depending on how you look at it, either almost two hundred years old or perhaps two thousand five hundred years.

I have attempted to introduce students to all the major notions of phonology – phonemes, allophones, processes, alternations, underlying forms, rule ordering and its contemporary competitor, and 'hyphenated' aspects of phonology – historical change, and first and second language acquisition.

Each time a new theoretical paradigm is introduced enthusiasts tend to reject everything that has come before, and this is certainly true in the history of phonology, from the rejection of historical phonology by early structuralists to the questioning of the traditional phoneme by some contemporary Cognitive linguists. As an introductory level textbook I feel it is my obligation to explain (actually 'teach') those concepts that have stood the test of time, as necessary providing what I believe to be a Cognitive Grammar explanation of what might cause language to act in a particular way. I think it is unlikely that linguists will ultimately reject the idea (which was actually 'discovered' by the Phoenicians roughly three thousand years ago) that speech is made up, in some mental sense, of a string of recurring segments, roughly twenty to fifty or so in number. It is also unlikely that Pāṇini's 4th century BCE concept of base forms with some kind of processual operations is completely off-base, despite recent attempts in several different frameworks to eliminate derivations. Comparable arguments can be made for concepts such as the syllable (on which many orthographies, both ancient and modern are based) and the foot (the basis for many systems of poetic meter).

In addition to the fact that these concepts have a long and honorable tradition there is the fact that a practicing linguist needs to be familiar with the basic concepts and know what the current questions are. This book will familiarize students with those basic concepts and introduce some, but by no means all the current controversies. It will teach students how to solve 'phoneme problems', which my first linguistics teacher, H.A. Gleason, Jr. used to say was the crucial linchpin of understanding how to 'do' linguistics. He felt that until students understood the basic methodology of complementary distribution, they didn't understand anything else in linguistics, at any linguistic level.

On the other hand, the book will not provide a thorough guide on how to use any particular current theoretical tool – complex optimality analyses or how to study minute frequency distributions that researchers such as Bybee and Kemmer argue are crucial to understanding historical change, or even storage issues. Along with the descriptive sections, the study questions are the most important part of each chapter, since they allow the user to test her understanding of the chapter and to apply the notions presented in it. The solutions to the study questions can be downloaded from the Benjamins website www.benjamins.com/.

This book would not have been possible without the assistance and valuable input of many friends, colleagues and students. At a minimum these include Jose Mompeán-González, Pilar Mompeán Guillamón, Anna Slon, John Taylor, Günter Radden, Eddie Capps, and numerous phonology classes at Southern Illinois University at Carbondale and Wayne State University. Evelyn Richter was enormously helpful in preparing the index. Margaret Winters made it possible in the first place by nursing the concept (and occasionally me) through many years of travail.

# Chapter 1

# Introduction to phonology

1.1 Preamble
1.2 A short history of phonology
1.3 The basic building blocks of phonology

## 1.1 Preamble

Phonology is the study of the organization and structure of the sounds of language. Like most areas of grammar, it deals both with universal and language-specific principles. All spoken human languages make all (or virtually all) their words with combinations of consonants and vowels, and all (or virtually all) languages group those sounds into units called syllables, and generally, group the syllables into larger groups called feet. These constitute universal aspects of phonology, although the reader will notice hedges even within these statements.

On the other hand, different languages make use of different sounds, and different languages choose the structure of their syllables differently. Some allow very complex syllables (the English word *strengths* is one of the most complex syllables in the world), while others, such as Hawaiʻian, only permit syllables consisting of a single consonant followed by a single vowel.

Similarly, some languages use enormous numbers of different sounds (some have as many as seventy) while other languages get by with tiny numbers (one language has only 13). There are enormous numbers of possible combinations of sounds, but in fact, languages tend to use a small common set over and over, and rare sounds are rare because only a few languages use them.

Students often are confused about the relationship between **phonetics** and **phonology**. **Phonetics** deals with all the possible human speech sounds – it is an inventory of possibilities, as defined by the human vocal apparatus, or the human perceptual system. Phonetics deals with what kinds of sounds humans *can* make. **Phonology**, on the other hand, deals with what *languages* do with those sounds – how they select certain sounds, how those sounds are fitted into their environments, and how they are constructed into larger and larger units, such as syllables, feet, words and so on.

We can make an analogy here with architecture and the study of building materials. Architects design buildings, using materials that they choose, but the nature of the materials determines what kind of use they can be put to. For example, glass is a good material for windows, since it is transparent, but it would make a poor material for a floor, since it is easily breakable. On the other hand, sand would make a very poor material for a wall, since it doesn't cohere, and doesn't support much weight. Phonetics is like the study of the nature of the materials used in building, while phonology is the study of the way in which those materials are actually used to construct buildings. Obviously, an architect must understand the structural properties of building materials (which ones can support weight, which ones resist the weather) in order to determine which materials would make good roofs or walls or floors or interior wall coverings. But there is more to architecture than simply listing the materials: there is also the question of design, and of certain minimum requirements (walls and a roof, for example). In much the same way, phonetics and phonology interact, with phonetics being the study of the raw materials used to create language, and phonology being the design principles that languages use to take those raw materials and build words out of them.

## 1.2  A short history of phonology

The synchronic study of phonological theory within a modern framework is probably the oldest part of modern linguistic theory. The study of syntax is of course, as old as the study of grammar itself, but it was only with the advent of a modern, scientific understanding of phonetics that linguists began to be aware of the problems and questions raised by the study of the behavior of sounds.[1] During the nineteenth century phoneticians such as Henry Sweet,[2] Paul Passy, Whitney, Sievers and others discovered what we now consider to be the keys to phonetic description – sounds can be completely described with the parameters of voicing, point, and manner of articulation (for consonants) and the tongue

---

1. I should mention here, although the name will reappear later as well, that there is one significant tradition of serious phonology that is much older than the one we will be studying in this book. That is the work of the Indian linguist Pāṇini, who composed a grammar of Sanskrit, an Indic language spoken around 1000 BCE. His great book *Aṣṭadhyāyī* contains a complete phonology of the Sanskrit language, and, with some training, can be read and used today. His intentions were not purely scientific, however, but rather he (and presumably the people with whom he worked, and who interpreted his grammar after him) wanted to preserve the accurate pronunciation of Sanskrit, which contained the sacred literature of the Hindu religion, since it was believed that prayers could only be efficacious if pronounced properly.

2. Sweet was a friend of George Bernard Shaw's, and Shaw may have modeled his Henry Higgins, the protagonist of *Pygmalion* (and *My Fair Lady*) on him. Many modern phoneticians and phonologists can claim direct (academic) descent from Henry Sweet, making us his great-great-grandchildren.

positions and lip setting needed for vowels. It was in the late 1800's that the International Phonetic Association was founded, and these scientists began cataloging not only the major European languages (French, German, English) but also looked at the lesser known ones, and began also listening in great detail not only to careful pronunciations of standard languages but also to the normal speaking rate of the dialects they found around them. As they did this, they discovered that things are not always as they seem.

The first person to discuss this fact explicitly was a Polish linguist named Jan Baudouin de Courtenay. What he was trying to explain was the fact that there is a difference between what the articulators are actually doing when we utter some word or phrase and what speakers perceive they are doing (and what hearers believe they hear). In other words, the highly trained phoneticians of the day could see, hear and feel details in their own speech, and that of others, that untrained native speakers of the language seemed to disregard. What was crucial for our story is that different languages seemed to disregard different details, so that this appeared to be a language-specific fact.

The other fact that was noticed was that units of a language appeared to change in form under different circumstances of use. This could vary from fairly unconscious changes (such as the fact that [s] often changes to [ʃ][3] when we say *Bless you*) to much more obvious ones such as the change in German from [aʊ] to [ɔɪ] when we make German *Haus* 'house' plural: *Häuser* 'houses', or the change from [ʊ] to [i] when we say the plural of *foot*.

Baudouin's idea was that we *perceive* and *store* sounds in one form, but adjust that form when we actually speak according to a set of phonetically-defined principles that he called 'divergences'. He also argued that when we hear others speak, we subconsciously 'undo' those divergences, hearing, in some sense, what the speaker intended to say – that is, what the speaker stored as well. Baudouin called the individual sound *intentions* '**phonemes**'.[4]

Baudouin's work was published in 1895, and that, in some ways, can be considered the beginning of modern phonology. Over the first half of the Twentieth Century linguists in a number of European and American centers developed the concept of the phoneme in various different directions, some of which were more compatible with the assumptions of Cognitive Grammar than others. Since a great deal of valuable phonological research has been published in all of these frameworks, it is necessary to understand the concepts and constructs proposed by all the major theories in order to be able to read work on languages you might be interested in. Consequently, I will be presenting some ideas that I don't believe are compatible with Cognitive Grammar, but have become so widely understood and recognized that anyone 'doing' phonology should be able to understand them. The basic

---

3   Phonetic symbols are explained in Chapter 2, so if you are not yet familiar with them you can return here after you have read that chapter, or guess from the context what they represent.

4.  Actually the word was first used in this sense by one of Baudouin's students, Mikołaj Kruszewski, but Baudouin's explanation of the idea is the most easily accessible explanation of this new concept.

concepts underlying how Cognitive Grammarians view the world, incidentally, will be discussed later in this chapter.

The first major innovation in phonological theory that has had a lasting impact is the notion that the variations in 'intended' sounds could be grouped into a set, with the phoneme itself functioning as the name of the set. Each individual variant was called an allophone (from the Greek αλλος 'other', plus φωνη 'voice'). Thus phonemes were sets of related sounds all classed as a single set. There was considerable discussion about the status of these sets. The American linguist Edward Sapir believed, with Baudouin, that these sets were modes of perception – that is, that speakers heard all the members of the set as if they were the same. He argued that we hear speech *phonemically*, and in a famous paper (Sapir 1933 [1972]) gave anecdotal examples of the action of this special kind of perception. For example, his Southern Paiute consultant, whom he had taught to transcribe, insisted on writing voiced consonants as voiceless because, although both the alphabet he was working with, and English have separate symbols, they are allophonic in Southern Paiute and his consultant couldn't perceive the contrast.

Other linguists working in this same period were more reluctant to ascribe mental activity to the facts that they were uncovering about language. A group of linguists centered in Prague (and consequently known as the Prague School) argued that psychological explanations were not the job of the linguist, who had to develop purely linguistic explanations, leaving the psychological interpretations to others. Classic references include Trubetzkoy (1968) and Jakobson (1968). Their ideas of the phoneme were based very heavily on the work of the great nineteenth century Swiss linguist Ferdinand de Saussure, the founder of the school of inquiry called Structuralism. Saussure believed that language was a self-contained system, where everything held together ('où tout se tient'), and argued that each distinctive unit in a language could only be defined in terms of its role in that language. Thus, every unit in language was only meaningful when contrasted with other units within the same system. To take an extreme example from an entirely different domain, consider the system of shoe sizes and jacket sizes. North American shoe sizes range from 2 to 15, while jacket sizes for men range from about 36 to about 50. Within each system we can compare, saying, for example, that a size 5 shoe is much smaller than a size 12. Similarly for a size 40 jacket and a size 50. But it is meaningless to compare a size 36 jacket to a size 9 shoe – the systems are not comparable. Saussure, and later the Prague school believed that it was as meaningless to compare the phoneme /p/ in French with the phoneme /p/ in English as it was to compare a size 15 shoe with a size 15 jacket (even if there were such a thing).[5]

The result of this 'autonomous' view was that the phoneme was removed from any connection to the speaker or hearer, becoming a unit with a life of its own without any necessity that it reflect the knowledge that the speaker or hearer had. Since phonemes

---

5. I am grateful to the late H.A. Gleason Jr. for this analogy, which really underscores the radical system-internal view that early structuralists had.

could only be defined relative to each other, if there were cases where only one sound is possible the result is something which is not a true phoneme. For example, in front of /t/ in English, the only nasal consonant possible is /n/, not either /ŋ/ or /m/ – there are no words like */kɪmt/ or */pæŋt/. Thus, in some sense we can't tell whether this sound is an /n/, an /m/ or an /ŋ/, only that it is a nasal. So the Prague school linguists proposed the idea of an *archiphoneme*, a sound that doesn't have all of its specifications. Since each feature in a sound only exists in opposition or contrast to each other feature, when there is no contrast possible, we can't 'tell' which one is there, and we must conclude that all that exists in such a situation is 'some kind of nasal'. However, native speakers can normally indeed identify which sound is occurring in a word, and if you are a native speaker of English (or German or Dutch, which have the same set of facts) you certainly don't find it strange that the word *hunt* or *paint* is spelled with the same letter used for both consonants in *nun*.[6]

A similar flight from concern about perception, production and storage of sounds occurred in North America during the 1940's and 50's. Even though Edward Sapir was an influential North American linguist, most North American linguists came under the influence of the predominant psychological school at the time, Behaviorism. Unlike the European Structuralists, American structural linguists did not reject psychological explanations, but rather they rejected the terms that Sapir and Baudouin had used, since they implied a level of cognitive processing that behaviorists had denied exists. Behaviorists were skeptical of the existence of notions like mind or thought, and viewed perception simply as the registering of a stimulus by an organism. Categorization consisted simply of a reinforced association between independent stimuli. In the case of phonemes and allophones this amounted to the view that humans were conditioned to respond identically to different allophones, and that was what made them members of the same phoneme. Because of this rejection of any kind of abstraction, they were also forced to reject the archiphoneme and similar constructs proposed by the European structuralists. The classic American Structuralist work is Bloomfield (1933), and arguments on many of these issues can be found in Joos (1966). The best-known textbook within this framework is Gleason (1961).

It should be mentioned that there are other traditions surrounding the phoneme, the best-known being the London school, represented by the classic work Jones (1967).

The European and American Structuralists dominated phonological theory until the late 1950's and early 1960's, when the Generative revolution began to affect linguistic departments throughout the world. Interestingly enough, a refugee from Nazi-occupied Prague, Roman Jakobson, who eventually ended up at Harvard University, across the river from MIT, had a significant influence on the development of the Generative version of phonology, even though Jakobson was himself one of the last living members of the

---

6. You probably also don't find it strange that the same letter is used to spell [ŋ] in *think* (or German *denken*), even though that letter is ⟨n⟩. But that's a much more complicated story we will deal with later.

original Prague School. Morris Halle and, to a certain extent, Noam Chomsky himself, with the collaboration (without, incidentally, the complete approval of Jakobson) developed the branch of phonology that could be roughly characterized as Generative Phonology, the theoretical framework that dominates most modern phonological theory. As with syntactic theory, the model has evolved greatly over the past thirty years, and is, even now, in considerable flux as a new paradigm has developed (one that we will examine in some detail later in the book). Some basic texts within this framework are Kenstowicz and Kisseberth (1979), which is based essentially on the Chomsky and Halle 1968 model, and Kenstowicz (1993) which includes more recent work on autosegmental and metrical phonology, discussed in Chapter 10.

The Generative Phonology paradigm began with the idea that all variations in the pronunciation of a morpheme (not only the allophones, but even phonemic variants, such as the /k/ ~ /s/ alternation between *electric* and *electricity* could be accounted for by positing a single underlying form, and deriving all variations through the application of phonological rules which systematically changed the features of the phonemes involved. While this general view has remained essentially the same over the past (roughly) forty years, pieces of the theory have gone in a number of different directions. Chapter 10 will discuss the current state of the theory.

## 1.3 The basic building blocks of phonology

A well-known and fundamental principle of Cognitive Grammar is that some linguistic units are most directly accessible to the naive native speaker of a language. These units are learned first, are the closest to being universal, and seem to be directly perceivable as such. Thus, we instantly recognize a dog, or a cat, while it takes expert knowledge to recognize an Alsatian dog or a Maine Coon cat on the one hand, or a canid, or even a mammal on the other. This principle that a certain kind of intermediate unit in the hierarchy of abstractness has immediate perceptual prominence is known as a *basic kind* or *basic level*. It is clear that something very similar to, if not identical to the phoneme as proposed by Baudouin, Sapir and others is the basic level unit of phonology. There is a great deal of evidence that speakers perceive segments directly,[7] and are easily able to make judgements about whether words start with the same sound, contain the same vowel and so on. This is true, of course, even if the words do not in fact contain the same sound – native speakers perceive the [æ] in *cat* and that in *bang* as identical even though they are quite different along at least three distinct phonetic dimensions – length, quality and nasality.

---

7. This is not to say that they don't also perceive larger units, such as syllables, feet, and perhaps pieces of the syllable, such as the rhyme. Whether features can be perceived directly (except through special training such as you are receiving) is much less likely.

Phonemes are naturally grouped into packages called syllables, and there are well-known and widely studied laws governing how syllables can be assembled. As with virtually all linguistic laws these are not absolute but take the form of prototypicality statements. All languages permit syllables consisting solely of a consonant and a vowel, but few permit syllables consisting exclusively of a stop followed by a fricative.[8]

Phonemes can be classified according to features, which are characteristics of sounds that seem to be perceptually salient in linguistic processing. Unlike phonemes these subsegmental characteristics are not normally available to the consciousness of native speakers in any direct way. This is why you learn feature-sized terms like 'voiced', 'velar' and so on in phonetics class, but no special training is needed to talk about a 'p-sound' or to notice that several series of sets of segments with successive sounds at the start sounds funny. Notice that the preceding alliterative sentence only works if the successive words start with the same sound, not with similar ones. 'Sister Suzy's sitting on a thistle' is alliterative, but 'Niece Lilly's dining on a tortilla' isn't despite the fact that every accented word begins with an alveolar consonant. Within the terms favored by Cognitive Grammar we would say that phonemes are basic level units, and hence easily available to speaker consciousness, while features are more abstract classifications not directly accessible to the untrained ear (or mouth).

Although speakers may not be aware of features, they are linguistically significant. That is, speakers behave as if facts about kinds of sounds determine their behavior. Thus all voiceless stops in English are aspirated at the beginning of words, all vowels in German are nasalized before a following nasal consonant and so on. This is not because speakers are performing some kind of abstract mental classification into rows and columns, but rather because features represent actual physical gestures (or at least the perceptual equivalent thereof). Thus it no more requires a belief in an abstract classification system to note that speakers treat similar sounds as the same as noting that hitting an object with an ax, a golf club or a baseball or cricket bat all require a strong windup to be effective. One could argue that aspirating a voiceless stop is as natural as adding a backswing before swinging a long heavy object or taking a deep breath before shouting. Again, it is not necessary to argue for some kind of abstract mental computation – long heavy objects are a certain way, and consequently one interacts with them in response to their characteristics. Similarly with phonemes. The fact that allophonic rules are language specific does not change this claim, since all allophonic rules are naturally motivated, it's just that different languages pick different ones to apply, something that we will see in detail later.

The framework that is presupposed in this book is that of Cognitive Grammar, a theory that was developed originally during the nineteen eighties, first by Lakoff and Langacker (see, particularly Lakoff (1987) and Langacker (1987)). Crucial to that model is the idea of categorization. Categorization is the human ability to recognize *kinds* of things – this is a

---

8. As we will see later in Chapter V, on syllables, such languages do indeed exist, although they are just extremely rare. But any English speaker can say Psst!

'dog', that is a 'tree', she is 'running' – placing individual instances of things and events (and abstractions as well) into categories. This ability is not solely a linguistic ability (and may not even be solely a human ability), but for the purposes of a book on phonology we will look exclusively at the linguistic aspects.

The traditional view of categories (frequently called the classical view) is that we place members into a category on the basis of shared characteristics. This is often called the **Aristotelian** view, since the first extended discussion of this area occurs in Aristotle's work. Under this view, all members of a category must share some defining characteristic (which constitutes its definition). Nothing in the classical view entails that members of a category can be differentiated from each other with respect to their membership – they are all equally either in or out. The standard method to symbolize this view is the Venn diagram, a circle with items either inside it (hence belonging to the category) or outside it (hence not belonging).

There are two ways in which the classical category appears not to correspond to actual human categorization behavior. The first is that not all categories have absolute boundaries. An entire school of mathematics, called **Fuzzy Logic,** has arisen around the view that actual membership in a category is gradable (one can, in principle, be only a little 'old'). Other categories, on the other hand, have absolute thresholds, such as being an American citizen, or, citing a classic saying, being pregnant. The status of boundaries will not be much of an issue in this book, as humans seem to behave as if sounds are always clearly a member of some category or other.

On the other hand, numerous researchers have found that not all members of a category are equal. Some are better members than others. This has been discovered through varying kinds of experimental research. One simple test is to ask a group of people (from the same speech community) to write down a list of, say, birds. Such lists are never random, and statistical analyses of such lists shows that certain birds are always at the top of the list, while others are rarely mentioned or occur at the bottom. For speakers of American English, birds such as the robin, sparrow and pigeon are listed at the top, but birds such as a chicken, penguin and ostrich are normally not what comes to mind first.

Even more persuasive are the studies that do not require conscious reflection (or actually measure how that reflection takes place). If we show subjects pictures of various birds, and ask them whether they are birds or not (we of course include non-birds as well, just to make it a real task), then measure how long it takes for the subjects to reply, we find that it takes significantly less time to recognize that a robin is a bird than it takes to recognize that a penguin is a bird. Note here that it is not a question of whether something is a bird or not, but just how 'good' a bird it is. Some birds fit our category better than others. These effects are called **prototype** effects, and they have been extensively studied by Rosch (see, for example Rosch (1975, 1978)),

The specific manner of categorization that Lakoff (1987) proposed was what he calls a **radial prototype category**, because the relationship among the members is similar to an image of spokes on a wheel. There is (or may be) a central member or members. Arranged around the central members are less central ones, which are similar to the central member, but differ from it in some respect. Growing out from the less central members are even less central members, differing from the less central members in other respects, and the process continues to the limits of the category (corresponding to the rim itself at the end of the spokes). The only disadvantage to the image of spokes on a wheel is that the actual 'shape' of a category is far from circular. What I imagine is a wheel whose circumference is distorted into the irregular shape of an amoeba.

To make this more comprehensible, let us examine a lexical example from Winters (1988). A *cup* is prototypically (at least in North America and the UK) a ceramic container for hot liquids. It has one handle, is bowl-shaped and sits on top of a saucer. If any of these characteristics are changed, the object may still be called a cup, but is a less good instance of one. For example, a more solidly built cup without a saucer (for which we also have the word *mug*) may also be called a cup. Or the handle may be missing (say, a Japanese or Chinese tea cup). Or further, it may be made of styrofoam or cardboard rather than ceramic. It could have two handles (as some infant cups do). A cup with two handles might also have symbolic value and not hold hot liquids – for example, the World Cup, which normally holds no liquids at all. On the other hand, in the English-speaking world, a cup may be stylized in another way, as holding a prescribed amount of liquid (or even solid). Thus a cup of oil means specifically 8 oz. (in England 10 oz.) of the oil. In fact, following a general organizing principle that has been dealt with extensively in the CG literature (metonymy), a cup of oil normally refers just to the oil, *not* to the container (via the standard metonymy of CONTAINER FOR AMOUNT OF CONTENTS[9]). Further, in North America, butter comes in quarter pound 'sticks' wrapped in paper. Each 'stick' is equal to 1/2 a cup, and consequently, a cup is understood by North American cooks as 'two sticks of butter', even though the butter never sees an actual container.

This example illustrates why we use the term 'radial' to describe categories – they are structured like (somewhat bent) spokes on a wheel. It also illustrates the principles governing the construction of these radial categories.

At the center, as best instance, stands the teacup. Leading out in one direction are modifications to the material and shape that retain the *function* (holding coffee or tea). Leading out in another direction (via the notion of standardization) are increasingly distant notions of quantity, until ultimately we are referring to solid objects wrapped in paper. Leading out in still another direction we find modifications in the *function* of the cup, retaining the general material and/or shape (same form, different function). Thus *cup* may refer to a prize for some contest. In fact, when we say 'That goal won us the Cup', *cup* refers not to the physical object itself (although physical possession of the actual cup is involved also) but rather to the prestige, money and fame connected with winning a championship. This connection between an object and the things normally associated with it is called 'metonymy', and is one of the ways in which nonprototypical members of a category are connected to the prototypical members. Both the use of *cup* to denote an amount, and its

---

9. I am grateful to Mark Johnson for pointing out to me the exact nature of this relationship.

use to mean 'championship' are examples of metonymic extension from the prototype, and there are also metaphorical extensions, such as *cup size* in a brassiere, or the *cup* that a golf ball goes into.

If we look at the overall structure of the category *cup*, we see its crucially *radial* nature. We cannot understand the connection between 'championship' and 'two pieces of butter wrapped in paper' except by following a trail along the spokes of our imaginary wheel back to the center – the teacup. Adjacent spokes do not necessarily have any relationship with one another, but only via a path that they can both trace back to the same center.

We will see below, in the chapter on the phoneme, that phonemes appear to be just such a kind of category, and, in particular, the problem that structuralist phonemicists ran into attempting to find a single set of distinctive features defining each phoneme can be solved if we do not take the classical view of the nature of the phoneme.

It is important to recognize, despite the long discussion in the preceding pages, that phonology is not only about phonemes and allophones. Phonology also concerns itself with the principles governing phoneme *systems* – that is, with what sounds languages 'like' to have, which sets of sounds are most common (and why) and which are rare (and also why). It turns out that there are prototype-based explanations for why the phoneme systems of the languages of the world have the sounds that they do, with physiological/acoustic/perceptual explanations for the preference for some sounds over others. Similarly, languages exhibit prototype gradience in syllable structure, with the 'ideal' syllable having simply a consonant and a vowel ('*ma*'), while much rarer syllable types appear to contain no vowels at all (*Srpsk* – a form of the Serbian adjective 'Serbian'), and some languages have words with no consonants at all (such as the Hawai'ian place name *Aiea*, or the Japanese word for 'blue' *aoi*).

Finally, there are areas of language where linguists disagree about whether *phonology* is involved at all. For example, when English adjectives such as *divine* [dəvaɪn] are converted into nouns through the addition of the suffix *-ity*, for many speakers both vowels in the word change – *divinity*. [dɪvɪnɪti] And even more radical changes happen when the adjective ends with a /k/-sound (sometimes). Thus *opaque* [oʊpeɪk] becomes *opacity* [oʊpæsɪti], with both a vowel and a consonant change. Some linguists have argued that the relationship between the two pronunciations of the root are due to similar processes to those which provide for 'aspiration' (the little puff of air after the first /p/ in *pop*), while others believe that the aspiration is produced 'on-line', automatically and unconsciously, while the vowel change and 'switch' of /k/ to /s/ should not even be described as a change at all. Still others maintain that there are no changes in speech production at all – everything is produced just as it is stored. I will argue in this book that the truth is somewhere in the middle – some details are computed on-line, while other details are stored permanently exactly as they are pronounced.

# Chapter 2

# A brief overview of phonetics

2.1 Basic classes

2.2 Manner of articulation

2.3 Points of articulation

2.4 Laryngeal and other features

2.5 Vowels

2.6 Suprasegmentals

2.7 Exercises

This chapter is not intended to serve as a substitute for a solid course in phonetics, nor for a good text on the subject. Good texts include Ladefoged (1993, 2005) and Rogers (2001) for general overviews of the entire field and Laver (1994) for the most thorough review of articulatory phonetics. Kent and Read (1992) is a readable introduction to acoustic phonetics in more detail than is covered in Ladefoged or Rogers, while Olive, Greenwood, and Coleman (1993) deals extensively with American English acoustic phonetics. The most recent complete study of the possible sounds of the world is Ladefoged and Maddieson (1996), a marvellous summary of the range of possibilities available to human language.

While enormous progress has been made in acoustic phonetics in the second half of the twentieth century, it is still customary to frame introductions to phonetics almost exclusively in articulatory terms. This is in part, I suspect, because while a few people can use spectrogram programs, everyone has a mouth, which makes learning about the articulators a real-time, experiential exercise.

## 2.1 Basic classes

We can divide the sounds of the languages of the world into two basic types, which we will call, for ease of use, consonants and vowels.[1] We can think of the vocal tract as a noisemaker

---

1. Earlier scholars distinguished between contoids and vocoids, which had a purely phonetic definition

at the bottom of a tube whose shape can be modified at will. The noisemaker is, of course, the vocal cords, which produce a buzzing sound when the vocal folds are held loosely together. When they are pulled apart either there is no noise, or, if the airflow is sufficiently heavy, there can be a hissing noise, as might be heard during a loud [h] sound.

The tube begins directly above the vocal cords, and exits at the mouth. There is an option for an additional exit through the nose (the exit is controlled by a valve called the velum). Most speech is produced with the nasal valve closed, producing **oral** speech, but if the velum is open and the mouth closed, the speech is said to be **nasal**, while if the mouth is open also, the speech is said to be **nasalized**.

If the vocal tract is relatively open the sound is characterized as a **vowel**, whereas if the vocal tract is relatively closed, the sound is a **consonant**. Sounds that are made with the vocal tract at an intermediate state are **approximants**. The closure can be complete, in which case the sound is a **stop** (also called **plosive**), or it can be sufficiently incomplete so that the air must be forced through, producing a turbulent airstream and a hissing noise. In this case the sound is a **fricative** (or **spirant**). It is also possible to combine a complete closure with a release of that closure sufficiently slow to result in hissing immediately following the release. This is known as an **affricate**.[2]

Vowels are, as I mentioned above, made with the vocal tract relatively open. Since vowels are normally voiced, the result is an amplified set of regular, systematic vibrations. Vowels are more like the brass or woodwind instruments in an orchestra, whereas the consonants are the percussion.[3] Not coincidentally, when we sing (in virtually any language or culture) it is the vowels that sustain the notes.

Approximants are sounds that share qualities of both consonants and vowels. While, like consonants, they have some kind of vocal tract closure *somewhere*, like vowels they also have some direct path from the vocal cords to the open air, leading to the open, musical quality we associate with vowels. For example, **nasal** consonants combine complete oral closure with a completely open nasal passage. **Lateral** consonants combine complete closure along the midpoint of the roof of the mouth with an opening on one side or the other of the tongue. Rhotic sounds are the most difficult to characterize, but seem to combine either intermittent closure (trills) or closure so short that it doesn't really 'count' (taps and flaps).

It is traditional to have two charts for displaying segments – one for consonants of all kinds, the other for vowels. The consonant chart is displayed with place of articulation

---

in terms of physical attributes, and consonants and vowels, which had *phonological* definitions based on the location of the sounds in question within a syllable – consonants are on the margins, while vowels are in the centers (nuclei) of syllables. We will consider this distinction later, and for now, ignore it.

**2.** From an acoustic point of view, consonants are **noisy** – they are characterized by random, irregular vibrations, or by complete silence, often followed by noise.

**3.** Those with greater musical expertise will note that in fact, consonants are actually like 'attacks', while vowels are the notes themselves, so the above analogy is not perfect.

across the top, and manner down the side. I include here the official IPA Chart as it appears in the Journal of the IPA (chart courtesy of International PhoneticAssociation:

1. IPA Chart

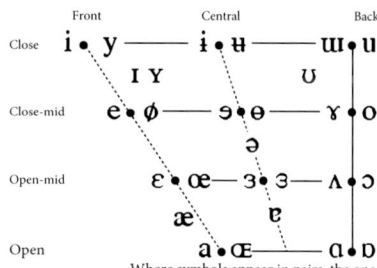
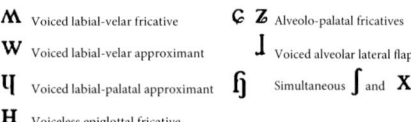

The chart recognizes eleven points of articulation, which most phonologists feel should be grouped into four main categories: **labial, coronal, dorsal** and **guttural**. Roughly, those sounds made with the involvement of the lips are labial, those made with the front part of the tongue (tip, blade) are coronal, while those made with the back of the tongue are dorsal, and those made with the root are guttural. Traditionally glottal stop, although not made with the root, is also in this last class.

## 2.2 Manner of articulation

**Stops** comprise plosives and nasals together. This is intuitively reasonable when we note that someone with a cold, whose nasal passages are blocked at all times, replaces all nasals with voiced stops. Note that affricates are not listed on the chart – the IPA believes that these should be represented as combinations of the appropriate stop plus fricative. Thus the initial sounds in English *church* and *judge* would be transcribed as [tʃ] and [dʒ]. However, most *phonologists* feel that there is a place for them, in that in those languages which have them, they act as if they were single units. In that case, special symbols are often used, such as [č] and [ǰ] for the sounds just discussed.

**Fricatives** are made by bringing a lower articulator close enough to an upper one so that when air is forced out a turbulent airstream results. Turbulence is perceived as hissing, so fricatives are noisy, hissing consonants. It is possible to superimpose the vibrations of the vocal cords on fricatives, giving voiced fricatives. Fricatives, of course, have points of articulation too, defined as the place where the narrowing of the vocal tract occurs.

There have been various ways of subclassifying fricatives, according to the shape of the tongue, or to the nature of the airstream. For example, sounds made with the tongue grooved down the middle are called **groove** fricatives, and may also be called **sibilants**. [s, z, ʃ, ʒ] are sibilants (although [ʃ, ʒ] are sometimes called **shibilants** in contrast with [s, z] a further division puts together [f, v, s, z, ʃ, ʒ] on the basis of the fact that the airstream produced by these sounds strikes two surfaces as it leaves the mouth. For example, for most speakers, [s] produces a jet of air from between the tongue tip and the alveolar ridge. However, the jet of air then impacts the lower lip, causing additional turbulence. That this is so can be seen by making an [s] and pulling the lower lip down out of the way – note how different it sounds. Sounds made with this additional source are referred to as **strident** sounds, as contrasted with, say, [ɸ, β, θ, ð, ç, j]. We will see later that stridency plays a role in the phonology of English.

Yet another way of classifying fricatives is between **slit** fricatives and **grooved** fricatives, a contrast that refers to the shape of the tongue as viewed from the front. If there is a groove down the center of the tongue, as there is with an [s] the term is 'grooved', and, obviously, slit fricatives involve the tongue in a relatively flat posture, as it takes in the English dental fricative [θ].

Sounds made with the articulators not as close together as they are to produce audible friction are called **approximants**, although it is not necessarily the case that the various kinds of approximant belong together as a phonological class. Since we are dealing with consonants, there is always some kind of contact involved with approximants, although the contact may be of radically different types. For example, **laterals** involve contact between the tip or front of the tongue and the teeth or alveolar ridge (or occasionally parts further back), but at the same time, the tongue sides do not make a complete seal against the gum ridges next to the side teeth, leaving a fairly sizable gap on one side or the other. This results in free air passage despite the closure in the center of the mouth. On the other hand, there is a class of sounds that consist of various kinds of rapid or intermittent contact between the tongue and the roof of the mouth, such as taps, flaps and trills. These sounds (the **rhotics**, or r-sounds) are also classed as approximants. Finally, there are sounds that consist, **articulatorily** of a vowel-like articulation, but which function within the syllable structure as onsets (that is, they serve to begin a syllable). These sounds, which are called **glides**, are again, quite different in articulatory properties from laterals and rhotics, but nonetheless are classed among the approximants.

Stops, fricatives and approximants constitute the complete class of consonants (as I mentioned above, there may also be a need to consider a class of affricates, although the IPA doesn't recognize such a class as a separate phonetic entity.)

## 2.3 Points of articulation

Sounds are classified also according to where in the mouth the obstruction is made (if there are indeed obstructions) or to where (in general) in the mouth the tongue is located (if there are no obstructions). In the case of consonants, the location of the obstruction is referred to as the point or place of articulation, while in the case of vowels the tongue position is referred to as vowel quality. As we will see later, there is considerable debate as to whether the placement of the tongue is the correct parameter to be using, with some suggesting that the relevant quality is acoustic rather than articulatory.

It is traditional to classify points of articulation from the front to the back of the oral tract (In the older tradition, often used to describe Sanskrit, the points are listed from back to front.)

Sounds made with an obstruction at the lips are referred to as **labial**, but there are two possibilities: either the obstruction involves both lips (**bilabial**) or the lower lip and the upper front teeth (**labiodental**).[4] Prototypically labial stops are **bi**labial, while labial fricatives are labio**dental**. Labiodental stops are extremely rare, perhaps even nonexistent (although there are labiodental nasals, symbolized by [ɱ], as in English 'emphasis'.) Bilabial fricatives [ɸ, β] are more common (they occur, for example, as variants of other sounds in Japanese and Spanish).

---

**4.** Ladefoged and Maddieson (1996) describe a **linguolabial** stop in a few languages spoken in Vanuatu in the south Pacific, but otherwise these sounds are not known to occur in language.

Almost all languages have bilabial stops [p, b], and many languages have labiodental fricatives [f, v]. Later, in our discussion of phoneme systems, we will see that some languages lack a voiceless labial stop, even though they have the voiced one.

Sounds made with the front, mobile part of the tongue are classified together as **coronal**s. These include sounds made by touching the tongue tip to the teeth (**dentals**) [t̪, d̪], the tongue tip or blade to the alveolar ridge (**alveolars**) [t, d], touching the tip (or even the underside of the tongue) to the area just behind the alveolar ridge (**retroflex**) [ʈ,ɖ]or touching the blade of the tongue to the post-alveolar area (**palato-alveolar**[5]). Many languages prefer to have only one set of consonants in this area, although they may well have stops of one kind and fricatives of another. For example, in Spanish, the stops are dental [ t̪, d̪] but the fricatives are alveolar [s, z[6]]. English, on the other hand, has alveolar stops and fricatives, as well as a set of dental fricatives [θð] but for affricates English uses the palato-alveolar point of articulation [tʃ, dʒ].[7]

Moving further back, we find sounds made with the center of the tongue against the hard palate (called, not surprisingly, **palatals**). Palatal stops are relatively rare, but occur, for example, in Hungarian, where they are spelled *ty* and *gy*: [c, ɟ]. On the other hand, the palatal nasal, [ɲ], is very common, occurring in French, Spanish, Italian, Malay and many other languages. Palatal fricatives occur in a few languages, more often as variants of other sounds. The voiceless one is quite common as a variety of /h/ in English 'huge' [çudʒ] and Korean [çʌndɛ] 'Hyundai'. In German it may be a separate phoneme (the debate on this question goes on and on). It occurs in words such as *ich* – 'I' [ɪç], *solche* – 'such' [zɔlçə]. The voiced one is, on the other hand, rather rare, but can be found in an emphatic pronunciation of /j/ in English 'you', [ʝ : u].

**Velar** sounds are made with the back of the tongue moving up to touch the velum. Stops [k, g] are the commonest, with fricatives [x, ɣ] being fairly common (although for some reason they are rare in many of the better-known European languages). The velar nasal [ŋ] is widespread.

A few languages have **uvular** sounds. Most commonly there are stops, although the voiced one is extremely rare [q, ɢ]. Some languages have uvular fricatives [χ, ʁ], and in a

---

5. Fairly recently the International Phonetic Association renamed this category 'postalveolar', but phonologists are not in general happy with this, as it obscures the connection between this class of sounds and, on the one hand, alveolars, and, on the other, palatals such as the palatal glide [j]. In this text I will continue to refer to these sounds as palatoalveolar. The term is actually retained in the IPA chart, but only for click sounds.

6. Note that the [z] in Spanish is only a variant of /s/, not a distinct sound.

7. The official IPA view of **affricates** is to treat them as a sequence of stop followed by fricative. As mentioned above, there is a common tradition within American linguistics (and there is considerable psycholinguistic evidence to back this up) that they ought to be considered *single* sounds, and are normally written as [č, ǰ].

few Northern European languages (and Israeli Hebrew) the voiced one counts as the /r/-sound. The uvular nasal [ɴ] is also very rare.

It is possible to make a consonant by pulling the tongue back so that the root approaches the back of the pharynx. These **pharyngeal** sounds are relatively rare among languages, but occur in Arabic, so they are made by lots of people. Arabic, and some dialects of Israeli Hebrew have both voiceless and voiced ones [ħ, ʕ]. These sounds are all fricatives – there are no pharyngeal stops. Some have suggested that there are a set of epiglottal sounds that are distinct from the pharyngeals, but this is still a controversial area.

Finally, it is possible to close the larynx shut, and treat this as a consonant – the glottal stop [ʔ]. While in English this is a variant of /t/ before /n/ (in catnip [ˈkæʔnɪp] for example) it is a true consonant in a number of languages, such as Hawaiʻian. In Hawaiʻi [hɑˈvɑiʔi] one can visit Kaʻaʻawa, pronounced [kɑʔɑˈʔɑvɑ].

## 2.4 Laryngeal and other features

Consonants can also vary along a third dimension in addition to place and manner of articulation, namely the state and activities of the larynx. The most common pairing is a set of voiceless and voiced obstruents. Voiceless consonants, roughly, are articulated without concomitant vibration of the vocal cords, while voiced ones are articulated with simultaneous vocal cord vibration. The exact nature of the timing relationship between vocal cord vibration and consonant articulation has been extensively investigated in the phonetics literature, where it generally goes under the heading of **voice onset time** often abbreviated **VOT**. There are actually three basic categories, one in which the vocal cord vibration begins well before the stop is released,[8] the normal **voiced** category, one in which vocal cord vibration begins immediately upon release of the stop (or shortly thereafter – a lag of roughly 30 msec. is common), which constitutes the **voiceless unaspirated** category, and finally one where the return to regular voicing is delayed for some time, sometimes as long as 100 msec. after the release. The period of voiceless airflow following the release is called **aspiration**. English has all three kinds of laryngeal settings. Aspirated stops occur (at least) at the beginning of words (*two* [tʰu]), unaspirated stops occur after /s/ (*stew* [stu]), while voiced stops occur between vowels[9] (*ado* [əˈdu]). Another variety of laryngeal setting involves using the larynx as an additional articulator. If the vocal cords are closed, the larynx can be used as a piston. If the larynx jumps upward, this adds an additional pop to the release (known as an **ejective**). Ejectives are symbolized by the

---

**8.** Voicing in fricatives is much more clear-cut – generally there is either voicing throughout the friction or there is none, but it resumes immediately with the vowel. A few languages delay the onset of voicing for some voiceless fricatives, leading to what are normally thought of as aspirated fricatives. Aspiration will be dealt with below.

**9.** Stops in other positions have more complex possibilities. This issue will be dealt with in more detail in later chapters.

placement of an apostrophe after the symbol: [p', t']. Alternatively, the larynx may be pulled downward during the closure, making the interior of the mouth a partial vacuum (like a suction cup being pulled away from the wall). The resulting inward rush of air as the stop is released produces the characteristic sound of an **implosive**. Implosives are symbolized as the voiced stop symbol surmounted by a hook: [ɓ, ɗ, ʄ]. Many West African languages have implosives (Hausa and Igbo being well-known examples). Caucasian languages and many native North American languages have ejectives – Navajo being a good example.

## 2.5 Vowels

Vowels are not classified in the same framework as consonants in traditional phonetics, because they are not made with a significant obstruction in the oral tract. Consequently, they do not have a point of articulation. How to classify vowels is one of the most controversial areas in all of phonology (and phonetics). The framework with the longest tradition argues that vowels can be described along two cross-cutting dimensions called **height** and **backness**.[10] The terms supposedly refer to the position of the highest point of the tongue. This definition of the features was used until extensive x-ray investigations showed that in fact there was no clean correlation between the traditional descriptions and the location of the highest point of the tongue. On the other hand, it turns out that there is a much clearer correlation between acoustic measurements and these dimensions.

A very brief description of formants is in order, but for a true understanding, consult one of the phonetics texts in the reference list, particularly, Olive, Greenwood, and Coleman (1993). Formants are emphasized harmonics in a periodic speech sound (such as a vowel or liquid). On a spectrogram, a visual representation of harmonics graphed against time, appear as dark horizontal bars. The height of the bar in the graph, measured in Hz (cycles per second) corresponds roughly to tongue position. Tongue height correlates very closely with the position of the first formant – a high vowel has a low $F_1$, a low vowel a high $F_1$ (you can hear this correlation by opening your mouth, closing your vocal cords by making a glottal stop and flicking your throat with your finger as you go from [i] through [e] to [a], or from [u] through [o] to [ɑ]). Backness, on the other hands, correlates roughly with $F_2$ – front vowels have a high $F_2$, back vowels a low one. (You can hear this too, by whispering [i ɯ] or [æ ɑ][11]). Some phoneticians believe that height and backness are actually acoustic properties, while others continue to argue for articulatory definitions. Yet others have suggested we are dealing with proprioceptive features (that is, features describing how we *feel* our tongue is acting). Finally, there is the possibility that the vowel features

---

10.  Interestingly, this term is not the best one, since the dimension is front:back, but there is no appropriate derived noun corresponding to this dimension. We will use the term **backness**, for simplicity. Other terms used occasionally are frontness, tongue advancement and tongue location.

11.  I have used all unrounded vowels because rounding vowels affects their formant structure.

are actually abstract perceptual ones, and that a purely physical definition might not exist. We will leave this question aside here, but will return to it when we talk about features in Chapter 5.

A sample spectrogram illustrating the author saying the vowels [i a u] is shown below.

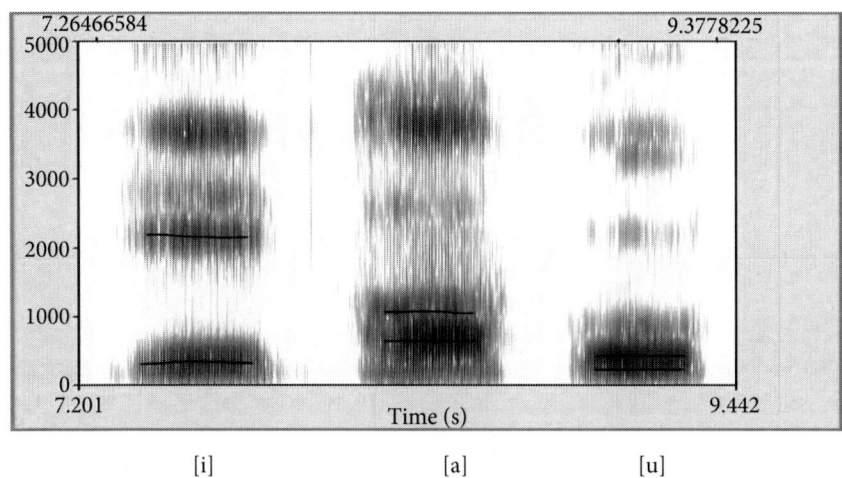

Spectrogram of [i, a, u] with center of first and second formant roughly marked as horizontal black line. Spectrogram created with PRAAT, Boersma and Weenink(2007)

Although we will use the terms **high**, **mid**, and **low**, which are probably the most common ones used by phonologists, the IPA uses an older terminology of **close**, **close-mid**, **open-mid**, and **open**. As we will see below, this also raises the question of how many levels there should be.

After that long preamble, we should add that there is another, uncontroversial feature, namely rounding, which has, of course, a purely articulatory definition, the rounding of the lips.

High vowels, then, are [i, y, ɨ, ʉ, ɯ, u], representing front unrounded, rounded, central and back unrounded and rounded. Virtually all languages have the first and last (for example in English *he*, *who*), while the others are relatively less common.

Mid vowels include [e, ɛ, o, ɔ] as in English *hat*, *yet*, *ought* (only in British English) and *oat* (and the front rounded and back unrounded correspondents [ø, œ, ɤ, ʌ], as in French *peu* [pø], *peur* [pœʁ], among others). Low vowels are [æ a,ɑ ɒ] as in [American English] *hat*,[12] Southern [American English] *I*, California English *hot* and Chicago *ought* respectively.

There is, in addition to the controversy about what the primary dimensions mean, a controversy about how many heights are necessary. This book will assume that only

---

12. As is always the case when we use key words to illustrate vowels, we need to be careful. If you speak American English, but live in the area surrounding the Great Lakes, you do not have a low vowel in words like 'hat', but pronounce something more like [hɛət].

three are needed – high, mid and low. The IPA assumes that four levels are better, but very few languages actually have four levels that are clearly distinguished only by height. Many languages subdivide the mid and high vowels into two sets (English and German are the most obvious examples) and there has been considerable debate about what to call this subdivision. One popular classification is to divide each set up into a higher, more peripheral version and a lower, more central version, giving the following sets:

(2)  Tense    Lax
     i        ɪ
     e        ɛ
     u        ʊ

The features Tense and Lax, then, differentiate related sounds at the same general height and backness coordinates. This allows for a number of additional 'heights', but correctly groups together sounds that languages appear to classify in the same way. For example, in English, only Tense vowels can constitute the sole vowel in a word if there is no consonant on the end of it (there are words like *tea*, *bay* and *toe*, but no words like *[tɪ], *[bɛ]).

As we have already mentioned, the feature Round is independent of Backness and Height, but there is a prototypical correlation between back and rounded, and nonback and unrounded. This will be discussed more thoroughly in Chapter IV on phonemes.

In a number of West African languages there is an additional feature, which seems somewhat similar to Tense, but works quite differently. This is the feature Advanced Tongue Root. In these languages, there are sets of vowels that are made with the root of the tongue shifted slightly forward, and other sets made without the forward shifting. X-ray investigations show that this dimension is quite different from the Tense feature discussed above, although the pairs *sound* somewhat like tense/lax pairs. As we will see in a later chapter, many West African languages make use of this characteristic in the phonologies of words, and in the morphological structure of the grammars.

There are a number of other characteristics of vowels that languages may choose to make use of. Quite a large number of languages have nasalized vowels (French, Portuguese and Hindi are well-known examples). More complex, and more poorly understood features include creaky voice and breathy-voiced vowels, which involve non-prototypical laryngeal settings.

One final set of characteristics, not of single vowels in the strictest sense, but nonetheless of great importance is that of length and diphthongization. Many languages differentiate between pairs of vowels that have the same articulatory features but differ in how long they last. Virtually all languages that make this distinction (normally known as long vs. short) make only one contrast, but there are a handful of languages (most notably Estonian) that have a three-way contrast. Japanese is a good two-way example, with minimal pairs such as

(3)  toː    'ten'      to     'door'
     suː    'inhale'   su     'vinegar'
     satoː  'sugar'    sato   'hometown'
     biːru  'beer'     biru   'building'
     meːsi  'card'     mesi   'meal'                    (Tsujimura 1996: 19)

A further complication for the classification of vowels is that many languages have *moving* vowels – that is, vowels of changing quality. English is a notorious example, in that, at least for American English, virtually all the vowels move in some way. The traditional name for moving vowels is **diphthong**, literally 'two-sound'. Diphthongs are normally classified by the beginning and ending sound, although they may well simply be a smooth path rather than a combination of two endpoints.

The most common kinds of diphthongs start out with a low vowel (often some form of [a]), and move in the direction of the two upper corners: [ai] and [au], as in *high, how*. These illustrate that most diphthongs begin with a lower vowel and trail off in the general direction of high glides. Diphthongs like these are called falling diphthongs, in that the most sonorous, or lower, part comes first. English also has a rising diphthong, where the most sonorous part comes last: [ju], as in 'unique', 'huge', 'cute'. Rising diphthongs are much rarer. Note that the terms 'falling' and 'rising' have nothing to do with vowel height, but rather with whether the 'center' of the vowel comes before the glide (falling) or after (rising).

There are also 'centering' or 'ingliding' diphthongs, and American English has these also, especially in the Midwest. These are diphthongs where the off-gliding vowel is schwa-like, rather than being related to the high vowels [i] and [u]. Good examples are American English pronunciations of *bad* [bæəd], *broad* [brɔəd]. These vowels give American English the characteristic that non-linguists refer to as a 'drawl'. British English also has centering diphthongs, but these derive historically (and perhaps synchronically also) from combinations of vowels plus /r/: *here* [hɪə], *there* [ðɛə].

Finally, in a few languages, including British English, there are actually **tri**phthongs, in such words as a careful pronunciation of *hour*: [aʊə] and *fire*: [faɪə].

## 2.6 Suprasegmentals

What is the difference between a diphthong and two vowels? It turns out that this is not, strictly speaking, a *phonetic* question, but rather a *phonological* one. A diphthong is a sequence of vowels contained within a single syllable, while two vowels is a sequence of vowels each constituting a separate syllable. While English doesn't provide really clear examples, a possible case would be the contrast in r-less dialects of British English between, say, 'fire' [faɪə], which is one syllable, and 'liar' [laɪ.ə], which most speakers would feel as two. Note the use of a period, a traditional way to express the presence of a 'syllable boundary'. Syllables are a controversial item in phonetics, although most phonologists recognize their existence as organizational units. Many of the restrictions on possible sequences of phonemes are best expressed as restrictions on which sounds can appear where within a syllable. And syllables seem to be the smallest independently pronounceable units – naive speakers cannot normally say individual phonemes, and consonants, particularly stops are normally said followed by the most basic vowel in the language. Ask a child to break a word into its component sounds and the child will either say [æ. pəl] or [æ.pə.əl].

We will discuss syllables at great length in chapter 4. Suffice it to say here that syllables are units that stretch across more than one segment, and so are traditionally called **suprasegmental** units.

Other suprasegmental units are pitch and stress. Pitch, which is loosely correlated with fundamental frequency[13] is used in three different ways in language. The easiest one to understand is its use as an emotional marker, but linguists generally don't study this particular use. Then, pitch patterns are used for syntactic/pragmatic purposes. For example, in most languages, falling pitch marks statements and rising pitch marks yes/no questions. A slight rise, repeated, marks non-terminal members of a list: 'six, seven, eight…' This use of pitch for syntactic/pragmatic purposes is referred to as **intonation**.

In over half of the languages of the world pitch has another function. Every word in the language includes not only some consonants and vowels but also a pitch pattern. Languages can have anywhere from two to eight or so distinct pitch patterns, each of which counts as a kind of phoneme, and it is necessary to learn which pitch pattern to use with each word, just as you need to learn which words start with /t/ or end with /u/. This use of pitch is known as **tone**, and languages which have distinctive tone are called tone languages. Tones can be simple levels (High, Mid, Low), or they may be moving (Rising, Falling, Low-Falling …). Recent phonological work suggests that moving tones can, in general, be considered sequences of level tones (so that falling tones could be represented as a sequence of High and Low).

Lastly there is stress. Stress is a feature that is easy to talk about but difficult to define with any degree of confidence. Traditionally it has been identified with loudness, but stressed syllables are not *necessarily* louder. If we measure stressed syllables and compare with otherwise identical unstressed syllables we see that they are, all other things being equal, *louder, longer* and exhibit a sharp pitch jump. Notice, however, that this feature is quite different from others we have discussed above. Features such as **alveolar, stop** and so on are absolute – either a sound is alveolar or it is not; either the vocal tract is closed or it is not. Stops are not defined depending on the relative degree of closure compared to other stops. But stress has exactly this characteristic – there is no absolute definition of a stressed syllable, but only one compared to surrounding syllables.

For that reason, linguists have gone outside of the purely physical realm of phonetics to talk about what stress actually *is*. One area of human activity that seems closely related to stress is that of rhythm. All living beings move in rhythmic ways (actually so do many inanimate objects, such as pulsars, but we can ignore them, since they don't speak to us). A rhythm is a recurring pattern, with one part of the pattern differing from the rest of the pattern. Consider, for example, the following *visual* pattern:

(4)   Xxx

---

13.   Fundamental frequency refers to the frequency with which the vocal cords vibrate, which is normally measured acoustically. It corresponds to our perception of pitch, as in a musical note.

if we repeat this pattern we experience it as a rhythm:

(5)   Xxx Xxx Xxx Xxx Xxx...

Notice that the larger X 'stands out'. Of course this could be because it's bigger, but notice that even a symbol that is the same size 'stands out':

(6)   xxo xxo xxo xxo xxo

even if it is third in the pattern (and thus a different rhythm from (5)). Stress seems to be the unit that 'stands out' in such a pattern. Now it is the case that languages normally mark the special syllable by giving it some additional phonetic substance – as mentioned above it is often longer, or louder, or the location for a sharp pitch jump. In addition, recent phonetic research has shown that the actual articulatory movements in stressed syllables are larger than those in the surrounding syllables. Furthermore, there is a well-known correlation between length and stress – in many languages long syllables are always stressed, to some degree. Lastly, *un*stressed syllables tend to have shorter articulatory movements, especially vowels. Specifically unstressed syllables tend to have more centralized vowels, and in many languages unstressed syllables have schwa [ə] – English, of course being a prime example.

Stress, on the other hand, tends to get 'stuck' on a particular syllable, often becoming lexically associated with that syllable, so that many languages stretch the rhythmicity of stress when words are strung together in phrases and sentences. Poetry, on the other hand, is the artful construction of rhythmic stretches in a pleasing manner, with cleverly placed disruptions to focus on particular words:

(7)   Is THIS a DAGGer THAT I see beFORE me
      The HANdle TURNed toWARD my HAND
      COME, let me CLUTCH thee (Macbeth)

Note the abrupt feel of the word 'come', which breaks the fairly regular iambic (xX) pattern. Rhythm has been studied for thousands of years, and the Ancient Greeks developed a series of terms for various patterns, at least three of which are commonly used in phonology as well. Each individual pattern is referred to as a **foot**, a term which, as we will see, is used in phonology as well. The pattern Xx (often referred to as strong-weak) is called a **trochee**, and such a rhythm is **trochaic**. An opposite pattern, xX is called **iambic**, the unit being an **iamb**. Another common unit is a **dactyl**, consisting of a strong and two weaks: Xxx.[14]

A classic example of how poetic rhythm works is Latin poetry. The great national poem of the Roman Empire, the Aeneid, is written in dactylic hexameter. That is, every line must consist of six dactyls. In place of some of the dactyls there can be a trochee. Latin poetry is based, not specifically on stressed syllables, but on syllable **weight**, a concept we

---

**14.** This somewhat clever name comes from the Greek for 'finger', which, of course, is made up of a long and two short bones.

will examine in great detail in chapter IV. Essentially long vowels and syllables that end in consonants are strong, and syllables that end in short vowels are weak. Here is the first two lines of the Aeneid, illustrating this patterning (long vowels are marked with the traditional Latin **macron** ā, ē etc. for length, short vowels are marked with the traditional **breve** (ĭ, ĕ etc.) and feet are divided by vertical strokes |):

(8)  Ármă vĭ|rúmquĕ că|nō Trōi|āe quī| prīmŭs ăb| ōrīs|
     Ītălĭ|ám fā|tō prŏfŭ|gús Lā|vīnĭăquĕ| vēnít|     (Skidmore 2008)

Notice that we have sets of dactyls and trochees to make a total of six per line. Compare it to the rhythm in example 7 above, based on English feet, which pay attention to stress rather than syllable weight in determining iambs.

When we discuss prosody in chapter V we will see that these terms have taken on a similar, purely phonological meaning in describing the sets of principles that govern stress patterns in language.

An additional complication that arises when we begin to talk about stress in a purely linguistic (as opposed to poetic) framework is that many languages seem to have multiple levels of stress. I should add at this point that the concept of multiple levels of stress is very controversial. There seems, in general, to be a geographic divide among linguists as to whether to talk about differing levels of stress. Linguists in Great Britain generally believe there is only one level of stress – stress is said to be **binary**, that is, either there or not. There may be other additional factors that mark some of those stresses, making them more prominent, but these do not constitute *degrees* of stress. On the other hand, most linguists in North America recognize multiple levels of stress, suggesting that English has at least three. At this point it makes sense to consider a concrete example. The following compound noun was suggested (in the nineteen fifties) to illustrate *four* levels of stress: primary, secondary, tertiary and weak:

(9)  élĕvàtŏr ôpĕràtŏr ($e^1le^0va^3tor^0$ $o^2pe^0ra^3tor^0$)

Note the use of the traditional accent marks acute (á), circumflex (â), grave (à) and breve (ă) to represent the descending levels of stress (strictly speaking, the breve marks no stress at all). A competing tradition uses numbers (represented as subscripts above), with the highest stress being one, with increasing levels representing lower levels of stress. This is supposed to capture the intuition that the first syllable of each word in the compound has the most stress (although the first word has stronger stress than the second), while the third syllables in each word are systematically lower than the first, and the schwa-like vowels are completely unstressed.

The British tradition rejects this theory of stress completely,[15] arguing that stress is purely binary. In the example above they would argue that the first syllable in each word

---

15. The clearest discussion of these issues (from the British point of view) can be found in (Ladefoged 115–18).

was indeed stressed, but that the third syllable (the [eɪ] vowels) are *not* stressed, but simply full (that is non-reduced, non-schwa-like) vowels. The differentiation between the two stressed syllables is that the first is the location of the strongest pitch jump – the place where the defining direction of the pitch jump occurs. Thus if the word is said as a question, the sharpest rise falls on the first syllable, and if it is said as a statement the sharpest fall falls on the first syllable. This particular syllable is referred to as the **tonic syllable**. Thus, within the British tradition what Americans call 'primary stress' is simply a stressed syllable which is also the **tonic**, while secondary stress is a stressed syllable that is not tonic. In the example of 'elevator operator', then, the relevant transcription would be something like

(10)    **é**levator óperator

where the bold underlined syllable is the tonic.

## 2.7   Exercises

1.   This textbook was not written to teach you phonetics – it is assumed that you are generally acquainted with the basics, including transcription. Just to help you remember the material, here is a wonderful poem illustrating the vagaries of the English spelling system. Make a broad phonetic transcription of at least three lines of the poem, which will force you to think not only about symbols and such, but also will give you a chance to think about the relation between spelling and pronunciation:

Hints On Pronunciation For Foreigners
[The origin of this poem is a mystery. It is attributed to T.S. Watt, George Bernard Shaw and Richard Keogh (or Krough)].

> I take it you already know
> Of tough and bough and cough and dough.
> Others may stumble, but not you,
> On hiccough, thorough, laugh and through.
> Well done! And now you wish, perhaps,
> To learn of less familiar traps.
> Beware of heard, a dreadful word
> That looks like beard and sounds like bird.
> And dead – it's said like bed, not bead.
> For goodness sake, don't call it deed!
> Watch out for meat and great and threat.
> They rhyme with suite and straight and debt.
> A moth is not a moth in mother,
> Nor both in bother, broth in brother,
> And here is not a match for there,
> Nor dear and fear for pear and bear.

And then there's dose and rose and lose
Just look them up--and goose and choose.
And cork and work and card and ward.
And font and front and word and sword.
And do and go, then thwart and cart.
Come, come I've hardly made a start.
A dreadful language? Man alive,
I'd mastered it when I was five!

2. Just to nail down your knowledge of phonetic symbols, read the following limericks and silly sayings, which are in several different dialects and write them out in standard orthography

    a.  ðə ɹeɪn ɪt ɹeɪnəθ an ðə dʒʌst
        ən ɔlso ɒn ði ʌndʒʌst fɛlo
        bət tʃifli an ðə dʒʌst bikaz
        ði ʌndʒʌst stilz ðə dʒʌsts ʌmbɹɛlə

    b.  ðɛɹ wɒz ə jʌŋ leɪdi neɪmd bɹaɪt
        huz spid wɒz mʌtʃ fæstə ðæn laɪt
        ʃi sɛt aʊt wʌn deɪ ɪn ə rɛlətɪv weɪ
        ænd keɪm bæk ðə prɪviəs naɪt

    c.  æn ɛpɪkjuə daɪnɪŋ ət kru
        faʊnd ə vɛɾi laːdʒ bʌg ɪn ɪz stju
        sɛd ðə weɪtə dəʊnt ʃaʊt and weɪv ɪt əbaʊt
        ɔː ðə ɹɛst wɪl bi wɔntɪŋ wʌn tu

    d.  ðɛə wʌ̃ns wɒz ən əʊld mæ̃n əv ɛsə
        huz nɒlɪdʒ gɹu lɛsə ɹən lɛsə
        ɪt ət last gɹu səʊ smɔɫ
        hi nju nʌθĩŋ ətɔɫ
        n̩d naʊ hiz ə kʰɒlɪdʒ pʰɹəfɛsə
        (from a now defunct website)

3. Take the first sound of each line in (2d) above and give its complete phonetic description (i.e. voicing, point and manner of articulation).

# Chapter 3

# Phonemes
## The fundamental category

> 3.1 Phonemes, allophones and other basic bits
> 3.2 How to find phonemes
> 3.3 Phoneme inventories
> 3.4 Phoneme discovery exercises

As discussed in Chapter I, phonologists have argued since the nineteenth century that units the size of segments constitute the basic building blocks of the phonology of a language. There have, from time to time, been phonologists who have argued against this concept, suggesting that perhaps features, or syllables are more basic, but overall a consensus has developed in favor of the segment-sized phoneme, however it is ultimately defined.

What everyone *does* agree on is that every language selects a set of basic sounds out of which it builds all its words. By and large these sounds all have the same status, although many languages have one or two marginal sounds that occur only in a few recently borrowed words (like the nasalized [ɔ̃] in American English *lingerie* [lɔ̃ʒəɹeɪ]) or occur only in words with specialized meanings such as onomatopoeic words.

As I mentioned in the introduction, there have traditionally been two different views of the reality of the phoneme. One, which originated in the nineteenth century, viewed the phoneme as a unit of mental storage and perception – phonemes are what we hear, and what we *believe* we are producing. This view, which has persisted as a thread throughout the history of linguistics contrasts with what we could call the structuralist view, that phonemes are ways in which language organizes itself, without making any kind of commitment to overt perception or production. This book will proceed on the assumption that phonology deals with how speakers actually process their language, and that the patterns and organization that we find are the result of ways in which human cognition is itself regular and follows general patterns.

## 3.1 Phonemes, allophones and other basic bits

The fundamental insight of phonology is that not all of the sounds produced by speakers of a given language are equal. Every language uses a (relatively) small number of sounds which are combined in relatively orderly ways. However, that small number of basic sounds are produced in a relatively large number of different ways. Put another way, the enormous numbers of different sounds that can be found in any given language can be classified and grouped into a small number of basic sounds, such that virtually any produced sound can be classified as belonging to one or another of the basic sounds.[1]

All the sounds that are grouped into a single category are called allophones, from the Greek αλλο, meaning 'other', plus φωνη 'sound'. The category itself is the phoneme. However, the phoneme is not merely the file folder into which all the variant sounds are placed – it is also the sound that we perceive in mental space, that we hear in our 'mind's ear'. It is also the form that the sound takes in long-term memory; the way the sound is stored. Massive evidence suggests that this is the case. One piece of evidence is that virtually no writing system known to us writes sounds that constitute different allophones. In English, for example, voiceless aspirated and unaspirated stops are allophones, yet no one has ever proposed a writing system in which [tʰ] and [t] in *tone* and *stone* respectively are written with different letters, and, as native speakers of English will tell you, it is very difficult to learn to hear the difference between those sounds, and beginning phonetics students normally do narrow transcription by the rule they learned in class ('This must be unaspirated; it's after an /s/') rather than by ear. There are, of course, writing systems that make even fewer distinctions, however. For example, English ⟨i⟩ represents a fairly large number of distinct phonemes. The point is that writing systems do not make subphonemic (that is, distinguishing among allophones) distinctions.[2]

Another piece of evidence that phonemes are the phonological 'coin of the realm' is that many (although not all) speech errors seem to involve the displacement of phonemes, which then behave as if they were 'in a new home', and come out as the appropriate allophone. For example, if, in aiming to produce *steel cage* the /t/ and /k/ are interchanged (a type of error so common it has a name: Spoonerism) the result is that the /k/ will be unaspirated (since it follows an /s/) while the /k/ will be aspirated:

---

1. We will see later that there may be cases where a particular sound is an instance of two other sounds. For example, many linguists have suggested that [ŋ] in English is not a basic sound, but rather the automatic instantiation of /n/ followed by /g/. This view is not universally accepted, but does explain a number of otherwise odd facts about English.

2. There is one somewhat controversial exception. Devanagari, the writing system of Sanskrit, has letters for sounds that were almost certainly allophones in Sanskrit. However, a good case can be made for the idea that devanagari was originally designed as a system of *phonetic* transcription, rather than simply a way of recording the language. It is certainly the case that Sanskrit scholars were very much concerned with the proper way of pronouncing Sanskrit.

(1) [stil kʰeɪdʒ] → [skil tʰeɪdʒ]

and, in fact, an alternative pronunciation:

(2) [*skʰil teɪdʒ]

would be inconceivable.

A similar example occurred when I overheard someone attempting to say 'whatever was out there', but instead said

(3) 'what was ever out there'

which came out

(4) [wɑʔ wəz ɛvɚ aʊʔ ðɛɚ]

The relevance for this example is that the /t/ in the intended utterance would normally have been said with a flap: [wɑɾɛvɚ], but instead came out with a glottal stop, as would be expected in its new, preconsonantal position. Clearly the word 'what' cannot have been stored with a flap, even though it was only part of the larger word 'whatever', but must have been stored with a /t/, which was then adjusted, on the fly, in real time, to a glottal stop. Again, this is strong evidence that phonological processes (whether couched in those terms or in some other metaphorical framework) apply in speaking, and are thus quite real.

It has been further noted that in any language activity carried out by non-phonetically-trained native speakers (rhyme and assonance in poetry, puns and other word play, language games) speakers behave as if allophonic variation is completely inaudible. Thus, in English, a glottal stop [ʔ] and a flap [ɾ] rhyme with each other if they both instantiate a /t/, but two instances of [ɾ] do not rhyme if one represents a /t/ and the other a /d/:

(5) Upon a mat      [əpɔn ə mæɾ]
    Upon a pad      [əpɔn ə pʰæɾ]
    A yellow cat    [ə jɛlo kʰæʔ]
    Serenely sat.   [sərinli sæʔ]

The first and second line do not rhyme, even though phonetically *identical*, but the first, third and fourth do, despite the fact that they are all phonetically *distinct*.[3]

As mentioned in Chapter I, this particular view of the phoneme was first proposed by Baudouin de Courtenay in the nineteenth century, but numerous other competing theories exist. Some of those other theories have contributed substantially to what we know about phonemes and how to study them, so what you will find in this chapter constitutes a synthesis of many competing theories.

---

3. This little poem, and the argument connected with it are due to the work of (Stampe 1987: 81).

One of the problems in studying phonemes is that we have defined a phoneme as a mental unit, and it is very hard to get inside of people's heads to find out how they have stored their sounds. Consequently, a set of tools have evolved for the purpose over the years, and although theories have come and gone, and views of the *true* nature of the phoneme have wandered everywhere, these tools have remained pretty much constant.

## 3.2  How to find phonemes

Consider what we find if we begin to study a language about which we know nothing. We are not native speakers – in fact, we are not speakers at all. So how do we know which sounds speakers categorize as the same? We essentially can get at the answer to this question from two different directions. First we can ask whether the speakers can hear the difference between two different sounds. This is accomplished by the method of **minimal pairs**. Second, we can see if the sounds are variants of a single sound. This leads to the method of **complementary distribution** and **free variation**.

Let us look at minimal pairs first. We know that two sounds constitute distinct sounds if native speakers can hear the difference between them. We can test this by finding two different words that are exactly the same *except for the two sounds in question*. Such a pair of words would constitute a **minimal pair**. For example, we know that /p/ and /b/ are distinct sounds in English because we can think of words that differ only in that one has a /p/ in some specified place while the other word is exactly the same, *except* that it has a /b/ in that place. The place can be anywhere in the word, and it is best to find examples in several different places. Here are some minimal pairs for English /p/ and /b/:

(6) pin : bin
    triple : Tribble[4]
    rip : rib

Each example must be a real, distinct word that native speakers can recognize as being distinct from the other word in the pair. This requirement then eliminates either of the following cases:

1. Sometimes a particular phoneme can be pronounced slightly differently without noticeable effect. For example, final stops in English can be released or unreleased, and the voiceless ones can be accompanied by simultaneous glottal closure, or that can be omitted. All possible pronunciations count as examples of the same word:

(7) [rɪpʰ], [rɪp̚], [rɪʔp] = *rip*

---

4. This example illustrates a common problem with the method of minimal pairs: it is often hard to find an example illustrating a particular sound in a particular place, given the requirement that each example must be a real, distinct word.

This is one kind of **free variation**. Some free variation is just plain free. However, other kinds of free variation seem to have sociolinguistic implications. Thus we can go to New York City and ask people to say the word *bad*. We can hear at least the following

(8) [bæəd]
    [bɛəd]
    [bɪəd]

but, while they all constitute instances of the 'same' word *bad*, they are markers of different social classes, formality levels, levels of social solidarity and so on. Extensive research on this issue has been conducted by Labov and his coworkers in numerous articles and books.

2. A second kind of free variation is much odder, and very little research has been done on it. This is variation in *which phoneme* a particular word contains. Here speakers can use either of several distinctive sounds, but don't seem to care very much which one they use. Thus we can say /ɛ/conomic or /i/conomic, or vary between /i/ther or /aɪ/ther:

(9) You say either,
    and I say either.
    You say neither
    and I say neither.
    Either either
    Neither neither
    Let's call the whole thing off.
    ©George and Ira Gershwin

While variations such as these are scattered throughout the language, they do not seem to have great theoretical significance, and have mostly come about through historical accidents of one sort or another.

Consequently, instances of free variation do not count as minimal pairs. That is, even though /niðər/ is heard as *sounding* different from /naɪðər/, it does not constitute a different word.

Thus, the first test of whether two sounds are distinct phonemes in a language is to find whether there are minimal pairs – pairs of words with a difference in meaning attributable to a single difference in sound.

However, it is often the case that we cannot think of examples of specific pairs of words illustrating the sounds we are interested in. In addition, if we are working with a language consultant who has not had linguistic training it may be difficult to convey what we are looking for. Consequently, an additional search tool has been developed. Since, in general, allophones of a single phoneme are similar to each other, we could make a list of all the similar sounds we can find, then look at the phonetic **environments** in which they occur, to see if their occurrence depends on their surroundings. We will look at why this should matter below, but for now, what we are looking for is **complementary distribution**.

Let's take a concrete instance. In Korean there are two sounds, [ɾ] and [l], which, for sake of argument we will say are similar (they are, in fact, both coronal approximants).

If we make a list of lots of words that contain each sound, the list would look something like this:

(10) kɯnɯl shade irɯmi name
 mul water kiri road
 pal leg kɯrəm then
 pʰal arm saram person
 ilkop seven uri we
 silkwa fruit jərɯm summer
 səul Seoul kəriro to the street (Gleason 1961: 57)

I have taken the liberty of arranging the words in columns – I need hardly point out that as you are investigating a language the data will not come in this format. It is extremely important when doing this task that you make sure you have each word transcribed accurately, and you must check and recheck your copying. It is incredibly easy to leave out a diacritic or to reverse letters, and if this happens you will never solve the puzzle.

What you are looking for is the phonetic surroundings of the sounds in question, and what you seek are unique phonetic identities for the surroundings of each sound. As you look at the above Korean examples you should be able to see that the [r] only occurs between vowels, while the [l] never does – it only occurs at the end of words or before other consonants. Thus, the distribution of the two sounds is **complementary**: the two sounds never occur in the same place.[5]

An analogy I like to use is of Superman and Clark Kent. If you wanted to investigate whether they were one and the same person, you could look for all the places where each of them can be seen. If you make a list, you will see that Superman is only seen at disasters and emergencies, but never in the newsroom of the Daily Planet, while Clark Kent is seen only at the newspaper office, but never at emergencies. Thus, their distribution is **complementary**. Since they are also physically similar, we can conclude that they are probably the same person. Precisely the same reasoning applies to allophones: if the sounds are somehow similar, and the surroundings that one occurs in are completely distinct from the surroundings that the other occurs in, we can conclude that the two sounds are allophones of the same phoneme.

One famous, non-psychological definition of a phoneme, in fact, is one or more phonetically similar sounds which are in complementary distribution.[6] Those linguists who are unwilling to take stands on the way in which sounds are *really* stored in long-term memory, or who believe that that is a question for the psychologists, not for linguists, normally use this definition. How is this purely **structural** definition related to the mental image conception that I argued for in the introduction and earlier in this chapter? The idea (which goes back to Baudouin's original idea of the phoneme as a psychic sound) is that we store phonemes as actual, mental sounds, but that in producing them, we *adjust* them

---

5. Note that the word is *complementary*, a concept taken from set theory, where the two distributions (between vowels and not between vowels) together make up the *complete* distribution of the sounds. Please note that the word is spelled with an ⟨e⟩ – we are not saying nice things about the sounds.

6. Normally the possibility of free variation is also included in the definition.

to fit their surroundings (what Baudouin called 'divergences'). Different surroundings will result in different adjustments. The result is that we have a small set of adjusted sounds depending on the phonetic surroundings, and, they will be in complementary distribution, since their existence can be attributed to their particular surroundings. They will all be phonetically similar, since they are all adjustments to the same basic phoneme, or mental sound. Thus allophones are the modifications that result when a particular phoneme occurs, say between vowels, or at the beginning of a syllable, or when stressed or whatever.

Within the generative tradition, the metaphor that is normally used is that the phoneme is an **underlying** sound, while the allophones are **surface** forms. This is borrowed from the now obsolete model of deep and surface structure originally developed to describe syntax in the 1960's, but despite being over forty years old, the terminology survives, as well as the idea that allophones are **derived** from phonemes through the application of phonological rules. We will discuss this view extensively below.

I should mention that there are other views of the phoneme that you should be aware of. Within the British tradition, Daniel Jones (best known as the father of the Cardinal Vowels) viewed allophones as members of a family of sounds, with the phoneme being the name given to the family itself, and the particular name for the phoneme being chosen as a matter of mnemonic convenience. Others have argued that the actual phoneme (that is, the unit of mental storage) is not an actual sound at all, but an abstract specification of only those features of the sound that make it different from all the other sounds in the language. There are several versions of this view around, including one developed in the nineteen thirties identified with the Prague School, and one popular within a recent generative school called Underspecification Theory. Again, these issues will be discussed below.

A further view, popular among some Cognitive Linguists, is that phonemes are abstract schemas for large numbers of individual stored instances of sounds, with schemas arising through repetition of production and perception of specific cases. This view will be discussed in a later chapter.

So, to sum up, phonemes are idealized mental sounds which are stored in long-term memory. As the sounds are produced, they are modified according to the phonetic environments that they find themselves in, resulting in allophones – the actual result of saying the words that contain the particular phonemes. The modifications that we make in producing sounds are dealt with in the chapter on **processes**.

## 3.3  Phoneme inventories

There is a further issue in dealing with the whole concept of phonemes that we need to examine, once we understand what the basic phonological building blocks of language are. Which ones do languages select among the thousands of possible sounds that human beings can make? It has been known in a kind of common sense way for a hundred years that some sounds are common throughout the world's languages, while others are very rare. For example, very few languages lack /t/, while very few languages have clicks, or ejective fricatives. Similarly, many languages have the vowel system /i e a o u/, and none have a system made up exclusively of high vowels, such as /i ɨ u/. There appear to be general principles guiding the set of phonemes that we find in languages around the world, and this section of the phoneme chapter will discuss some of those principles. The original classic work on this subject, incidentally is Trubetzkoy (1939 [1969]), and the basic contemporary reference is Ladefoged and Maddieson (1996).

A major guiding principle seems to a preference for **symmetry**, that is for the phonemes of the language to line themselves up in neat rows and columns. Of course, speakers don't consciously arrange their phonemes in phoneme charts, they just produce them in words, but it *is* the case that when we place the phonemes of languages on phonetically motivated charts, they overwhelmingly converge on the familiar kind of chart with points of articulation across the top, and manners along the side, with there tending to be stops, fricatives, voiced and voiceless sounds all appearing in the same place column. In addition, there is a strong tendency to find at least three points of articulation, roughly labial, coronal and velar. If there are more there are always at least this minimum. For example, no language has labial, labiodental and dental as the sole set of places – there are no languages with the following stop phoneme set:

(11)  p pf θ
      b bv ð

These general tendencies were first explored in depth in a classic book by Jakobson (1968), where he examined ways in which children acquired the set of sounds in their language, the ways in which language was impaired in patients experiencing aphasia.[7] He noted that the order in which children seemed to acquire sounds mirrored the relative frequency in which one can find sounds in the languages of the world. Thus, [θ] is quite rare around the world, and is very difficult for English-speaking children to acquire. Similarly, [y] is relatively rare, and French-speaking children learn to produce it after they have mastered [i] and [u]. Jakobson believed that there was a hierarchy of difficulty among sounds, and that the inventories of the languages of the world reflected that hierarchy.

Since that time,[8] phonologists basing their research on his pioneering efforts, have developed the concept of **implicational laws**. For instance, if a language has ejective stops it has plain stops, and if a language has back unrounded vowels it strongly tends to have rounded vowels.[9]

---

7. Aphasia is the language deficit produced by specific kinds of damage to the brain. Some of these kinds of damage produce phonological disorders.

8. The date of the English translation of his book does not reflect the fact that he wrote it during the Second World War, and that he lectured to Harvard and MIT linguistics departments on these issues extensively during the fifties on through the seventies, which accounts for the pervasiveness of his ideas throughout the latter half of this century.

9. A surprising counterexample to this claim is the set of lax vowels in Midwest American English. Here we find [ɯ] in place of [ʊ] (good is pronounced [gɯd]), [ɤ] (somewhat backed – think

The reasons for these tendencies are varied and complex, although some have argued for a single dimension that would describe (and perhaps account for) the facts. The original proposal for a dimension came from the same Prague School linguists who were originally headed by, among other people, Jakobson. The Prague School linguists thought that whenever we find a pair of sounds, one of which is easier, or more common than the other, the 'harder' sound tends to have one more characteristic, or **feature** than the other. For example, languages with voiced stops always have voiceless ones too. The suggestion is, then, that voicing is an *extra* feature, or **mark**, and the voiced stop is **marked** compared to the **unmarked** one. Similarly, front rounded vowels are marked relative to front unrounded ones, and the rounding is the **mark**. In general, the extra feature is the marked feature, and the sound with the extra feature is marked, the one lacking that feature being unmarked.

This terminology has evolved from this somewhat technical sense to a much broader one in which marked characteristics in language are the unusual, special or rare, relative to the unmarked ones. In fact, the terms are often used outside of phonology proper to mean anything expected (or unexpected) in some setting. A classic illustration is dress. At a formal party, wearing a tuxedo or evening gown is unmarked, but wearing SCUBA gear is highly marked. Note that these definitions are contextual. On a diving boat over a tropical reef, cummerbunds and stiletto heels are marked, bathing suits and diving masks are unmarked. Analogously, for stops, voicing is marked – voiced stops are harder to acquire and rarer around the world (although only slightly so). However, for nasals, voicing is unmarked – *voiceless* nasals are very rare, and acquired very late by children speaking languages that contain them, while almost every language in the world has voiced nasals, and no language has voiceless nasals without also having voiced ones.

Markedness is often connected with **naturalness**. In this book, naturalness will be used to refer to processes, which will be discussed in the next chapter. Essentially, the ways in which sounds adapt to their environment are more or less **natural**, to the extent that they are phonetically motivated, a concept that will be explored later.

Markedness is also related to the concept of **prototypicality**. Recall the discussion of this concept in Chapter I. Just as there are better and worse birds, there seem to be better and worse vowels and consonants. Phonologists working within this paradigm believe that once we understand the function of phonemes, we can see why some fulfill that function better than others. We would anticipate that some sounds make better *language* sounds than others.

In order to understand this we need to have some conception of the function of phonemes in the first place. This is a question we have sidestepped up till now, but in order to understand why languages make use of the sounds that they do we need to think about what sounds are for in the first place.

---

of the country-western singer's pronunciation of *love*) and [ɑ] in place of [ɔ] – in Chicago often actually [a].

Speech (at least from the purely phonetic standpoint) has a number of functions, all related to the concept of communication.[10] Speech must be audible, and must contain enough distinctions to encode all the possible words of the language, preferably with a minimum of confusion. But in addition, speech must be produced by our vocal tracts.[11] Our vocal tracts consist of more and less easily movable parts, one of which, the jaw, has a natural periodicity of movement which makes itself felt in other oral activities, such as sucking and chewing. In addition, the entire body has a natural rhythm, which can be experienced just by asking people to tap their feet. That these motions are connected can be seen by asking people to tap their feet and to sing along. It is virtually impossible to sing at a different rhythm from that which we are tapping with our feet or fingers.

Speech is simply built on top of this natural rhythm, with phonological feet[12] corresponding to the rhythmic beats that we get with foot tapping (or hand clapping). Consequently we find speech designed to produce ideal beats. If we assume, for a moment, that each beat corresponds to a syllable (the situation is somewhat more complex, but we will make this simplifying assumption here), we should ask what makes a good beat. It should have an abrupt onset and a slow decay. That is, its shape should be roughly:

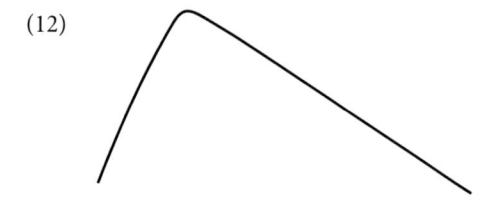

(12)

The loudest point of the beat should come immediately after the sharp onset, and the sound should die away slowly in time for the next beat. Implementing this in speech sounds we would expect to find short, sharp-sounding consonants immediately followed by vowels, which are the loudest sounds. Consequently, a prototypical syllable should be a simple CV syllable (see chapter IV for more discussion). Since in voiced consonants the voicing merges with the voicing for the vowel, we would expect that voiceless consonants make better consonants – that is, demarcators of each beat.

However, making rhythmic sounds is not the sole function of speech. Speech, of course, has a crucial semantic function, and the semantic function is fulfilled by having enough *different* consonants and vowels to encode all the words in the language differently. This can be accomplished, of course, either by having lots of different consonants and vowels or by having long words and fewer distinct segments. Each alternative has advantages

---

10. There are undoubtedly other functions of speech, such as the encoding of thought, but these are not relevant to the nature of phonology itself.

11. There are undoubtedly analogous principles for Signed Languages, but I have no expertise in those areas, and will leave the relevant discussion to others.

12. The concept of **foot** is introduced in the next chapter.

and disadvantages. Having lots of consonants allows for short words, but requires fairly great precision in making each consonant, since similar consonants could potentially be confused with one another. If a language, for example, has voiced, voiceless, ejective, implosive, unaspirated and aspirated coronal stops, any ambient noise could make it harder to hear the difference between them. Similarly, languages tend to avoid having very similar points of articulation (few languages contrast dental and alveolar stops, for example).

On the other hand, people are in a hurry, and tend to be lazy, and long words are an annoyance. It has long been known that short words are more efficient (an old principle called Zipf's law shows that there is an inverse relationship between word length and frequency – frequent words are shorter). Thus languages have an incentive to use lots of different consonants and vowels, since then words can be shorter.

Clearly, the design of any particular language will be a balancing act,[13] but we now can understand why syllables consist, minimally, of CV, and why languages need differences among consonants and vowels.

Given the need for difference, we can then look to articulatory and acoustic facts to account for what constitutes being different. Presumably we want sounds to be maximally different from each other, but not so different that they require complex articulatory gyrations to be made 'on the fly', while trying to warn someone about the approaching tiger. Recent research by Stevens (1989, Stevens & Keyser 1989) suggests that there are significant regions in the mouth where small differences in articulator placement are relatively inaudible, and other places where a small movement makes a big acoustic difference. These architectural facts about vocal tract acoustics add up to the fact that the primary points of articulation tend to be bilabial, coronal (either dental or alveolar) and velar (and not, say palatal or uvular). Hence, no language in the world lacks consonants made at each of these three places.[14]

Similarly, vowels are louder (and hence more audible) the more open the mouth, which leads us to expect that every language will have an open, unrounded vowel [a]. Furthermore, the formant pattern of an [a], with a high $F_1$ and a mid-level $F_2$ is therefore maximally different from two other possibilities – low $F_1$ with high $F_2$ (the high front vowel /i/) and low $F_1$ and low $F_2$ (the high back rounded vowel /u/). Thus the maximally distinct vowels are:

(13)   i       u
          a

---

**13.** Just to forestall any possible misunderstandings, it is clear that languages are not *designed* in any case, but inherited from the parents of the current speakers. But all languages are subjected to the constraints being discussed, which limit and channel all possible sound changes in the directions being discussed. The fact that these changes lead in different directions explains why languages do not all sound the same, and will be considered extensively in chapter 7.

**14.** Hawai'ian lacks an alveolar *stop*, but has an /l/ and an /n/.

with an additional possibility being two additional vowels with intermediate values for the first two formants, yielding what is well known to be the most popular vowel system

(14)   i       u
       e       o
            a

Now it is certainly the case that there are vowel systems throughout the world that do not conform to this general triangular pattern, and there are similarly some very oddly shaped consonant patterns, but the vast majority of the phoneme systems of the world conform to the general principles that I have been discussing – the vowels prefer to hug the outside of the vowel triangle, and the consonants cluster around the three major points of articulation, coming in pairs (either of voicing or of some other glottal involvement such as ejectives or implosives). The stops and fricatives generally line up vertically as well, although a language may have more stops than fricatives (some languages actually have no fricatives at all) or more fricatives than stops:

(15)   Nauruan (Micronesian/Austronesian)
       p    $p^w$    t    k    $k^w$
       b    $b^w$    d    g    $g^w$
       m    $m^w$    n    ŋ    $ŋ^w$
       m:   $m:^w$   n:   ŋ:   $ŋ^w$:
            r  ř  j  w

(16)   English
       p    t         k
       b    d         g
            č
            ǰ
       f  θ  s  ʃ
       v  ð  z  ʒ
       m    n         ŋ
            r  l  j  w

Again, as with stops, there are never more voiced fricatives than voiceless ones.

It is not possible to give absolute threshholds on size of phoneme inventories. The smallest known inventory is that of Rotokas, a Papuan language (Ladefoged & Maddieson 1996: 367):

(17)   p    t    k
       β    ɾ    g
       i         u
       e         o

On the other hand, there are languages with huge inventories. For example, a famous example is Kabardian (a Caucasian language spoken in Russia, Turkey and Israel) (Maddieson):

(18) Kabardian consonant inventory (from Colarusso 1992: 44) (North Caucasian, Russia)

| Labial | Alveolar | Alveo-Palatal | Lateral | Palato-Alveolar | Palatal | Velar | Uvular | Pharyngeal |
|---|---|---|---|---|---|---|---|---|
| p | t |  |  |  | c | kʷ | q qʷ |  |
| b | d |  |  |  | ɟ | gʷ |  |  |
| p' | t' |  |  |  | c' | k'ʷ | q' q'ʷ |  |
| f | s | ҫ | ɬ | ʃ | ç | xʷ | χ χʷ | ħ |
| v | z |  | ɮ | ʒ | ʝ |  | ʁ ʁʷ | ʕ |
| f' |  |  | ɬ' | ʃ' |  |  |  |  |
| m | n |  |  |  |  |  |  |  |
| w | r |  |  |  | j |  |  |  |

Here are some words in Kabardian (Colarusso 1992: 44):

(19) [qɛpˈɬaʁʷʁʷaːs] 'You saw him'
 [səqˈqʼɛbdokˈʷkˈʷɛns] 'I shall go with you (some time)'

Another example is Thompson, also called Ntlakapmxw, a Salish language of British Columbia, Canada:

(20) p'  t'  tɬ      tʃ'  k'  k'ʷ       q'ʷ
 p   t        ts   tʃ   k   kʷ   q   qʷ   ʔ
                ɬ    s    ʃ    ç   xʷ   χ   χʷ   h
 m   n   l   z   j   ɣ   w   ʕ   ʕʷ
 m'  n'  l'  z'  j'  ɣ'  w'  ʕ'  ʕ'ʷ

Here are some sample words in Thompson ([ntɬakapmxʷ]):

(21) [kəɬqintijxs] 'they take the top off it'
 [səlketetuze] 'you people turn him around' (source: unpublished class notes from Larry Thompson)

Again, because these principles are shaping *tendencies*, rather than absolute constraints, we find that languages overall have a moderate number of consonants and vowels, with extremes at either end. Since prototypicality effects show up everywhere else in language, we should not be surprised to find them in the shape of phoneme systems either.

Sometimes we can let the fact that phoneme inventories come in regular rows and columns influence our decision about how to treat a sound. For example, French has dental stops [t̪ d̪ n̪ l̪], but alveolar fricatives [s, z]. A narrow phonetic chart would put them in different columns, but a phonemic chart would assign them to the same column, calling them something more neutral, such as 'Coronal'. A similar decision will put French palato-alveolar [ʃ, ʒ] in the same column as palatal [ɲ], especially since no language distinguishes between palato-alveolar and palatal nasals (in fact, there isn't even an IPA symbol for a palato-alveolar nasal). From a cognitive point of view we can assume that there are basic phonetic feature types (such as palatal), but that for articulatory or acoustic reasons some manners of articulation are 'better' at one subdivision within that type, while others are better elsewhere. Thus many languages have palatal nasals but few have palatal fricatives, and similarly, many have palato-alveolar fricatives, but there are no palato-alveolar stops. However, there are palatal stops. On the other hand, there are palato-alveolar *affricates*, [tʃ, dʒ] in many languages. Recent phonetic research has shown that making contact with the tongue at the palato-alveolar area and releasing it instantaneously (that is, making a stop) is quite difficult, and this problem can be solved either by shifting the stop further back, to the palatal region (i.e. [c, ɟ]) or by delaying the release (i.e. [ tʃ, dʒ], or perhaps more accurately [č, ǰ]. As with many other cases we have seen and will see, an idealized target will be adjusted to fit the exigencies of the vocal tract or be enhanced to provide a better acoustic signal.

Overall, then we can argue that the phoneme systems of the world reflect language-specific compromises among a number of conflicting demands. There must be enough different sounds to permit all the words of the language to be distinguished, but those sounds must be pronounceable in real time (and so be relatively easy to articulate). They must be audible against a background of noise, and easily segmentable (that is, must be discernable within the general speech stream).

None of these requirements is consciously or overtly taken into account, as I mentioned above. Speakers just speak what their parents speak, and continue to try to match the way that people around them speak, but with all the conflicting pressures (including pressures of both conformity and individuality – see Keller (1994) for extensive discussion). But the overall result is a set of preference structures such that some sounds are most 'popular', while others are very rare. In a sense, phoneme *systems* also have a prototype structure, such that there are more or less prototypical sets of vowels or consonants.

## 3.4 Phoneme discovery exercises

In each of the following sets of data there are words in a phonetic transcription. The exercise begins with the word 'focus', meaning that you should consider the sounds in the list and attempt to determine whether they are allophones of one (or, in some cases, more than one phoneme) You should follow the method outlined in the chapter. These exercises are taken from Whitley (1978).

(22)  Italian (Romance language spoken in Italy and elsewhere)

Focus: [n], [ŋ] (accents = stress)

| néro | 'black' | njénte | 'nothing' | dipíndʒere | 'depict' |
|---|---|---|---|---|---|
| sapóne | 'soap' | úŋgja | 'claw' | língwa | 'language' |
| bjáŋka | 'white' | ónda | 'wave' | téŋgo | 'I have' |
| tornáre | 'return' | stáŋko | 'tired' | lúŋgo | 'long' |
| dʒɛnte | 'people' | invɛ́rno | 'winter' | fíne | 'end' |
| nɔnno | 'grandfather' | dántsa | 'dance' | frantʃéze | 'French' |
| áŋke | 'also' | fáŋgo | 'mud' | kwantúŋkwe | 'although' |

I will guide you through the answer to the Italian problem. Begin by making two columns of words, one with all the words containing an [n], the other with all the words containing an [ŋ]. If you have graph paper (or want to try using a spreadsheet) line the words up so that all the [n]'s are directly above one another and similarly all the [ŋ]'s.

Once you have done this, simply look for commonalities, either to the left or to the right. In this case you should see immediately that the [ŋ] only occurs before velar consonants, while the [n] never does.

Write up your answer in a formal manner following this format:

[ŋ] occurs only when followed by velar consonants /k/ and /g/: [fáŋgo], [stáŋko]
[n] is never followed by velars, but only by vowels [nɔnno] or alveolar consonants: [dántsa]
[n] and [ŋ] are both nasal consonants differing only in point of articulation.
Therefore they could constitute a single phoneme, /n/.

Formal Description:
/n/ has two allophones:

[ŋ] before velar consonants
[n] elsewhere.

Important Points:
Be careful to distinguish between square brackets for unclassified sounds and allophones, reserving slant brackets solely for phonemes
Test your hypothesis against a few words after you are finished.
In reporting the solution in a formal description, be sure to put the 'elsewhere' condition last:

condition 1
condition 2
condition 3
…
elsewhere

Don't include all the data in your answer (particularly, don't include any graph paper solutions), but do give a couple of examples to illustrate each condition.

(23)   **Daga (New Guinea)**

Focus: [s], [t]

| jamosivin | 'I am licking' | urase | 'hole' | topen | 'hit' |
| jamotain | 'they will lick' | sinao | 'drum' | use | 'there' |
| asi | 'grunt' | wagat | 'holiday' | tave | 'old' |
| anet | 'we should go' | simura | 'whisper' | siuran | 'salt' |
| senao | 'shout' | otu | 'little' | tuian | 'I kill' |

(24) **Russian** (Slavic language spoken throughout Russia)

Focus: [i], [ɨ] (accents = stress)

| sudʲítʲ | 'judge' | ptʲítsɨ | 'bird' | ílʲi | 'or' |
| ískra | 'spark' | mɨlʲi | 'they washed' | lʲáktʲi | 'lie down' |
| bɨtʲ | 'be' | vɨsókə | 'high' | ʒɨná | 'wife' |
| sitɨ | 'sated' | sudí | 'courts' | kʲinó | 'movie house' |
| jidá | 'food' | rʲiʃitó | 'sieve' | nɨl | 'moaned' |
| xʲimʲík | 'chemist' | bʲítʲ | 'beat' | sʲílʲnə | 'strongly' |

(25) **Papago** (Uto-Aztecan, now known as Tohono O'odham)

Focus: [t], [d], [tʃ], [dʒ] (consider the latter two single sounds, č and ǰ)
also: voiceless nasals and vowels

| dʒihsk | 'aunt' | daʔiwuhʃ | 'run outside' | huɯtahsptʃu̥ | 'make it 5' |
| dɔʔaʔk | 'mountain' | dʒuɯuhkɔh | 'remove hair' | âaʔdʒiwih | 'swim' |
| tʃuːli̥ | 'corner' | ʔahidaʔk | 'year' | dʒuːʔw̥ | 'rabbits' |
| tʃuâaʔgi | 'clouds' | dɔhaʔihtʃuhk | 'will be anything' | huɯdʒuli̥ | 'self' |
| âahtʃum̥ | 'drown, dive' | tʃuhti̥ | 'name' | stɔḁ | 'white' |
| taht | 'foot' | dʒumali̥ | 'low' | tʃihkpan̥ | 'work' |
| ʔiːdḁ | 'this' | tɔnɔm̥ | 'be thirst' | stahtɔnɔmːah | 'thirsty times' |
| muɯduɯdam̥ | 'runner' | ntɔçi̥ | 'I'll go' | piwuɯhɔ̥ | 'not true' |

(26) **Zulu** (Niger-Congo, spoken widely in South Africa)

Focus: [e], [ɛ]; [o], [ɔ]. Analysis should be valid regardless of stress. Try to find a single rule/generalization for all cases. For a hint, look at the footnote.[15] (Phonemic tone is omitted, and accents = stress)

| àɓelúːsi | 'herdsman' | bɔ́ːna | 'see' | ɛ̀nduɛléːni | 'in the path' |
| lóːlu | 'this' | isíːmɔ | 'shape' | ɫàbɛléːla | 'sing' |
| uː\|éːzu | 'slice' | ɛláːkʰɛ | 'his' | ùmlɔ́ːmo | 'mouth' |
| iɲóːni | 'bird' | ‖éda | 'finish' | iːt'wéːt'wɛ | 'apprehension' |
| ezíːɲɛ | 'others' | iːɓéːlɔ | 'pasture' | boɲ\|úːla | 'pull out of mud' |
| \|oɓíːsa | 'worry' | \|ɔ́ːla | 'relate' | nɛŋ‖ɔ́ːla | 'and the wagon' |

---

15. Sometimes assimilation operates at a greater distance than just one segment away.

# Chapter 4

# Syllables, feet, words
## Phonological constructions

4.1 Groups of sounds
4.2 The internal structure of the syllable
4.3 The sonority hierarchy
4.4 Between syllables
4.5 Feet
4.6 The word as a unit
4.7 Exercises

## 4.1 Groups of sounds

The fact that sounds do not come out of our mouths one segment at a time has been known for a long time. In fact, many people have argued that segments per se actually only exist as abstractions, because it appears that the smallest piece of sound we can comfortably produce is larger than a single segment. If you think about it, when you try to say a consonant, and particularly a stop, you are most likely to say [tʰə] or [gə], and it's really very hard to say [g] in isolation.

Furthermore, although the Roman alphabet (which is the basis for most writing systems in the world) expresses segments directly, many other writing systems don't, but instead express units consisting of (at least) a consonant and a vowel together, and may also include a following consonant. In the Japanese syllabaries *hiragana* and *katakana*, and the Sanskrit and other writing systems based on the Brahmi script each symbol stands for a consonant and vowel in an indissoluble unit.

The term used to describe this suprasegmental unit is the well-known term **syllable**. There has been an enormous controversy about the status of this unit, with opinions varying between those, on the one hand, who argued that it was an unnecessary addition to the inventory of linguistic units (this was most strongly argued for in Chomsky & Halle

(1968), but other American Structuralists also felt this way) and others, on the other hand, who have argued that segments are inventions of linguists spoiled by the unnatural Roman writing system, and that syllables are the smallest real linguistic units.

One of the problems with the concept of the syllable is that it is not a purely physical entity (like a vowel or a consonant), in the sense that it does not correspond to any single physical gesture of the articulators, nor to any single stretch of sound. This has led phoneticians to be skeptical of its existence~ – one cannot see syllables in a spectrogram, nor in a waveform. Similarly, syllables do not appear in x-ray films of people speaking. Of course, for cognitive linguists (and in fact, for most linguists of any stripe) language is not a physical event in any case but a cognitive one, so that the inability to define a purely physical unit like the syllable is not a drawback.

Normally the easiest part of thinking about syllables is recognizing them in words. If we take a word like *anthropology* we can easily see that it has five syllables, and when we learn to spell (at least in English) we learn how to divide the word into syllables: *an-thro-po-lo-gy*. Of course, things are rarely that simple. The syllable division rules that we learned in school were *orthographic* rules – rules for dividing the spelling of words. For example, we divide *sitting* as *sit-ting*, but, of course, there aren't two phonetic /t/'s in the word, only two spelled ⟨t⟩'s. One of the facts that we find about syllables is that while we often know how many syllables there are in the word, and can say the word syllable by syllable, we find some difficulty in saying exactly where one syllable ends and the other begins. Try saying *satire* one syllable at a time and you will happily say [sæ.tʰaɪr].[1] On the other hand, if you divide our earlier example *sitting* you might be less comfortable with [sɪ.tʰɪŋ]. Perhaps you said [sɪt.tʰɪŋ], with a double [t], reflecting the spelling, curiously enough. But of course neither pronunciation reflects the undivided pronunciation of the word, which is without any kind of [t]: [sɪɾɪŋ]. The problem is that we can't say either [*sɪɾ.ɪŋ] or [*sɪ.ɾɪŋ]. So where does the syllable divide? Later we'll see that both before and after as well as in the middle of the flap have been proposed as answers to the question.

Most linguists argue that syllables are *organizational* units of sound. That means that they unite individual segments into constituents, much the same way as words are organized into phrases, and phrases into clauses and so on. Thus, it is argued, syllables have a hierarchical structure. This organizing principle recurs not only in syntax (where clauses are made up of phrases which are made up of words) but also in morphology, where words are made up of suffixes and prefixes: *deny* (a verb) suffixed with *-able* makes a new adjective, and then *-ity* can be added to make a new noun out of the new adjective: *deniability*.

The traditional pieces of the syllable are the **onset** and the **rhyme** (sometimes spelled **rime**). The onset consists of every segment up to but not including the vowel, while the rhyme includes the rest of the syllable. The term rhyme is, of course, familiar from poetry,

---

1. The period is normally used to divide syllables. Other symbols that are found in the literature are the dollar sign $, and more complex notations representing tree structure. We will discuss these below.

where it refers to the fact that ends of lines must have the same **rhyme** (in the technical syllable sense – recall that we talked about this in Chapter III on Phonemes):

(1)  Hickory dickory d**ock**
     The mouse ran up the cl**ock**

Notice that it is only the vowel plus all following segments that must match – what precedes is irrelevant.

The rhyme is divided into the **nucleus** and the **coda**. In the most simple terms, the nucleus is the vowel and the remaining consonants are the coda. In the above example, the nucleus is /ɑ²/, the coda is /k/. What complicates the matter in English is that both the nucleus and the coda can be rather more complex (as can, for that matter, the onset). In a word like *tasks* there are three consonants in the coda, and in **sixths** there are four: [ksθs]. English, incidentally, is relatively unusual in permitting so many consonants in the coda. Four is near the top permitted in the languages of the world, and in fact, in many languages the limit is zero. A well-known language that has such a limit is Hawai'ian. If you think of Hawai'ian words (you probably know half a dozen) you will notice that every consonant is followed by a vowel:

(2)  Ho.no.lu.lu
     Ha.le.a.ka.la
     Ki.la.u.e.a
     Ma.u.na Ke.a

We can classify the phonology of languages with respect to exactly what they allow in their codas, with languages like Hawai'ian representing one extreme (zero consonants in the coda), and languages like English (up to four) representing the other extreme. Other languages appear part way along this continuum. One interesting set of restrictions is not on the number but on the *kind* of consonant permitted in the coda. For example, in Japanese, there can be one consonant in the coda, but there are heavy restrictions on what that consonant can be. It can be either a nasal (*Hon.da, Shim.bun*) or a consonant identical to the consonant following: *tep.pan, Nip.pon, gak.kai*. No other consonants are permitted in the coda. Mandarin permits only nasals /n/ and /ŋ/, and in some dialects, /r/.

In general, languages make no restrictions on what can occur in nuclei, except that it should be a vowel. Two vowels in a nucleus constitute one definition of a diphthong, although defining a diphthong this way doesn't distinguish between rising and falling diphthongs (the /ju/ in *cute* vs the /aɪ/ in *bite*). The one complication involving nuclei involves whether things other than vowels can occur in the nucleus. In some languages, such as English and German, nasals can occupy the nucleus in unstressed syllables:[3] *hidden* [hɪdn̩], German *geben* [gebm̩]. In other languages the restriction is not quite so strict.

---

2.  Depending on your native dialect or language, you may have a different vowel in this word, of course.

3.  Under such a circumstance the consonant is said to be **syllabic**, and, as you recall, is marked in IPA with small vertical stroke under the consonant: l̩, s̩ etc.

In Czech /r/ can be a stressed nucleus: the city of *Brno* [ˈbr̩no]. A language that has been the subject of much recent inquiry is Imdlawn Tashlhiyt Berber (spoken in North Africa) where apparently *any* consonant can be the nucleus of a syllable. Some famous examples are /txznt/ meaning 'you stored', which is syllabified [tx̩.zn̩t] and /tftkt/ ('you suffered a strain'), which comes out [tf̩.tk̩t] (Prince & Smolensky 1994). This is, of course, a highly unusual case – languages greatly prefer relatively open segments to count as the center of syllables.

As I mentioned above, a common assumption is that the parts of a syllable have a hierarchical structure:

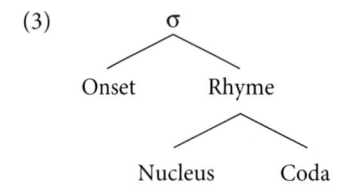

(3)
```
            σ
           / \
        Onset Rhyme
              / \
          Nucleus Coda
```

The reasons for this assumption include the fact that many languages have rhyme (in the poetic sense) as a linguistic device. Other languages have alliteration, which involves identity among Onsets. Old English was famous for this device. In any line of Old English poetry there had to be at least two stressed words with the same onset in one of their syllables (one in each half of the line):

(4)    Stræt wæs stanfah, stig wisode[4]
       gúmum ætgædere. Gúðbyrne scan[5]

However, there doesn't seem to be any language whose poetry requires identity between words which are identical in Onset+Nucleus while ignoring the coda.

In addition, there are many cases in languages where there are restrictions between the nucleus and the coda. For example, in English /ŋ/ forbids a preceding tense[6] vowel: [*iŋ, *eŋ] etc. However, onsets normally do not set restrictions on what follows – any consonant in English can be followed by any vowel. There are a few exceptions, all involving what appear to be some kind of constraint on too many identical segments.[7] For example,

---

4. The rules for complex onsets were somewhat variable. Sometimes the whole onset had to be identical, and for other poets the alliteration was solely with the /s/.

5. The road was stone-bright, the road led on the gathered men, warhelmets shone.

6. The concept of 'tenseness' was discussed in chapter 2.

7. This constraint, which has been extensively investigated within the framework of analysis called autosegmental phonology, is referred to as the obligatory contour principle (OCP).

a number of languages seem to resist the sequence /ji/ or /wu/ (although English permits both: *ye, woo*).

## 4.2 The internal structure of the syllable

One of the main reasons for arguing that we need a syllable as a linguistic unit is that many phonological patterns appear to pay attention to syllable structure. For example, it is simplest to describe the operation of aspiration in English by making it sensitive to syllable structure. Consider the following data

(5)  pie      pʰaɪ         spy        spaɪ
     pacific  pʰə.ˈsɪ.fɪk  specific   spə.ˈsɪ.fɪk
     appear   ə.pʰir       aspire     ə.spaɪr

Note that whether the /p/ begins an accented or unaccented syllable, as long as it is at the beginning of the onset it is aspirated. If something else precedes it (and, of course, that something could only be an /s/) in the onset it is unaspirated.

Similarly, in German, obstruents are devoiced syllable-finally:

(6)  abgehen      ˈap.ge.ən       'walk away'
     wegfahren    ˈvɛk.fɑr.ən     'drive away'
     Burgmeister  ˈbʊrk.mai.stər  'mayor'

One additional issue that has been extensively discussed in the phonological literature deals with how many consonants are permitted to occur in onsets and codas. We have already seen the limiting case above – none, along with the fact that many languages permit only limited kinds of (single) consonants in codas. Every language permits at least one consonant in onsets. In fact, there are languages which forbid empty onsets – Arabic requires that every syllable begin with a consonant, although some have argued that syllable initial glottal stop is simply an empty consonant fulfilling the function of being an onset.

## 4.3 The sonority hierarchy

More interesting is the question of the *maximum* number of consonants permitted in onsets and codas and how they may be arranged. We have seen that many languages permit only one, and may even restrict what kind of consonant may occur, especially in codas. But some languages do permit multiple consonants in onsets and codas, and there appear to be fairly strict requirements on what kinds, and in what order they may occur.

If we begin with a language which has a fairly simple set of possibilities, we can note that French never permits more than two. Here is a representative sample of French words, with phonemic transcriptions:

(7) psychiatre   psikjatʁ   psychiatrist
    pneu        pnø        tire
    pleut       plø        rains
    preuve      pʁøv       proof
    pois⁸       pwa        pea
    *           *fs-
    FNAC        fnak       acronym for discount department store
    fleuve      fløv       river
    frère       fʁɛʁ       brother
    fois        fwa        time
    *           *ls-
    *           *ln-
    *           *lr-
    loi         lwa        law
    *           *rs-
    *           *rn-
    *           *rl-
    roi         rwa        king
    *           *ns-
    *           *nl-
    *           *nr-
    noix        nw-        nut

As you could probably tell, I have carefully massaged the data to help you see a pattern. In particular, I have set the data out in groups based on the kind of consonant that comes first, followed by the kind of consonant that comes second. You can first note that we began with initial stops, then moved to initial fricatives, then initial liquids, and finally, initial nasals. This ranking of first members of initial consonant clusters (**glides** > **liquids** > **nasals** > **fricatives** > **stops**) is known as the sonority hierarchy, and recurs in a number of places in principles of grammatical organization. Relative to this, notice that I didn't even bother to give examples with the initial segments reversed (for example, there are no examples like *rp-, *lf-) This is because they are all resolutely impossible. French (and, as we will see, most other languages) wants sonority to increase within an onset. Syllables are preferably sonority hills, with the sonority increasing from the beginning in the onset, peaking at the nucleus and decreasing towards the coda. Recall the diagram of an off-center hill above showing an ideal beat.

If you think about comparable words in English (or German, if you know some German) you will realize that this generalization holds for all those languages – in onsets, sonority must increase. Furthermore, the *slope* of the increase is subject to some fairly strong

---

8. This case, and more complex ones, such as *trois* /tʁwa/ raise the crucial question of how French syllables are organized. Specifically, is /wa/ a sequence of onset glide+nucleus or is it a complex rising diphthong? We will leave this question till later.

constraints in most languages. That is, the difference between the sonority of the first and the second consonant must be fairly great. So we have stops plus liquids, or glides, but stop plus fricative (ps-) is unacceptable in English (although French, as we can see, has less restrictive rules).

You have probably already noticed that there is one fairly serious exception to this generalization: /s/. Both French and English have lots of words where /s/ is *followed* by a consonant of lower sonority: French *sport, schizophrène, station* begin with sp-, sk- and st- respectively. Similarly, German permits /ʃ/ to combine with initial stops and liquids: *Schlange, Schmuck,* [ʃlaŋə] 'snake', [ʃmʊk] 'jewelry'.

There doesn't seem to be any good explanation for this exceptional treatment of /s/ (or, in German, /ʃ/), but the fact that it recurs in lots of languages suggests that we just haven't yet found the reason. Suffice it to say that this is an area that needs more research.

We have only been looking at two-consonant clusters so far. Look what happens if we look at three-consonant clusters. If you make a list of all the possibilities in English, you find the following[9]

(8) spl-
spr-
str-
skl-
skr-

By now, you should be able to see something quite general here – what is allowed after the /s/ is exactly what is allowed in two consonant clusters (other than those already containing an /s/). What this means is that we don't in general have to allow for three consonant clusters in English (or French, or German), but instead have a general rule for *two*-consonant clusters, but permit an /s/ to be preposed to any onset. Since, in general, onsets are limited to two positions, this will permit a maximum of three consonants, but only if the first one is an /s/.

Interestingly enough, the peculiar and somewhat exceptional nature of /s+C/ clusters appears in other languages as well. For example, in Spanish, clusters like /kl-/ and /pr-/ are permitted, but /sC-/ clusters are forbidden. When speakers attempt to pronounce words with such clusters, they 'fix' them by inserting an initial /e/, thereby making the /s/ the coda of an initial syllable, and eliminating the problem:

(9) Snoopy → /es.nu.pi/

This 'solution' is an old one, one that the language apparently went through with all its words several hundred years ago. Notice that there are native Spanish words such as

---

**9.** There is a controversy here that I am avoiding by not including *skew* and *squeeze*, which have [skj-] and [skw-] respectively, because not all linguists agree that the glides are actually *in* the onset. This certainly seems to be true for the [ju] pairing, which seems to be a unit phoneme. The [w] is less clear.

(10) España /es.pa.ɲa/ 'Spain'
escuela /es.kwe.la/ 'school'

We know that these words derive from Latin words with /sp-/ and /sk-/ clusters, so presumably at some point in the history of the Spanish language the speakers began feeling the need to resyllabify these words without the (now illegal) /sC-/ clusters. Every word in the language that had that configuration was modified, and this constraint remains in the language, so strongly in fact that it applies even when Spanish speakers attempt to speak English or other languages that do not have the constraint. The result, as we have seen, is the addition of /e/'s to any word.

Similar 'solutions' have been adopted by speakers of various dialects of Arabic, which has the same constraint. A nice discussion of how these differences affect these Arabic dialects English can be found in Broselow (1983, 1992). Speakers of Japanese, who have a much stricter constraint on syllable structure, use a different 'repair strategy'.[10] In that language (and in many others like it) there can be no consonants at the end of syllables at all (there is actually a special exception to this, but we will ignore it for now). In Japanese, vowels are inserted after every consonant that is followed by another consonant (or that occurs at the end of a word. Thus, when Japanese borrows the word 'strike' it 'repairs' it by inserting vowels after the /s/, the /t/ and the /k/

(11) sutoraiku 'strike' (baseball)
sutoraiki 'strike' (labor dispute)[11]

Just as there are restrictions on the onsets of syllables, there are restrictions on the coda of a syllable as well. The simplest kind of restriction is not to permit one at all. Many languages have exactly this structure, where all syllables are said to be **open**. An open syllable is one without a coda. All Hawaiʻian words, for example, consist simply of a consonant and a vowel:

(12) ka.la.ni.ʔa.na.ʔo.le 'name of a highway on Oʻahu'

---

10. The term 'repair strategy' is used by phonologists like Carole Paradis in a more general sense to describe what happens when the language, for whatever reason, finds a sequence of segments that cannot be made into a legal syllable. In her work she argues that not only borrowing words from other languages, but even assembling new words by adding suffixes and prefixes may trigger repair strategies. We will look at this idea when we get to the morphophonemics section of the book.

11. These words raise many other interesting questions about how languages treat loan words. The choice of different final vowels connected with a semantic contrast lacking in the donor language may be purely arbitrary. Otherwise Japanese normally inserts /u/ as its epenthetic vowel. The use of /o/ after the /t/ has a separate motivation. The phoneme /t/ has an affricated allophone [ts] before /u/, and the use of /u/ would have produced something like [sutsuraiki], which seems to be too far from the source word. More could be said about why /u/ is the most common epenthetic vowel, with /i/ coming next and /o/ available for use after /t/, but this footnote is already too long.

Again, repair strategies will be brought into effect if a word with a consonantal coda is borrowed into the language. The name *Bill* has been borrowed, and comes out /pila/, since no syllable may end in a consonant.

The simplest situation is one where there are no codas at all, but many languages permit a single consonant in the coda. Most Western Austronesian languages permit any consonant to end a syllable, but permit only one at a time. Malay, for example, has words like *tidak, boleh, rumus, kalang* [kalaŋ]. Other languages, however, have stronger restrictions on codas. Spanish, for example, permits only coronal consonants /s,d,l,r,n,θ[12]/ but not /t/: *dos, verdad, arból, tener, tambien, paz*. Even stronger restrictions are common. Many languages permit only sonorants, or even only nasals.

Another commonly-found restriction on codas is slightly different in nature. Italian and Japanese, for example, permit virtually any consonant in a coda, *but only if it is identical to the consonant in the following onset*. Thus Italian has words like *fat.to, non.na*, and Japanese has words like *ip.pon, kat.ta*, but not words with non-identical consonants (no *\*fak.to, \*kaw.ta*[13]).

English, of course, is one of the more liberal languages with respect to codas. We can find not only one, but two-consonant clusters: *task, rest, tax, ellipse, burp, tank*. Again, as with onsets, there seem to be principles governing the possibilities. If we exclude combinations containing /s/ (again!), we find a familiar-looking set:

(13) lift
lump link, cant
curt, curve, darn, Carl
ilk, elf, elm

If you pause to think about the pattern exhibited here what we find is the converse of the onset restrictions: sonority must decrease. The slope of the sonority decrease, on the other hand, can be much gentler than the slope of an onset. In fact, English codas permit us to very finely divide the sonority hierarchy. Notice that even /l/ and /r/ are different: we find cases of -rl but never -lr: Carl but *Calr.

At this point you may object that there are in fact even more than two consonants permitted in a coda, and at first glance this seems right. We can find three: *lumps, next,* or four: *sixths, nexts, lengths*. But this profusion of extra consonants is illusory. Notice that in all of these cases the extra consonants are at the end, not only of a *syllable,* but of a *word*. Inside a word multiple consonants are never assigned all to a coda; in fact no more than two are ever in the coda:

(14) Barn.stable, Bax.ter, birth.day, Thorn.burg, Wolf.burg

---

12. / θ / occurs only in continental Spanish in words such as **paz** [paθ].

13. I chose these particular examples because they appear to be the historically earlier forms of the Italian 'done, fact' and Japanese 'bought'. Both situations are the result of a historical process of assimilation that applied to all instances of non-homorganic consonant clusters.

Notice, incidentally, that many of these words are not even prototypical words, but proper names or compounds (or both). It is very difficult to find words in English that have multiple consonants inside, but even if you do (try to find some – *extraneous* is an example) and then divide them into syllables, you will find that virtually all the consonants go into the onset (obeying the rules, as discussed above, of course). Thus my previous example is [ɛk.streɪ.ni.əs], and not even [ɛks.tʰreɪ.ni.əs] – note the lack of aspiration on the /t/.

So what are we to do with *fifths*, *exists* and their ilk?[14] Notice first of all that these extra consonants all occur at the end, not only of syllables, but of words. So perhaps there's something special about the end of words that allows extra consonants. But notice also something odd about the permitted consonants. Without exception they are coronals: /s/, /t/, /θ/. And almost without exception they are also independently meaningful: they are expressions of present tense, plural or nominalizations, or a combination of these: six-th-s. This is a fairly odd set-up for a language, but the facts seem to be as I have presented them, and all we can say is 'Here it is.'

From a descriptive point of view we say that at the end of a word English syllable structure permits an **appendix**, which can consist of one or two coronal obstruents, each of which must be a separate morpheme. The complete English syllable structure can thus be diagrammed as follows

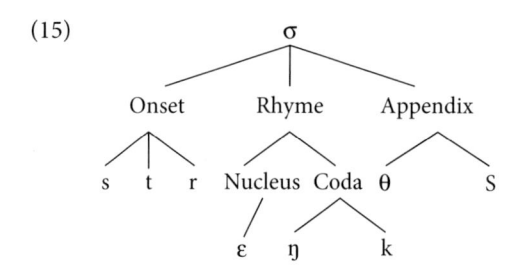

(15)
```
                    σ
        ┌───────────┼───────────┐
      Onset       Rhyme      Appendix
      ╱ ╲         ╱ ╲          ╱ ╲
     s t   r   Nucleus Coda   θ   s
               ╱    ╱ ╲
              ɛ    ŋ   k
```

One other possible way of dealing with this would be to argue that the appendix doesn't attach to the syllable node, but rather to a higher level node, the word node. This would correctly encode the fact that the appendix can only occur at the end of the last syllable of a word. This would require a more elaborate tree in which the syllable nodes are connected together in a higher constituent. The simplest case would be to make them daughters of a **Word** node, but, as we will see in the next section of this chapter, there is a level intermediate between the syllable and the word, namely the **foot**. This would force us to set up a fairly complicated tree structure that looks like this:

---

14. It has been suggested that *angsts* [ɑŋksts] may exhibit a string of five consonants – probably the most extreme case, although how often do we need to talk about more than one?

(16)

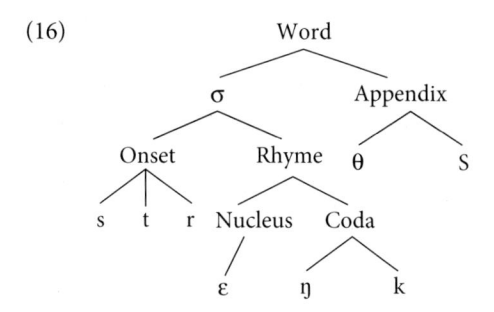

```
                    Word
                  /      \
                 σ       Appendix
               /   \      /    \
           Onset   Rhyme  θ     s
           /|\      / \
          s t r  Nucleus Coda
                   |     / \
                   ɛ    ŋ   k
```

Finally, we have put aside the issue of /s/. Try to figure out what the rules are for two-consonant clusters in codas, one of which is /s/. You will see that we can't just treat /s/ as an example of an appendix.

## 4.4 Between syllables

One further issue remains in talking about the structure of syllables, and that is what happens when we find consonants between vowels. In such a case, there is often a competition for syllable membership. In most languages the result of the competition is normally easy to determine. For example, in Hawaiʻian only syllable onsets are permitted, so when we find a single consonant between two vowels there is only one syllabification permitted:

(17)    ono: o.no

But what happens in languages where there are both onsets and codas? Theoretically, in such a language we could expect to find alternative possibilities:

(18)    ono: o.no OR on.o

Interestingly, however, we find, in language after language, that languages seem to prefer their consonants in their onsets whenever there is a choice. This has come to be known as the **Maximal Onset Principle**, and it can easily be illustrated in English as well:

(19)    a.part
        a.pply[15]
        a.stride

---

15. Note that the orthography doesn't like this choice, insisting that geminate *letters* be split. Interestingly enough, geminate *sounds* insist on being syllabified in different syllables also. Below we will see why this is so.

More than three consonants will, of course, force a split into coda and onset, but again, with the maximal number of consonants going into the onset:

(20)  in.struct    *ins.truct[16]
      ar.thritis   *arth.ritis
      ac.tress     *act.ress
      e[k.s]tra    *e[ks].tra

Here, where we have a choice, we see that the one with the maximal number of onset consonants is what is chosen. A particularly cute contrasting example is the pair 'attractive': 'Atlantic'. The Maximal Onset Principle would call for the following:

(21)  ə.træk.tɪv
      *ə.tlæn.tlɪk

but this would lead, in the second case, to the impermissible onset *tl-, and you can check for yourself that the syllabification is instead:

(22)  ət.læn.tɪk.

A clue to the syllabification is the particular allophone of /t/ that you get. Compare the /t/ in 'attractive' with that in 'Atlantic'. In my dialect I have something virtually identical to [tʃ] before /r/, but [ʔ] before /l/, because it is syllable final. This is a classic illustration of the interaction of the maximal onset principle with the constraints on possible onsets. Essentially the rule is 'make onsets as large as possible, while not violating onset rules'.

This is best illustrated by an even more complicated example with four consonants between two vowels. Divide the word 'express' into syllables and you will find that the correct division is [ɛk.sprɛs]. As a check of this, incidentally, you can ask yourself whether the [r] is devoiced (i.e. whether the /p/ is aspirated).

## 4.5  Feet

There is ample evidence that syllables are not simply strung together to make a word, but that, for most languages, they are grouped into larger divisions traditionally called **feet**. The concept of foot originates in the analysis of poetry, and is a very old concept. Ancient Greek poetry, for example, required that each line of poetry consist of a series of similar patterns of stressed and unstressed syllables. Each foot, then, is a combination of one stressed and a small number of unstressed syllables. You may have learned about iambic

---

16.  If you are not sure about whether I have divided the syllables correctly, check the state of aspiration or voicing of the consonants in each case – you will note that it behaves. Furthermore, many speakers would have an affricated allophone of /t/ here if it were syllable-initial, sounding almost like [tʃ], as in *truck* [tʃrʰʌk]. We don't get this here. We find [ɪnstrʌkt] not *[ɪnstʃrʰrʌkt] or *[ɪnstrʰrʌkt] for example.

and trochaic feet in studying English poetry. Remember that Shakespeare often wrote in "iambic" verse, in which each foot consisted of an unstressed syllable followed by a stressed one:

(23)   (Shăll Í) (cŏmpáre) (thĕe tó) (ă súm)(mĕr's dáy)
       (Thŏu árt) (mŏre lóve)(ly ánd) (mŏre tém)(pĕráte)

Traditionally the breve (ĕ) is used to represent an unstressed syllable, while the acute (é) represents a stress of any kind. Another way of representing stressed and unstressed syllables was to refer to the stressed ones as **strong** (S) and **weak** (W).

Classical Latin poetry was also foot-based, but depended on feet defined by syllable length, rather than syllable stress. As we saw in Chapter II, in Latin a syllable was long if it contained a long vowel, a diphthong or was closed by a consonant. The Aeneid, for example, was built entirely on dactylic feet, which have the pattern āăă:[17]

(24)   (Ārma vi)(**rum**que ca)(nō Troi)(**ae** quī) (**prī**mus ab)(ōrīs)

Although the concept of feet originated in the discussion of poetry (and specifically Indo-European poetry at that – there are no iambs or dactyls in Japanese Haiku, which simply counts syllables of all types as the same) it has turned out to be very useful to describe languages of all types using the same inventory of foot types. There is no complete consensus on exactly which feet are needed, but a very popular proposal can be found in (Hayes 1995). He suggests that languages assemble the syllables of words into two different types of trochees, syllabic and moraic, or into iambs. These could therefore be abbreviated as SW (trochee) and WS (iamb).

English is a very poor language to use to introduce this concept, since principles governing the division of English words into feet are very complex. However, there is no doubt that we need feet to talk about English phonology. The simplest case illustrating this is a famous phenomenon involving taboo words. In all dialects of English it is possible to insert a taboo word *inside* another word:

(25)   Ala !@#$ bama
       Kalama !@#$ zoo
       pon !@#$ toon

What is interesting is that there are absolute restrictions on where the insertion can take place:[18]

(26)   *A !@#$ labama
       *Alaba !@#$ ma
       *Ka !@#$ lamazoo
       *Kala !@#$ mazoo

---

**17.**   An option in this style of verse was to replace some of the dactyls with spondees: āā).

**18.**   There is an extensive literature on this phenomenon, but the definitive description was done by McCarthy (1982).

The rule is really quite simple: the insertion can only take place between feet:

(27)  (Ala)(bama)
      (Kalama)(zoo)
      (pon)(toon)

Consequently, if a word does not have more than one foot, you cannot insert anything:

(28)  *(bă !@#$ lóon)
      *(só !@#$ fă)
      *(băná !@#$ nă)

and if a word has three feet, there are two insertion sites:

(29)  Appa__lachi__cola

While the feet we have been discussing are relatively accessible, and apply exclusively to English, much research over the past fifteen to twenty years has shown that it is possible to describe the stress patterns of many languages with the idea that languages choose some foot type (generally either iambic or trochaic, SW or WS) and then overlay on all words. Languages then have a further 'choice', whether to start at the left or right end of the word.

## 4.6 The word as a unit

Most languages assemble their feet into **phonological words**, which do not always correspond to syntactic or morphological definitions of 'word'. We have to have a unit of word from a phonological point of view because there are phonological facts that apply exclusively at the phonological word level. Consider, for example, the phenomenon known as English **contraction**. From a phonological point of view, the following are single words:

(30)  let's
      he's
      they're

yet from a syntactic point of view they are made up of words belonging to phrases that are separated by the primary sentential branch: NP + VP (at least for the latter two cases).

Many languages restrict certain phonological phenomena to operate within the domain of the word. In Russian, for example, obstruents must be voiceless at the end of words:

(31)  gorot (NOM.)      goroda (NOM. PL.)

In many languages, the word is the domain of stress assignment. This means that there can be one stressed syllable (or only one primarily stressed syllable) in any word. There are many languages which we call 'fixed stress languages', where the stress occurs only on the first syllable of a word (as in Hungarian and Finnish) or the last syllable (as, essentially, in French. A very common pattern is for stress to fall on the second last (called **penultimate** syllable). This is, with some additional qualifications, the pattern in Latin and Classical Arabic.[19] In all of these cases, we could not specify where stress fell unless we could talk about the word as a phonological unit.

Current generative phonology maintains that it is important that every level of analysis be made up exclusively of units of the lower level, and that there be nothing left over. Thus, there can be no segments that are not in a syllable, no syllables that are not in feet, and no feet not incorporated into words. This is known as the strict layer hypothesis.

There turn out to be some principled exceptions to this theory, and English is a particularly good illustration of some of the exceptions. One of them has already been discussed: the final syllable of a word may contain an appendix. For example, English syllable codas have only two slots within a word:

(32)   Baxter   [bæks.tər]
       arctic   [ɑrk.tɪk]

but at the end there may be as many as two additional consonants:

(33)   sixths     [sɪksθs]
       strengths  [strɛŋkθs]

it seems useful to argue that the final [θs] combinations are not a part of any syllable, but simply attached to the word itself, which would constitute a violation of the strict layer hypothesis. A similar question can be raised about some odd cases in English stress patterns. Generally speaking an English word can be exhaustively divided into feet:

(34)   (Talla)(hassee)
       (Missi)(ssippi)

but if a word begins with a lax vowel in an open syllable,[20] that syllable cannot stand as a separate foot:

(35)   ba(nana)
       pre(diction)
       su(pposedly)

---

19.   Actually stress is on the penultimate syllable in Latin and Arabic unless that syllable is *weak*, in which case it's on the **antepenultimate** syllable, the third last. And there are additional quirks, but the main point should be clear.

20.   Strangely enough, another systematic exception is proper names beginning with the prefix *Mac*, such as McDonald, McTavish and so on.

Words like these contrast clearly with words in which the initial syllable is closed, even if it is lax:

(36) (in)(spection)
(ec)(static)

This contrast has traditionally been called the 'banana/bandana' rule (another nice pair is 'capacity/captivity'). In any case, if we attempt to exhaustively divide these words into feet, we are left with an initial unfooted syllable, and while we *could* suggest that 'banana' is a special foot consisting of weak-strong-weak, that particular type of foot is very rare among the languages of the world (there is actually a name for xXx – amphibrach), and we should be hesitant to propose it for English, which seems to be primarily trochaic in structure. This leaves us with the alternative of suggesting that the initial syllable doesn't actually belong to any foot but is simply glued on to the beginning of the word, as a kind of downbeat ('a one and a two …'). Again, this would violate the strict layer hypothesis.

## 4.7 Exercises

1. Using the appropriate tree structures, provide syllable structures for the following words:
    a. merchandise
    b. instrumentation
    c. nightingale
    d. bowdlerize
    e. drawbridge

The second syllable of d. and e. begin with similar sequences of segments but have quite different syllable structures. Justify your solution.

2. The two English words *Saturn* and *satire* usually have different allophones of the /t/ phoneme in the middle:

ˈsæˌtʰaɪɚ
ˈsæɾən

The first example has primary stress on the first syllable and secondary stress on the second, while the second example has only a primary stress. Using concepts in this chapter construct an explanation for what might cause the /t/ to be aspirated in one case and flapped in the other.

3. The word *twelfths* is an ordinary English word, but its 'syllable' structure is quite complex. Using all of the concepts we discussed in the sections on syllable, foot and word structure, account for the presence of each segment in the word (you will have to transcribe the word first, of course). Do the same thing for the bisyllabic word *triumph* and the trisyllabic word *anapests*.

# Chapter 5

# Processes – The forces shaping phonology

5.1 Introduction to processes and features
5.2 Major class features
5.3 Manner features
5.4 Point of articulation features

## 5.1 Introduction to processes and features

It is obvious that speech sounds are not unanalyzable units – they have phonetic characteristics that are relevant to how they behave – sounds with similar characteristics behave similarly. Even in basic phonetics we see this, noting, for example that when we begin to learn about English aspiration it is pointed out that only voiceless stops have aspiration. The idea that similar sounds behave in similar ways, and that those similarities should be studied and cataloged originated with the Prague School, who invented the concept of **distinctive features** and **markedness**, as we saw in the previous chapter. Sounds can be described in lots of different ways, but linguists generally try to find those characteristics that seem to be cognitively real. The primary clue to cognitive reality is the fact that relevant sounds behave in a similar way, telling the investigator that the language itself seems to consider that they share some **feature** in common. Thus features are linguistically significant characteristics of sounds. An alternative view is that features are labels for lists of sounds. This particular view is useful in trying to implement phonological rules in simple computer programs, but we will take the view that features are cognitively real characteristics of sounds.

It is important here to emphasize that although we are arguing that features are cognitively real, that does not necessarily mean that they are open to introspection. There is good reason to believe that phonemes are basic level units (a term familiar to Cognitive Linguists). They are immediately graspable by naive users of the language, and are the size and shape of units that naive speakers can manipulate, and with which they interact. Thus phonemes are the units of rhyme, of puns and similar language play.

This is not to say that we cannot become aware of finer features. However, it takes expert knowledge to know about those features, just as it takes expert knowledge to know about different dog species, bird species or computer fonts. In the end, though, the basic unit of awareness is at the level of the phoneme, not at the level of its defining characteristics. There are many linguists who have argued that only the features are cognitively real, the phonemes being handy abbreviations for lists of features. This seems to be an error, however. Phonemes are the real, graspable units (note the use of metaphors of manipulation), but we subconsciously categorize phonemes according to their characteristics, in much the same way as we categorize other objects that we handle – we pick up a golf ball differently than we pick up a bowling ball or an apple. That does not deny the reality of the soccer ball or apple, nor does it deny the reality of such things as diameter, material, or surface characteristics. But the fact that these balls have such attributes does not mean that they do not exist as balls as well.

It should be pointed out here, however, that other Cognitive Linguists have not been persuaded that features have any cognitive reality beyond the linguists who work with them. For further on this view see Bybee (1999, 2001).

Features, then, are ways of categorizing sounds based on linguistically significant attributes of those sounds. Within contemporary Linguistics there is a generally agreed upon set of features that have emerged over the past fifty years.[1] Although some of them are more controversial than others, they are sufficiently standardized that any phonologist needs to be aware of them, even if he or she doesn't necessarily agree with each detail. We will go over the features in groups, then summarize how they are used to express the operation of processes.

## 5.2 Major class features

The first task is to classify sounds according to their most basic characteristics: consonants, vowels, obstruents, liquids, glides and so on. The features that are used for this purpose are [sonorant], [consonantal], and [approximant].

### 5.2.1 Sonorant

Sonorant sounds are those that are produced with the vocal tract open enough that air can flow freely without obstruction at any point. Thus, vowels, glides, laterals (except for lateral *fricatives*), rhotics and nasals are sonorants, since in each case, there is a clear, uninterrupted path for the air to follow. As a result, sonorants have a formant structure, and you can *sing* a sonorant – singing a nasal is called 'humming'.

---

1. The first set of formal features was introduced in Jakobson Fant and Halle (1963). The current version emerged from work started in Chomsky and Halle (1968). Any comprehensive contemporary phonology text can be consulted for the debates over some of these features.

One thing to remember when dealing with features is that they are designed to 'crosscut' traditional categories, so note that both vowels and some consonants are sonorants.

The remaining consonants are [–son].[2] There is a traditional name for [–son] consonants, which are the stops, affricates and fricatives: they are called **obstruents**, but obstruent is not a feature in most standard works. Instead it is simply a label for the class of [–son] sounds.[3]

### 5.2.2 Consonantal

**Consonantal** sounds are, in a sense, almost the opposite of sonorants, in that they are defined as sounds having a significant obstruction *somewhere*, even if some other part of the vocal tract is open. Thus, the only sounds that are not **consonantal** are vowels and glides. Laterals have an obstruction in the center of the mouth, rhotics have obstructions either at the alveolar ridge or at the uvula.[4] Nasals have the entire mouth closed (even though the nasal passages are open), and of course, stops, fricatives and affricates are all, by definition, obstructive sounds, and therefore [+consonantal].

#### 5.2.2.1 *Approximant*

Approximants are sounds that involve insufficient obstruction to create noise. Thus, vowels, glides and liquids (rhotics and laterals) are approximants, while nasals and obstruents are non-approximants. Together with [sonorant] and [consonantal] these three features define the major classes of sounds:

(1) $\quad$ stops $\qquad$ vowels $\qquad$ liquids $\qquad$ glides $\qquad$ nasals

$$\begin{bmatrix} -son \\ +cons \\ -appr \end{bmatrix} \begin{bmatrix} +son \\ -cons \\ +appr \end{bmatrix} \begin{bmatrix} +son \\ +cons \\ +appr \end{bmatrix} \begin{bmatrix} +son \\ -cons \\ +appr \end{bmatrix} \begin{bmatrix} +son \\ +cons \\ -appr \end{bmatrix}$$

## 5.3 Manner features

The remaining manner features define kinds of consonants in greater detail, and all involve details of the kind of constriction or obstruction taking place in the vocal tract, or the location of that constriction when it defines a *kind* rather than a point of articulation.

---

2. There are traditional three-letter abbreviations for every feature. Note also that features are enclosed within square brackets, and are preceded by a plus or minus value.

3. Occasionally an author will make the opposite choice and choose [± obstruent] as the feature making this distinction, but you will never see a system with both **obstruent** and **sonorant** as features.

4. The English /r/ is an exception, and many people have argued that articulatorily it's not a consonant at all, but rather a glide, both phonetically and phonologically.

### 5.3.1 Continuant

Continuant sounds involve a continuous airflow, while [–cnt] sounds have the airflow cut off somewhere. In its simplest incarnation, [–cnt] sounds are stops, and [+cnt] sounds are fricatives. In addition, nasals (which are frequently considered stops in any case) are [–cnt]. Affricates, since they *begin* with complete closure of the vocal tract are, of course non-continuants, and vowels and glides are [+continuant]. The liquids are somewhat trickier. It seems clear that all kinds of r-sounds are continuants, but laterals are a puzzle. In some languages they appear to act as if they were stops, while in other languages they behave as continuants. Since laterals involve complete closure at the center of the mouth, but an opening on the side of the tongue, this dual nature should not be surprising.

### 5.3.2 Nasal

This feature is relatively self-evident: sounds made with a lowered velum are [**+nasal**], those made with the velum raised are [**–nas**]. Nasal consonants are the most obvious examples, but nasalized vowels are also [+nasal], and a few languages have nasalized glides.

### 5.3.3 Strident

**Strident** sounds are relatively 'noisy', as you might guess from the name. This feature has limited applicability – it only applies to sounds that involve friction, which is to say, to fricatives and affricates. All fricatives involve a constriction of the vocal tract sufficiently tight to produce a noisy stream of air. The turbulence caused by forcing air through a narrow opening constitutes the 'hissing' sound that we associate with fricatives (and with the final portions of affricates). However, as we saw in the chapter on Phonetics, that jet of air can be either simple or complex. When we make a [ɸ/β] or a [θ/ð] the air goes straight out from our lips. But when we make an [f/v] the jet of air is directed against the lower lip. You can test this for yourself by pulling your lower lip down out of the way. If you make an [f] or [v] with the lip pulled down and then permit it to return, you will hear a radical difference in the sound, but this does not happen with [ɸ/β]. Similarly, make an [s] or a [z] and compare that with [θ/ð]. The sounds made with the additional surface for the airstream to contact are **strident** sounds, the remaining sounds are non-strident. Thus [f, v, s, z, ʃ, ʒ, pf, ts, dz, tʃ, dʒ] are all strident, and all other sounds are non-strident.

### 5.3.4 Lateral

Sounds made with the side of the tongue lowered, while the tip remains in contact with the roof of the mouth (dental, alveolar, palatal or retroflex regions) are [**+lateral**]. All other sounds are [–lateral]. Thus any sound represented in the IPA with some variant of the letter ⟨l⟩ is a lateral: [l, ɫ, ɬ, ʎ, etc.].

## 5.4 Point of articulation features

The next set of features divides up the upper articulators, but in a different way from the traditional list running from labial to uvular. Since the features were originally all binary in nature they tend to lead to a view of the vocal tract as something more structured than simply a set of contiguous regions, and recent research has shown that we need to think of the roof of the mouth as consisting of three (and, for some languages four) primary regions, with further subdivisions within each one. The primary regions are normally considered to be represented by unary features, often expressed in all caps. Within each region there are additional features that may or may not be present, and which themselves tend to be binary. We will, as is normal, work from front to back.

### 5.4.1 Labial

Labial sounds, as you might guess, are made at the lips. Labial sounds include labials (stops, fricatives etc.), labiodentals (only fricatives exist in this category) and rounded sounds, including labiovelars such as [w], and doubly-articulated sounds such as [k͡p]. We can distinguish between the subdivisions of LABIAL for the fricatives with the use of the feature [strident] – labiodentals are strident, bilabials are nonstrident.

### 5.4.2 Coronal

**Coronal** sounds are made with the tip or blade of the tongue. This is probably the most diverse region of the mouth, probably because the blade of the tongue is capable of very precise and quick movements. The tongue can touch the teeth, the alveolar ridge and behind it, both with the tip and with the blade. Phoneticians have a six-way classification involving apical and laminal tongue positions and dental, alveolar and post-alveolar points of articulation, but phonologists have generally not classified coronal sounds in this way. Instead they define CORONAL as normally involving the tongue-tip touching the alveolar ridge. If the tongue tip touches the teeth an additional feature is needed, and if either tip or blade touches behind the alveolar ridge a different additional feature is used.

Thus within CORONAL there are additional features:

#### 5.4.2.1 *Distributed*
To express the difference between alveolar and dental the feature [distributed] has been proposed, although it is rarely used. Roughly, [+distributed] sounds are laminal (made with the tongue blade) while [−distributed] sounds are made with the tongue tip (apical). Since almost no languages distinguish between dental and alveolar stops, the feature is rarely needed, – [strident] is used to distinguish fricatives in these regions.

#### 5.4.2.2 *Anterior*
The feature [**anterior**] was introduced in the *Sound Pattern of English*, and originally divided the entire vocal tract into a front and back half, with the dividing line just behind

the alveolar ridge. Since it was recognized that the three major place features are needed, [anterior] has been downgraded to a subdivision of CORONAL, with sounds made at the alveolar ridge or teeth being [+anterior], and those made behind it (retroflexes and palato-alveolars) being [–anterior]. Thus [θ] and [s] are [+anterior], while [ʃ] and [ʂ] are [–anterior]. If we need to distinguish between palato-alveolar and retroflex, palato-alveolars are laminal (and thus [+distributed]) while retroflexes are [–distributed].

#### 5.4.2.3  *Strident*
Although strident counted as a manner feature, it also has application as a place feature, as mentioned above.

### 5.4.3  Dorsal

The feature DORSAL denotes sounds made by the back of the tongue touching the palate, the velum and the uvula. The vast majority of languages have only one sound in this region, but some languages do have palatal stops and/or uvular sounds. These sounds are distinguished using the same features that we will use for vowels, since both DORSAL stops and vowels involve the raising and/or backing of the whole tongue body. We will postpone discussion of these distinctions until we get to the section on vowel features.

### 5.4.4  Guttural

GUTTURAL sounds include pharyngeals and glottals. Some languages (particularly in the Semitic family) treat this group as a class, which has led some phonologists to believe they share a point of articulation.

## 5.5  Basic vowel features

In addition to a set of features for the primary points of articulation, there is a set of features that are used for vowel characteristics, although they secondarily have consonantal consequences, so I will introduce them here.

These features refer to the placement of the body of the tongue, and are based on the assumption that there is a neutral position for the tongue, and that therefore each positive specification for one of these features is a deviation away from that neutral position.

The assumption (which stems from SPE) is that [ɛ] is the least marked vowel (in the specific technical sense of being specified as minus for all vowel features). If the tongue body is raised above [ɛ], the vowel is [+**high**], so that would include [i, u, y, ɨ, ɪ, ʏ, ɯ]. If the tongue body is lowered below [ɛ], the vowel is [+**low**], which would consist of [a, ɑ, ɒ, ɔ (perhaps)]. All remaining vowels are [–high, –low]. Note that this essentially allows only three levels of height, a point we raised in Chapter 2 and to which we will return shortly.

Even more different from the standard phonetics assumption is the theory that [ɛ] is neutral, and therefore back vowels are considered [+**back**]. Therefore, [u, ʊ, o, ɔ, ɑ, ɒ, ʌ, ə, ɨ] are all *back*. There is no category of 'central' within this feature system. Thus, it is impossible to distinguish between central and back unrounded vowels [ɨ, ɯ], or between [u, ʉ]. The theory is that there are no languages which make such distinctions. Some dialects of Swedish have been proposed as counterexamples to the latter pair, but the two vowels in question have other differences besides simply tongue retraction, so the theory may in fact be correct.

The one last feature that is needed to achieve the standard five-vowel set (and a few more) is the feature [**round**]. It has the obvious interpretation that rounded vowels are [+round], unrounded ones are [–rd]. Consequently, [ɨ], for example, is [+hi, +ba, –rd], which is identical to [ɯ]. Central vowels, to reiterate this point, are back unrounded vowels. within this feature system. This extends, incidentally, to schwa, which would be [+ba, –hi, –lo, –rd].

It would probably be useful here to provide a chart showing how these vowel features carve up the vowel space:

(2)

|  | –back |  | +back |  |
|---|---|---|---|---|
| +high | i |  | u |  |
|  | e |  | o |  |
| +low | a | ɑ | ɒ |  |
|  |  |  | +round |  |

This system easily permits the standard five-vowel system, and more, as you can see, but it doesn't suffice for languages that seem to have additional degrees of height. Here is an interesting case where the phoneticians and the phonologists disagree, and since phonology is about how native speakers perceive and categorize sounds, not simply how the sounds can be described objectively, we will go with the phonological solution.

Those languages that have additional heights almost always have pairs of vowels that are adjacent in each of the primary zones found in the above chart. English and German, for example, have both [i] and [ɪ] as well as [u] and [ʊ]. Similarly, many languages have [e] vs. [ɛ] and [o] vs. [ɔ]. Chomsky and Halle proposed that these pairs of sounds are differentiated by the feature [**tense**], with the higher, more peripheral vowels [i, e, u, o] being [+tns], and the more centralized, lower vowels [ɪ, ɛ, ʊ, ɔ] being [–tns].[5] The reason this feature is unpopular among phoneticians is that it is very difficult to substantiate the articulatory meaning evoked by the term. However, one argument for the tense (vs. relaxed, i.e. *lax*) view is that in teaching these contrasts to native speakers of languages that lack them, emphasizing holding the mouth tight and hard, vs. relaxing the articulators (and the rest of the body) seems to work very well.

---

5. The opposite of tense is **lax**, but since only one opposition is needed, lax is a synonym for [–tns].

The result of the addition of the feature [tense] is a five-height system, which Ladefoged & Maddieson (289–90) propose is all that is needed:

(3)

|       |       |   | −back |       | +back |       |   |
|-------|-------|---|-------|-------|-------|-------|---|
|       | *y*   | **i** |       |       | **i, ɯ** | *u* |   |
| +high |       |   | ɪ     |       | ʊ     |       |   |
|       | *ø*   | **e** |       | ə     | *ɔ*   | *o*   |   |
|       | *œ*   |   | ɛ     |       |       |       |   |
| +low  |       |   | a     |       | ɑ     | *ɒ*   |   |

**Bold = + tense**
*Italics = + round*

There are two additional features that affect vowels in some languages. In quite a few West African languages vowels again come in pairs, but the articulatory definition of the pairs is much clearer, and has been confirmed by extensive x-ray studies. In these languages (which include Igbo and Akan) there are pairs of vowels that are differentiated by the forwarding of the root of the tongue, independent of what the body of the tongue is doing overall. Thus each major vowel position comes with the tongue body either advanced or not. The feature [**advanced tongue root**] [±ATR] is used here. It would be very convenient if this feature turned out to be equivalent to [tense], since [+ATR] vowels sound to English or German ears very much like tense vowels, while [−ATR] vowels sound lax, but unfortunately the features behave in very different ways in the patterning of the languages. For example, in Germanic and Romance languages there is a close relationship between tenseness, length and open syllables (and conversely, between laxness, shortness and closed syllables). On the other hand, tenseness almost never assimilates from one syllable to another.[6] However, ATR is not at all connected with length or syllable structure, but almost all languages that use ATR have processes ensuring that all vowels in a word are either all [+ATR] or all [−ATR]. This behavior, which is called **vowel harmony**, will be discussed at length below. What is particularly annoying about this disjunction between [tense] and [ATR] is that [+ATR] vowels *sound* like tense vowels to those who speak languages with that feature.

The other common feature used in vowel systems is one we have already discussed – [**nasal**]. Nasalized vowels are, of course, [+nasal].

Now we need to return to the question raised above in talking about the feature **DORSAL**. That feature included palatal, velar and uvular stops, but didn't distinguish them. There are languages, however, that have all three, and many languages that have two of the three. If we look at x-rays of these sounds (or even standard diagrams), we can see that in

---

6. Although the French Canadian variety of French does indeed exhibit tenseness spreading, which we will examine in our discussion of **vowel harmony**.

order for the dorsum of the tongue to contact the velum the tongue body must be moved up and back in a 'northeasterly' direction. To contact the uvula, the tongue moves straight back, while it must move simply straight up to contact the hard palate. These directions are, of course, just exactly the primary vowel features [high] and [back]. Thus palatal sounds are DORSAL [+high, −back], velar sounds are DORSAL [+high, +back] and uvular sounds are DORSAL [−high, +back].

## 5.6 Translation equivalents

This set of features can thus be used to divide the entire range of points of articulation in language, although the points are not arranged in the linear scale that the IPA suggests. Here is a summary of the most common points of articulation:

(4) Bilabial: [LABIAL, +distributed]
Labiodental: [LABIAL, −distributed]
Dental: [CORONAL, +distributed, (−strident, for fricatives)]
Alveolar: [CORONAL, −distributed (+strident for fricatives)]
Retroflex: [CORONAL, −distributed, −anterior]
Palato-Alveolar: [CORONAL, +distributed, −anterior]
Palatal: [DORSAL, +high, −back]
Velar: [DORSAL, +high, +back]
Uvular: [DORSAL, −high, +back]
Pharyngeal: [GUTTURAL]

### 5.6.1 Laryngeal features

The original view of laryngeal features was that the only feature needed was the obvious one, [**voice**], and for most languages this is still true. However, a number of other laryngeal settings need features to describe them, and two basic ones have been proposed and have gained wide currency in addition to [voice]:

#### 5.6.1.1 *Spread glottis*
**Spread glottis**, as its name implies, involves the back edges of the vocal folds being spread apart. This happens when sounds are aspirated, so that feature is expressed as [+s.g.].[7]

#### 5.6.1.2 *Constricted glottis*
[**Constricted glottis**] refers to the vocal folds being held tightly together. The phonetic effect depends, then, on the voicing of the sound in question. [+c.g.] sounds in conjunction

---

7. Actually, of course, the *phonetically* precise definition of aspiration is for the time during which the glottis is spread to overlap the beginning of the following vowel after the stop, so that aspiration could be considered a timing rather than a purely articulatory feature, but we will ignore that issue here.

with a voiceless stop are ejectives, while [+c.g.] sounds in combination with voiced sounds are implosives. This seems to meet with our intuitions that one way of emphasizing voiceless stops (i.e. of making them 'super-voiceless') is to make them ejective. In English we find this in syllable-final emphatic pronunciations such as 'nope' [nop'] or 'What?' [wɒt']. 'Super' voiced stops, on the other hand, are imploded – think of the exasperated kindergarten teacher: 'Now [ɓ]oys and [ɠ]irls!'

## 5.7 Stress patterns

As we have seen in the chapter on phonetics, stress is a relative term, essentially defined by being a place in a regular pattern, although it may be expressed phonetically by the presence of increased phonetic substance, such as additional length, loudness, or an increase in the distance up or down that the pitch movement occupies. Originally it was thought that we needed simply the feature [±**stress**], but this won't do for languages that have more than one degree of stress (but remember from Chapter II that not everyone believes there *are* degrees of stress.) The idea of a stress feature also forces us to say that stress is a feature of a vowel, but it seems more likely that stress is a **suprasegmental** feature.

To describe the patterns that stress seems to show we need to look at large numbers of languages, since stress patterns seem to differ wildly across languages. However a great deal has been learned in the past fifteen years about ways to think about stress patterns, and what we will be learning is a distillation of real progress in our understanding of how languages build up their stress patterns.

The simplest patterns we can describe are those in which there is a single stress on each word, and that stress always occurs in the exact same place in that word, as we discussed above. Thus, in Hungarian and Finnish (among other languages) stress always falls on the first syllable in the word:

(5) **Hungarian**
gyakorlatok     ˈjakorlatok     'exercises'
nyakkendők     ˈɲakːendøːk     'ties'
közmondás      ˈkøzmondɑːs    'proverb'

(6) **Finnish**
laatikko        ˈlaːtikːo       'box'
sanomalehti     ˈsanomalehti    'newspaper'
Kalevala        ˈkalevala       'Finnish epic poem'

On the other hand, French has stress only on the last syllable (unless that syllable happens to be a schwa, in which case stress falls on the immediately preceding syllable):

(7) French
Montpellier     mɔ̃pɛlˈje       'city in southern France'
impossible      ɛ̃pɔˈsiblə      'impossible'

| | | |
|---|---|---|
| télévision | televiz'jɔ̃ | 'television' |
| importante | ẽpɔʁ'tɑ̃tə | 'significant' (f.) |

The 'unless' clause in the immediately preceding sentence is extremely typical of stress rules in languages. It is quite rare for languages to assign stress to the same position in every word. Among those that do, the most common places are initial (first syllable), final (last syllable), and, the most popular – the second last syllable. As is often the case, incidentally, there are commonly used Latin terms for these syllable positions. **Initial** we have already met. Final position is **ultimate**, and the last syllable is the **ultima**. Second last is **penultimate**,[8] and there is also third last: **antepenultimate** (again note that the noun lacks the -te suffix: **antepenultima**, sometimes also **antepenult**). Very occasionally you will find reference to the fourth last syllable (words have to be pretty long to need this word, but you will see **preantepenultimate** occasionally).

Continuing in the vein above (and, as mentioned briefly in the preceding chapter), we often find stress rules are of the form: 'Put stress on X syllable if you can, otherwise on Y syllable, and failing that on Z. A classic example of such a stress pattern is the Latin Stress rule (which also turns out to be the Classical Arabic stress rule, and is found in a number of other languages, including, to a certain extent, English).

In order to understand the Latin stress rule we need to remember the principles of syllable construction (see chapter IV). In Latin there are five vowels (i, e, a, o, u – the five vowels of the Roman alphabet, of course), but they come in phonemically distinct long and short varieties (length is traditionally marked with a bar, or **macron** over the vowel). Heavy syllables consist of nucleus containing a long vowel or diphthong, or of a nucleus plus a coda, regardless of the length of the vowel. Light syllables consist of a short vowel with no coda.

If the penultimate syllable is heavy, stress falls there:

(8) ma.**gis**.trēs   'teachers'
    por.**tā**.mus   'we carry'
    li.be.**rō**.rum   'of children'
    a.**des**.te   'come (imperative)'
    fi.**dē**.les   'the faithful ones'

On the other hand, if the penultimate syllable is light, stress falls one syllable to the left, on the antepenult:

(9) a.**gri**.co.la   'farmer'
    **pro**.pe.rat   'he hurries'
    Bri.**tan**.ni.a   'Britain'
    **ar**.ti.bus   'by the arts'

---

8. Note that a popular language change, at least in the US is to use the word 'penultimate' to mean not 'next to last', but rather something like 'extremely last' – i.e. the very latest or final word on something. That meaning has not yet leaked into phonology.

Just to make it somewhat more complicated, if the word has only two syllables, stress falls on the first syllable, regardless of its weight (presumably it has no place else to go):

(10)   **ter**.ra    'land'
       **e**.nim    'however'
       **fu**.git   'he puts to flight'

One curious point to notice: stress *never* falls on the last syllable, regardless of its weight. Even this rule has an exception – there are a few Latin words that consist entirely of a single syllable, and, of course, stress falls on that syllable:

(11)   **nox** 'night'
       **vōx** 'voice'

Here are some Classical Arabic words illustrating the same principles (Wright 27)

(12)   **Penultimate**
       ya.ˈquː.lu
       qaː.ˈnuː.nun
       fi.ˈrin.dun
       ya.quː.ˈlan.na

(13)   **Antepenultimate**
       ˈka.ta.buː
       ˈtˤa.la.bun
       ka.ˈtab.tu.maː

Summing up, then, a very common stress pattern is for the stress to fall on the second-last syllable if it is heavy, and otherwise on the third-last syllable.

One way to describe this, incidentally, is to recall the foot terminology and suggest that the languages put **trochees** on the end of words, with the caveat that the strong part can't occur on a light syllable (consonant and short vowel), so you have to shift one syllable to the left in that case. If you play with this you will see it will give you exactly the right result.

There is an additional complication about stress that makes the description of stress patterns much more involved. This is the fact that in many languages there appears to be more than one stressed syllable in each word. Many languages have several stressed syllables per word, with one of them being more prominent than the others. When such a situation occurs the language is said to have both primary and secondary stress. I will assume here that the model in which languages like English are said to have several levels of stress is correct, but recall from Chapter II that there are linguists who disagree with this model, and argue that levels of stress are actually something quite different – a combination of stress, full vowels, and the location of the tonic syllable.

Languages that have multiple levels of stress normally arrange the secondary stresses in alternating syllables, giving a kind of up-down, back and forth feeling. Here are some English words which illustrate primary and secondary stresses:

(14)   rèconcìliátion
       Wìnnebágo
       pròpagánda

Notice that these words all consist of alternating stressed and unstressed syllables, and that the last stressed syllable is the location of the primary stress. As mentioned above, one theory about how to describe the stress pattern that these words illustrate is to say that English words, like lines of poetry, are made up of a series of **feet**, specifically trochees (see Chapter 2 for poetic terminology on stress patterns). Essentially we lay a series of trochees on the word, starting at the *right* edge, then make the rightmost foot stronger than the others. Thus English has a template for stress that looks something like this:

(15)   X x . X x . X́ x

This pattern is, however, a gross oversimplification of the English facts. First of all, English stress pays attention to the *kind* of syllable involved. Specifically, English has inherited so many words from Latin that it has remnants of the Latin stress rule scattered all about the language. Since there are so many words that follow this pattern, we can be confident that these patterns have some kind of reality for English speakers, although they certainly don't have the kind of automaticity that allophones have.

For this reason, English words often illustrate the same kind of sensitivity to syllable structure that we discussed in Latin. Recall from Chapter II that stress in Latin falls on the penultimate syllable just in case that syllable is either long or closed (a kind of syllable traditionally called **heavy**). If the syllable is not either long or closed, stress falls on the preceding syllable, regardless of its weight. English words that illustrate these patterns include *América, marginália, agénda, aróma*. The sensitivity of stress to syllable type is called **quantity sensitivity**, and is a very common fact about stress systems.

Virtually the only type of quantity sensitivity we find in languages is sensitivity to syllable weight as defined by the structure of the rhyme. We can understand why only the rhyme (i.e. the second half of the syllable) should define the weight of the syllable by thinking about how we perceive length in general. Consider, for example, Morse Code, which consists entirely of two signals, a short pulse and a long one. How do we know whether we have heard a long or a short beep? We certainly don't know when the beep begins, since both short and long begin the same way. It is only after the 'second half' of the beep that we can tell whether it is long or short. Analogously, it is only the shape of the rhyme that will define the length (or weight) of a syllable.[9]

One way of dealing with the concept of syllable weight in a quantitative way has been to suggest that there is a unit of weight for syllables, called the **mora**, from a Latin word meaning 'delay'. Short vowels in open syllables constitute one mora, and coda consonants

---

[9]. Of course, virtually no generalization in language is ever perfect. Everett and Everett (1984) have shown that in Pirahã, a South American language, stress is sensitive to the voicing of the onset consonant.

constitute a second mora, as do the second half of long vowels and diphthongs. So [ta] is one mora, and [taː], [tai], and [tat] would all have two morae.

## 5.8 Processes

The idea that sounds are changed to fit their surroundings is a very old one, dating back to the nineteenth century, but has also had its detractors, at least since the mid nineteen thirties. Baudouin was the first to conceive of phonemes as mental targets, and stated that sounds change to fit their circumstances. He classified processes (which he called 'divergences') according to whether they were phonetically motivated (which he called 'physiophonetic') or conventionally or historically motivated (which he called 'paleophonetic'). Edward Sapir, in the nineteen twenties and thirties also argued that speakers adjust the sounds they produce according to rules of their language, not noticing that they do so (Sapir). But the anti-psychologistic views of the [American Structuralist]s challenged this idea, claiming instead that allophones were simply groupings of sounds according to principles proposed by linguists acting as scientists, with no claim that anything particular was going on in the heads of speakers.

In the late nineteen fifties and early sixties the first generative phonologists returned to the view that there were basic sounds that were adjusted in the process of speech, but rejected the distinction first proposed by Baudouin between those adjustments that were phonetically motivated and those that were remnants of historical changes. Thus in the classic *Sound Pattern of English*, Chomsky and Halle placed rules inserting aspiration on voiceless stops on the same footing as the rules changing /k/ to [s] in *electric* when the suffix '-ity' is added.

Stampe, in his Natural Phonology argued that some adjustments are psychologically real, operating in real time as we speak, while others simply reflect historical relationships (or perhaps morphological ones) between related forms of words. He proposed a terminological distinction between **processes** and **rules** to reflect this contrast. Later versions of Generative Phonology adopted a similar distinction, although the basis for the classification was somewhat different. In that theory the terminology was a contrast between **lexical** and **post-lexical** rules.

Under any name, the process-oriented view holds that a set of target sounds are successively deformed by language specific processes, each process producing a new form slightly different from the preceding one. The succession of forms is referred to as a **derivation**. One way to imagine this succession is to think of a word as pronounced one century after another as sounds change one by one, although the process model would argue that this is a metaphor for a similar process actually occurring in the mind of a speaker as s/he constructs an utterance.

Recently linguists have become very suspicious of process metaphors in general, for reasons that have to do with issues arising out of the philosophy of science, rather than from psychological questions. It is felt by those in the Generative school that 'derivations' (that is, sequences of representations created by successively applying processes to the same form) are a device that is too powerful (in the technical philosophy of science sense). As a result processes have been abandoned in place of a view of permissible deviations between intended target and output which apply all at once. This idea, called Optimality Theory, will be discussed in Chapter 10. Cognitive Grammar, on the other hand, rejects derivational models because it believes that there is no evidence for the intermediate stages, and perhaps even for the original target form as well. I will argue in this chapter that this view is mistaken, and that speakers actually construct novel ways of pronouncing words in real time as they speak, following phonetically motivated constraints that their language has adopted.

So, to return to the original subject of this chapter, within the theory of Cognitive Grammar, what is a process? Let us make this notion somewhat clearer by thinking about a totally different domain, namely semantics. Here I will borrow from the work of Claudia Brugmann (as reported in Lakoff (1987)) on the meaning of the word *over*. If you imagine a picture of this word you are likely to think of some object located above another.[10] Thus, we can say that the light hangs *over* the table, or that the UFO hovered *over* the city. But we can also imagine a hole in the wall, *over* which we have placed some wall paper. In fact, we could even imagine a hole in the ceiling, *over* which we have placed a patch. Here the relationship of 'above' and 'below' is completely reversed, yet we do not feel we have uttered a contradiction. What we did, instead, was to mentally rotate our perspective until we are looking down on the ceiling, in which case we are still placing the patch *over* the hole. Such a mental rotation of perspective is called an Image Schema Transformation (Lakoff 1987: 440), and these transformations are a regular part of mental functioning.

Or consider a rather different domain – reaching for something. If we reach for a glass, our hand moves out directly towards the glass. But suppose that there is another glass in the way. In such a case, we adjust our reaching gesture to avoid the glass that obstructs our access to the one we want. *This* is what I mean by a process – the adjusting of a gesture to accommodate some obstruction or hindrance. It is not a mysterious psychological construct, but rather a natural response of the body to physical limitations. Notice, incidentally, that reaching around the unwanted glass is not a deterministic response. We could instead move the offending glass, or, if we are clumsy, or in a hurry, simply reach through it and knock it over.

To bring the idea of process even closer to home, consider how speech is affected when the articulatory organs are otherwise engaged. For example it is perfectly possible to talk with a cigarette hanging from one's mouth (although these days this is a rare experience). It is even possible to talk with food in one's mouth. A careful transcription of such speech shows that there have been a number of substitutions made. The substitutions are the

---

10. We could be technical and talk about orientation with respect to the pull of gravity and so on, but I'll keep the informal nature of this discussion for now.

processes we are talking about – they are 'calculated' in real time as we speak, completely unself-consciously.

It is crucial to remember here that the kinds of process we are talking about in this section are the automatic, phonetically-motivated processes that govern allophonic variation and rapid speech reductions (and, for that matter, careful speech overarticulations). Alternations that are found in the language because of the residue of historical events do not have this kind of status. How can we tell the difference? Normally morphophonemic alternations that are simply historical relics are the kind of thing that would appear in a table of irregular verbs in a language textbook, or that have to be taught in a native language classroom (some of you may remember learning that the letter 'c' is 'soft' before 'i' or 'e', or that vowels have their 'long' sound when followed by a silent 'e'). If you violate a 'rule' (a historical relic) you may sound uneducated, or silly, or jocular. But if you violate a true process, you will sound like a foreigner, or as if you have a speech impediment. Consider what an American would sound like who didn't aspirate voiceless stops, or who didn't nasalize prenasal vowels, or who didn't substitute flaps for alveolar stops. Quite different from someone who said [dəvaɪnɪti] or [ilɛktrɪkɪti].

Processes are automatic and exceptionless – English doesn't have a few words with unaspirated t's, or a few vowels that aren't lowered and backed before tautosyllabic /l/ (compare the /æ/ in 'Al' with that in 'ab' or 'ad'). But there are exceptions to the shortening 'rule' that gives us lax [ɪ] in *divinity, salinity* etc: *nightingale*.

Processes, on the other hand, are occasionally optional, and have stylistic effects. Some Americans actually *do* stop substituting flaps for voiceless alveolar stops, because that makes them sound 'English' (we'll leave the sociolinguists to worry about why they might want to do that.) Those processes that govern casual speech (omitting schwas and flaps in English, omitting schwas in French) and that govern supercareful or emphatic speech (making sonorants syllabic: [gɹeɪt], [pl̩iz]) are obviously also optional.

Processes apply to anything at all – borrowed words, nonce words, slips of the tongue, a foreign language until such time as we can 'do better' – that is, until we can learn to overcome our native habits. While aiming at 'skin pigmentation' I once said [spɪŋ kɪdmɛn]. (I caught myself saying it before I could finish). Notice that the /p/ is not aspirated, the /k/ is, and the /n/ assimilated to the following velar stop. None of these pronunciations could have been stored, since I had never said this before, nor heard anyone else say it either. I must have created this 'on the fly'. This is what processes look like.

I am spending a considerable amount of time focusing on this issue because the notion of phonetic processing (specifically, modifications to underlying intentions) in real time has had some bad press lately, and many linguists, particularly Cognitive ones have become very skeptical. I am arguing that phonology is different from syntax (and perhaps morphology) in that the process metaphor ought to be alive and well.

The strongest advocate for the view that processes are real-time mental events, Stampe (Stampe 1969, 1979, 1987; Donegan & Stampe 1978; Donegan 1986), argued that there are fundamentally two classes of processes, **fortitions** and **lenitions**. Others have suggested other labels – Dressler (1984) prefers **foregrounding** and **backgrounding**, for example, but I will retain the traditional labels for this book. We will discuss each kind of process in turn.

### 5.8.1 Fortitions: The selection of basic sounds

The name for this class of processes originates with the nineteenth century view that sounds could be ranked along a hierarchy of 'strength', with stops being strongest, fricatives next, nasals next, with glides weakest next to vowels. Within current views this idea of strength has been subsumed under the sonority hierarchy discussed earlier (although note that **sonority** and **strength** are essentially opposite qualities). Thus, a process that moves a sound higher on the strength scale was called a **fortition**. Such changes would include fricatives becoming stops, voiced stops becoming voiceless and glides becoming fricatives or even affricates.

The work of the Natural Phonologists (Stampe, Donegan and Dressler, particularly) have broadened the use of the term **fortition** to include any process that increases the distinctiveness of a sound, either in isolation or relative to surrounding sounds. In my work I have suggested that this is equivalent to movement within a network of sounds from the periphery to the center of a radial network, making sounds more prototypical (Nathan 1999, 2006, 2008). The ultimate idea is that fortitions define a set of ideal sounds, and thus define the least marked sound systems. Thus, for front vowels, [i] is 'better' than [ɪ] or [ɨ], and the process, allowed to operate, will replace the latter two with the former. Similarly, as mentioned in chapter 2, there is a prototypicality relationship between non-low back vowels and lip rounding. Rounding emphasizes the lowered F2, making back vowels even more distinct from front ones. Thus prototypical back vowels are rounded (and prototypical round vowels are back). We could interpret this in process terms by saying rounded vowels are backed, and back vowels are rounded. Thus speakers find it hard to say front rounded vowels [y, ø] in languages that lack those sounds and they will 'correct' them by unrounding them to [i, e].

Although lenitions are generally the kind that come to mind first when thinking about processes, fortitions are an important source of phonological structure and behavior as well. Fortitions generally seem to fall into three major categories. The first are the formative obligatory processes that define the overall structure of phonemic systems. These are the processes that can be thought of as the implementation of prototypicality effects on individual phonemes. They enhance the perceptibility of the features that define particular sounds, by eliminating or 'toning down' contradictory features. Thus vowels are (i) not nasal, (ii) are preferentially high or low (or, if necessary, also purely mid), and (iii) front vowels prefer to be unrounded, while nonlow back vowels prefer to be rounded. Taken together these three processes,[11] allowed to 'run amok', that is, to apply without restriction on any input whatsoever, will output a vowel system that looks like this:

(16)  i    u
       e    o
          a

---

11. Just for the sake of the formalization, these processes could be written this way:

(i) V → [−nasal]
(ii) V → [+high] OR [+low]
(iii) V[−low] → [α back, α round]

There is an extensive discussion of these kind of prototypicality statements viewed as processes in Donegan (1978, 1986). Similar processes would apply to consonant inventories, yielding systems that prefer the three major points of articulation, stops required with fricatives additionally greatly preferred (and, for example, /s/ preferred over, say, /θ/). Among stops, voiceless are preferred to voiced. Taken together these prototypicality statements amount to a restatement in process terms of the Jakobsonian preference laws discussed in Chapter 10.

Fortitions also define some of the incipient changes that apply to produce certain classes of sound change. For example, in many Southern American dialects, low lax vowels have developed off-glides – palatal for /æ/ and labiovelar for /ɒ/, so we get [bæɪd] for 'bad' and [dɒʊg] for 'dog'. Once the glide is inserted, further fortitions can generate an entire additional syllable, so that both Southern English and African American Vernacular have two syllables for 'bad': ['bæjɨd]

The similar changes that led to part of the [Great English Vowel] shift and are recurring in American and Australian dialects:

(17)   i   →   əɪ   Australian 'me'
       o   →   ɛʊ   Philadelphia 'go'

are primarily dissimilative in nature, in that they break a tense (and thus long) vowel into two parts, one with a more sonorant center, and the second with a palatal or labial off-glide.

This kind of fortition that can also be seen in ongoing language change (and, of course, its results can be seen in historical change) in famous examples of vowel shifts, such as the Great English Vowel Shift discussed earlier, and in the current ongoing vowel shift in the major cities of the United States surrounding the Great Lakes. In that shift the lax vowels /ɔ ɑ æ ɛ / in words such as 'wrought' 'rot', 'rat' 'set' respectively, shift in a clock-wise rotation as follows:

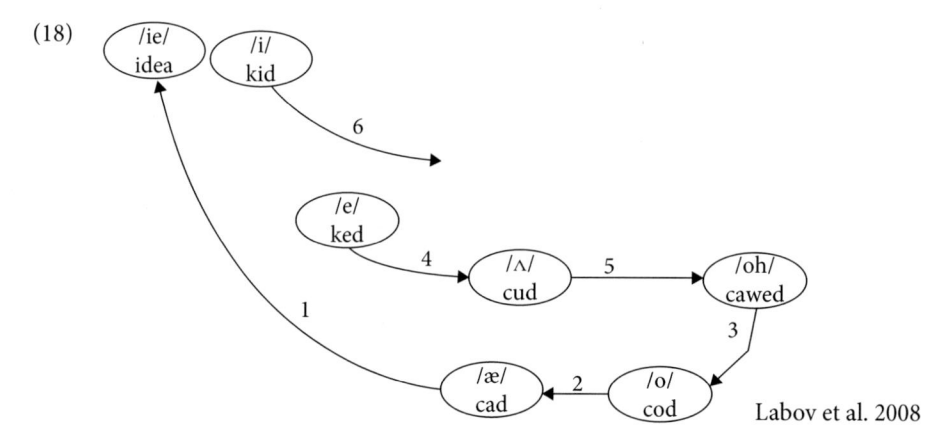

(18)

Figure 1. The northen cities shift.

While a great deal more can be said about fortitions and their role in shaping the phonologies, and particularly the inventories of languages, that topic must be reserved for a more advanced text.

### 5.8.2 Lenitions: The implementation of speech

One of the things you find immediately when looking at lenitions is that they are processes that have been known for so long in linguistics that they have fancy Latinate names that go back to the nineteenth century. And you probably do need to learn the names, because everyone still uses them and expects others to know them. Lenitions in general can be divided into assimilative and reductive processes. Assimilative processes are the easiest, and we will go through them one a time.

#### 5.8.2.1 *Assimilations*

Assimilations all involve a sound becoming more like its neighbor. Phoneticians often refer to this process as **coarticulation**, which emphasizes the idea that sound gestures are executed simultaneously, rather than sequentially, but we will continue to use the term most preferred by phonologists.[12] Assimilations can occur either in anticipation of a following sound or by maintaining some feature into the next sound. In keeping with my comment above about terminology there are three different ways of talking about directionality. When a sound anticipates some feature of the upcoming sound it is said to undergo **anticipatory** assimilation, or **regressive** assimilation (because the feature is said to be moving 'backwards' through the word), or simply **leftwards** assimilation. When a feature continues 'forward' from the causing sound to the affected sound it is said to be **perseveratory** assimilation (the feature 'perseveres'), or **progressive** assimilation (the feature moves 'forward' through the word) or again, simply, **rightwards** assimilation.

Almost any feature can be assimilated, but some kinds of assimilation are so common that that they have their own special name. We will examine each one in turn.

#### 5.8.2.2 *Nasal assimilation*

The most common phonological process in the world is nasal assimilation. Prototypically, a coronal nasal changes its point of articulation to match the point of articulation of a following stop. A classic illustration is Spanish, where all syllable final /n/'s assimilate to a following stop:

(19)  un hombre  [un ombre]   'a man'
      un beso    [um beso]    'a kiss'
      un factor  [uɱ faktor]  'a factor'
      un gato    [uŋ gato]    'a cat'

---

12. Some even make a principled distinction between these two terms (assimilation and coarticulation), but for our purposes we can disregard this distinction.

English also has an active process of nasal assimilation, which can be seen in phrases such as *ten men, in case* [tɛm mɛn, ɪŋ keɪs] but in English it is optional.[13] This process occurs in almost every language that linguists have examined (although it is said not to occur in Russian, so that the word 'bank' is actually pronounced [bank]). The most common case is for a coronal nasal to assimilate, but there are cases of both velars and labials assimilating also. It is also most commonly triggered by a following stop, but cases of assimilation to fricatives or even sonorants are attested. Note that nasal assimilation is a regressive/anticipatory/leftwards assimilation.

It should be added that while nasal assimilation is the most common kind, assimilation of place/point of articulation is extremely common, occurring frequently in English casual speech, so that *bad boy* is often pronounced [bæbbɔɪ].

### 5.8.2.3 *Voicing assimilation*

In many languages it is not possible to produce a consonant cluster with different voicing values for the consonants, particularly if the consonants are obstruents. This is certainly the case for English if the two (or more) consonants are both in the coda. Thus the form that represents, simultaneously, the noun plural marker, the singular present tense and the possessive (probably underlyingly /z/, but nothing rides on this choice here) always agrees in voicing with the preceding obstruent consonant:

(20) dogs [dɔgz]
cats [kæts]
plays [pleɪz]

Russian has a similar voicing assimilation process, applying leftwards across word boundaries. The past tense of the copula, 'was', *был*, pronounced [bɨɫ], 'spreads' its voicing leftwards to preceding obstruents (and all obstruents in Russian are voiceless in word-final position) in the word *брат*, [brat] for example:

брат был [bradbɨɫ] (compare [brat] in isolation) 'brother was'

This process applies even in Russian-accented English. A Russian speaker of my acquaintance used to say that something '[maɪdbi] true'.

These cases of voicing assimilation, of course, are rightwards and leftwards respectively.

### 5.8.2.4 *Nasalization*

Another frequently encountered case of assimilation is nasalization (not to be confused with nasal assimilation, discussed in section (a)). In many languages vowels and even

---

13. There is another instance of nasal assimilation in English, but it is a rule, not a process. That one is illustrated in examples like '**im**possible' (as opposed to '**in**operative'). However, this rule is limited to the negative prefix, and an identical prefix with the meaning 'inwards' does not assimilate in this way: 'input', 'inbound'. Note that it is possible to say these words with an assimilated version, but it is optional. It is, however, never correct to say *i[n]possible.

liquids acquire nasal qualities when preceded by a nasal consonant. In English, for example, vowel, liquids and glides nasalize before any nasal:

(21) borrowing [bɔ̃r̃õw̃ĩŋ]
     film       [fĩlm]
     iron       [ãĩə̃n]

Recently it has been discovered (Cohn 1993) that this kind of nasalization is different from the nasalization found in languages that have nasalized vowels as phonemes, in that it appears the velum simply gradually lowers from the end of the oral obstruent until the nasal consonant. In a language such as French, which has phonemic nasal vowels, the velum drops immediately after the obstruent and remains down until an oral consonant is reached:

(22) bonté [bɔ̃te] 'goodness'

### 5.8.2.5 *Palatalization and other assimilations*

There are many other kinds of assimilation that we could discuss. For example, a high front vowel /i/ or a glide /j/ often has an effect on a coronal, or, in some cases, on a velar. In each case the consonant is moved towards the 'palatal' vowel/glide. In modern English, for example, all coronals are palatalized into the corresponding palato-alveolar by a following /j/:[14]

(23) 'what you see …'     [wɑtʃəsi]
     'did you know him'   [dɪdʒənoʊɪm]
     'bless you'          [blɛʃu]
     'as you are aware …' [æʒuɑɹəweə̆]

Although in English this process is triggered only by the palatal glide, in Japanese a similar process is triggered both by the glide and by the high front vowel /i/. Similar changes take place, so that /s, z, t, d, n/ become [ʃ ʒ tʃ dʒ ɲ] respectively (a separate process merges [ʒ] with [dʒ]). The writing system reflects this palatalization, so that the syllabary does not have a way of writing 's+i', but the slot in the grid where we would expect to find it has something pronounced [ʃi] instead, so that the row of syllabary characters beginning with /s/ is recited [sa ʃi su se so].

Another kind of palatalization involves the movement *forwards* of a velar under the same influence. Many languages have a simple palatalization that produces a palatal stop or fricative (English 'keep', 'geese' are pronounced [cip ɟis], for example, and Greek /xi/ is pronounced [çi]). In many languages, however, the resulting palatal stops are somewhat unstable (due, probably to the difficulty of making a single stop and release along the roof of the mouth with the back of the tongue), and tend to go on to become affricates [tʃ, dʒ],

---

14. It should be pointed out that not all linguists agree that this kind of palatalization results in actual mergers (i.e. that the [ʃ] involved is actually the same entity as the one in *shave*. See Zsiga (1995) for discussion.

either as part of a series of processes, or, very commonly, as part of a series of historical changes. The Slavic languages have an extensive series of morphophonemic alternations in which nouns and verbs that end in velars have alternate forms with palato-alveolar affricates or fricatives:

Russian Consonant Alternations

(24) | Velar | Gloss | Palatalized | Gloss
--- | --- | --- | --- | ---
 | plaˈkatʲ | 'cry' (inf.) | plaˈtʃu | 'cry' (I sg.)
 | noˈga | 'leg' | ˈnoʒka | 'leg (diminutive)'
 | naˈxatʲ | 'plough' (inf.) | naˈʃu | 'plough' (I sg.)

Palatal quality is not the only feature that can be passed from vowel to consonant. Labial quality can also be assimilated, although this is much less frequently noted. But, for example, all English consonants are rounded before a rounded vowel (so, for example, [tʷu] 'two', [kʷuɫ] 'cool').

There are many other kinds of assimilation we could illustrate. For example, the Italian word *atto* [atto] 'act' derives from pre-Latin *ag-tus* ('do-past participle') via a sequence of voicing assimilation (discussed above for Russian) followed by **total assimilation** where the newly derived [k] is completely assimilated to the following consonant yielding a double (or geminate) consonant. The whole sequence then is

(25)    *gt > kt > tt

A quite different kind of assimilation is found in Quechua, where there are three vowel phonemes, [i a u], but the two high vowels are lowered when following uvular consonants. Remember that velars are [+ high] but uvulars are [– high]. A similar situation occurs in Inuit (also known as Greenlandic and Eskimo). Thus we find [ikusik] 'elbow' but [seʁmeq] 'glacier'.

### 5.8.3 Deletions

A more extreme process is the complete deletion of a segment. There is, again, a set of Greek-based terms for all possible deletions. Fairly rare is deletion at the beginning of a word (referred to variously as **aphesis** or **apheresis**). Probably the use of 'way' as an intensifier (as in 'way cool', 'way over the mountain' derives from the deletion of the initial schwa in 'away' (itself derived historically from the word *way* with a prefix). Similar cases include Shakespearean *pon my word* (from *upon*), and *'tis* from *it is*.

A very common kind of deletion is deletion of a vowel in the middle of a word. This is referred to as **syncope** (pronounced [sɪŋkəpi]). This process is very common in English, leading to consonant clusters, sometimes even 'illegal' ones:

(26)    'every'    [ɛvri]
        'family'   [fæmli]
        'communication'   [kmuŋkeɪʃən] (twice!)
        'deficit'  [dɛfsɪt]
        'potato'   [pteɪɾoʊ]

Consonants can be deleted too, as in

(27) lastly [læsli]
    mostly [moʊsli]

Lastly there is deletion at the end of a word – **apocope**. This occurred in the history of English, leading to all the written 'silent e's' in our writing system – they used to be pronounced as schwas.[15] Word final t's and d's in English delete when part of a consonant cluster, particularly when a consonant initial word follows[16] as in

(28) 'left behind' [lɛfbihaɪnd]
    'raised Cain' [reɪzkeɪn]

### 5.8.4 Insertion

Not only can segments be deleted, sometimes they can be inserted instead. There seem to be two basic reasons for insertion: preventing clusters of consonants that violate syllable structure constraints in the language, and easing transitions between segments that have multiple incompatibilities. We'll deal with each kind in turn. Again, there are Greek-based terms for insertions at the beginning, middle and end.

Insertion at the beginning is observed in Spanish, where the language does not permit /sC-/ onset clusters. Words that are inherited from Latin with such clusters changed to have an initial /e/ inserted:

(29) especial [espesial] 'special'
    estudiante [estuðiante] 'student'
    escuela [eskwela] 'school'

This process even affects recent borrowings and Spanish-accented English, so that Charlie Brown's dog 'Snoopy' is named [esnupi]. Insertion of a segment at the beginning of a word is called **prothesis**.

Similar insertions can take place inside a word if syllable structure requires it. In English stop+nasal onsets are prohibited, so place names like Pnomh Penh are pronounced [pənɔm pɛn] in English. Insertion inside a word is called **epenthesis**. There is a special kind of epenthesis which involves inserting a schwa between a liquid and another consonant. This occurs in non-standard English between [θ] and /r/ or /l/ in words such as the following

(30) arthritis [aəθəraɪɾɪs]
    athlete [æθəlit]

---

15. Actually, not all final ⟨e⟩'s in English were originally schwas – some ⟨e⟩'s were added simply to mark that the preceding vowel was pronounced tense, as a spelling-pronunciation guide. English spelling has been modified many times over its history.

16. In African American Vernacular English (AAVE) this process is much more widespread, and is not limited to coronals in clusters, and may apply if the cluster is followed by a vowel: 'I [lɛf] all the apples on the table'.

and can also be seen in 'film' [filəm]. This was an active process in Sanskrit, and the process has a Sanskrit name: **svarabhakti**.

Segments can also be inserted in final position, particularly in languages that do not allow final consonants, where a final vowel is inserted to 'protect' a final consonant that would otherwise be deleted from a borrowed word. Hawai'ian often inserts final vowels

(31)  'Bill'   pila
      'John'   keoni[17]

as does Japanese, which also inserts vowels between any pair of consonants (remember that Japanese permits no consonant clusters except nasal+stop or geminates):

(32)  'baseball'  beisuboru
      'strike'    sutoraiki

A particularly strange, but well-known kind of insertion is the famous 'intrusive/linking r' of British and some dialects of [American English]. In these dialects a historical /r/ has been deleted in word-final coda position, but when the word is followed by vowel-initial words under complex and not-completely-understood circumstances, the /r/ reappears. In other cases the /r/ reappears even when there was never an /r/ there in the first place (this is known as 'intrusive r'). Typical examples of 'linking r' are

(33)  rear       [riə]
      rear end   [rirɛnd]

while an example of 'intrusive r' is

(34)  idea [aɪˈdiə]
      idea is [aɪdiərɪz]

All of the examples we have seen so far involve insertion of vowels to break up sequences of consonants that violate syllable structure constraints. But there is a different kind of epenthesis that is fairly wide spread, involving the insertion of a stop between a nasal and a voiceless fricative. Since movement from a nasal stop to a voiceless fricative involves three simultaneous articulatory changes (lift velum, release closure, open vocal cords) languages often prefer to sequence the three gesture changes as follows: lift velum and open vocal cords simultaneously, then release closure. This amounts to inserting a voiceless stop after the nasal. This change is an ongoing process in English, and has also been a historical change. Here are some synchronic examples:

(35)  'warmth'     [wɔrmpθ]
      'hamster'    [hæmpstɚ]
      'strength'   [strɛŋkθ]
      'youngster'  [jʌŋkstɚ]

---

17. The /ke/ is an attempt to deal with the palatal in a language that lacks coronal stops.

Historically we also find 'thunder' from Old English 'þunor'. Here the transition is between an /n/ and an /r/, and the insertion of the voiced stop again eases the complex transition. Historical examples parallel to the synchronic ones above include 'Hampstead' and 'Hampton' from *ham* 'home' + 'stead' or 'town'.

## 5.9 Writing 'Rules'

A standardized notation has been developed for writing processes. It was originally developed within the framework known as Generative Phonology in the early nineteen sixties, but is still widely used by almost all phonologists of whatever theoretical persuasion as a kind of short form. The basic principle is to express rules in the form:

(36)   X → Y / W ___ Z

This means that a basic **X** gets some change, **Y**, when it is preceded by **W** and followed by **Z**. Either W or Z can be omitted if they are irrelevant – that is, if nothing on that side affects the process. So, for example, a process changing /t/ to [č] before front vowels would look like this:

(37)   CORONAL → $\begin{bmatrix}-\text{ant}\\+\text{str}\end{bmatrix}$ / ___ $\begin{bmatrix}+\text{syll}\\-\text{ba}\end{bmatrix}$

Similarly, a process devoicing a sonorant after an aspirated stop would look like this:

(38)   $\begin{bmatrix}+\text{con}\\+\text{son}\end{bmatrix}$ → [−voi] / $\begin{bmatrix}-\text{cont}\\+\text{spr.gl.}\end{bmatrix}$ ___

Ends and beginnings of words are treated as if they were segments, and are expressed with the special symbol #, or occasionally as bold square brackets (especially if a particular part of speech is referred to: ]N for nouns, for example)

Thus, final devoicing of obstruent consonants would be represented:

(39)   [−son] → [−voice] / ___ #

If some segment is optional (that is, it doesn't matter whether it is there or not), it can be placed in parentheses: (C). Sometimes you can have any number of segments of some type, including none. That is expressed as $C_0$ (and pronounced 'c sub-zero').

There are abbreviations for kinds of segments that are commonly used. Consonants and vowels can be referred to with **C** and **V**.

In general there are strict rules for what should go into the feature list for X and for Y. For X all and only the **distinctive features** for that class of sounds should be listed. Thus you should check each feature to see if it can be eliminated, and try to use the fewest number possible to capture the group of sounds that undergo the process.

On the other hand, in Y you should put all and **only** the features that change. Do not list a feature if it remains the same. In general put whatever seems to be necessary into the environment, particularly whatever feature is *causing* the change.

Here are some sample rules and their interpretation:

(40)  C  →  $\begin{bmatrix} +\text{high} \\ -\text{back} \end{bmatrix}$  /  ___  $\begin{bmatrix} V \\ -\text{back} \end{bmatrix}$

'palatalize a consonant when it is followed by a front vowel'

(41)  V  →  [–tns]  /  ___ CC

'lax a vowel when it is followed by two consonants'

There are more complex rule conventions that can be used, but are somewhat controversial. For assimilation rules there is a way to make a sound take the *same value* as something in the environment. Instead of a plus or minus we put a Greek letter, and somewhere else in the rule there must be a matching Greek letter. You can have more than one Greek letter, one for each feature. For example, if a language simply copies the voicing value of a following sound we could write two rules:

(42)  [–son]  →  [+voice] /  ___ [+voice]
AND
      [–son]  →  [–voice] /  ___[–voice]

or we could simplify these to

(43)  [–son]  →  [α voice] /  ___ [α voice]

Similarly, if a sound assimilated both voicing and aspiration, we could write

(44)  [–son]  →  $\begin{bmatrix} α \text{ voice} \\ β \text{ spr.gl.} \end{bmatrix}$  /  $\begin{bmatrix} α \text{ voice} \\ β \text{ spr.gl.} \end{bmatrix}$

An additional need we have is to insert and/or delete segments. We do this by treating 'nothing' as a kind of segment, symbolized by the mathematical zero symbol Ø. An insertion is represented as zero becoming something:

(45)  Ø  →  ə  /  C ___ C

while a deletion is the opposite:

(46)  t  →  Ø  /  C ___ C

Finally there is a way of writing 'either/or'. This method is quite unpopular now, because it amounts to a claim that things have nothing in common (if they did, there would be a single feature and we wouldn't need this). Nonetheless, you still occasionally see the notation of brace brackets { }, especially in older work. The most common place to find them was in the expression

(47)　__ C $\left\{ \begin{array}{c} C \\ \# \end{array} \right\}$

This is interpreted as 'followed by either two consonants or one consonant and a word boundary.' This turns out to be one of the spurious generalizations, because the configuration is exactly the same as 'syllable boundary'.

## 5.10 Exercises

1. For each group of sounds, identify the odd one out, and state the feature that differentiates it from the other sounds in the group:

   a. [q, x, ʁ, ɣ, r]
   b. [β, s, z, t, d, n]
   c. [i, ɛ, æ, ɔ, ɑ]
   d. [i, ɛ, y, œ, ɯ]
   e. [t, d, n, ɲ, ʃ, x]

2. Answer these questions based on the following phoneme system

| Consonants Place/Manner | Labial | Alveolar | Palatal | Velar | Glottal |
|---|---|---|---|---|---|
| Stop | p b | t d | c ɟ | k g | ʔ |
| Fricative | f v | s z |  | x ɣ | h |
| Nasal | m | n | ɲ | ŋ |  |
| Liquids |  | l r |  |  |  |
| Glides | w |  | j |  |  |

| Vowels | Front | Central | Back |
|---|---|---|---|
| High | i | ɨ | u |
| Mid | e | ə | o |
| Low | æ | ɑ |  |

List the features required to identify the following groups of sounds:

   1. /e ʌ o/
   2. /p b t d c ɟ k g ʔ/
   3. /i e æ/
   4. /k g x ɣ/
   5. /n l r/

3. For the following changes, describe first the class of sounds on the left, using as few features as you can, then list all and only the features that change.

   a. /l, r/ → [l̥, r̥]
   b. /e, o/ → [ɛ, ɔ]
   c. /p, t, k/ → [f, θ, x]
   d. /t, d/ → [t̪, d̪]
   e. /β, ð, ɣ/ → [b, d, g]

4. For each of the phoneme problems in previous chapters, rewrite your answers in process format, giving input, output and environment with the correct format, first using informal symbols, then using formal feature notation. For each one, try to make the number of features in the set on the left of the arrow as minimal as possible. Make sure that only features that change value are in the list to the immediate right of the arrow.

5. For each of the phoneme problems in previous chapters, discuss what kind of process is illustrated (fortition vs. lenition, kind of lenition).

# Chapter 6

# Alternations

6.1  Introduction
6.2  An extended example
6.3  Exercises on alternations

## 6.1   Introduction

So far in this text, all phonological processes have dealt with allophonic relations between sounds. That is, each process operated on some basic sound to produce a variant of that sound fitted to a particular environment, but the 'created' sounds generally didn't correspond to other target sounds pre-existing in the language. Generative Phonologists refer to such processes as 'structure-preserving', as they do not create 'structure' (that is, do not create new phonemes, but rather expand the range of existing phonemes within the language). The traditional name for this kind of process is 'allophonic', of course.

However, not all processes of the kind we have been discussing in the previous chapter (automatic, phonetically-motivated ones) are as well-behaved. Sometimes an automatic, natural process pushes a target sound into the territory of one of its neighbors. In such a case, one phoneme can come to sound just like another. Such a process is described as 'morphophonemic'. When we see examples we will see why the concept of the 'morpheme' is brought into play in such cases.

Morphophonemic processes have a much more controversial history in the study of phonology than do allophonic ones, exactly because their results are accessible to native speakers. When one phoneme 'sounds like' another, that means we can hear it happening (the 'we' being non-linguists). A classic example of such a process is the flapping process in American (and Australian) English. An extremely oversimplified account of this process would state that the coronal stops /t,d,n/ become flapped (strict IPA terminology would say 'tapped') following a stressed vowel immediately before an unstressed vowel. Examples include words such as 'pretty' [ˈprɪɾi], 'trading' [ˈtreɪɾɪŋ] 'running' [ˈrʌnɪŋ].[1]

---

[1]. The facts are much more complicated than indicated here. Notice examples such as 'infinity' [ɪnfɪnɪɾi] (the /n/ is also flapped, but that is irrelevant here.) Similar oddities include the fact that, in

The result of the application of such a process is that words with /t/ and /d/ are pronounced the same, and minimal pairs such as 'latter':'ladder', 'waiter':'wader' can be pronounced identically, no longer being minimal pairs.[2]

When American Structuralist linguists first began looking at these issues, they felt that morphophonemic processes were in some sense fundamentally different phenomena from allophonic ones, because they appeared to transform one phoneme into another phoneme, rather than just specifying the allophonic variation within a single phoneme. As a consequence, morphophonemic processes are often only visible when we compare different forms of the same word. If we consider the words discussed in the preceding paragraph, a strict structuralist would ask how we knew that the [ɾ] in 'latter' needed to be treated any differently than the same sound in 'ladder' – in fact, the spelling is the only clue. But for the other pair, we have the information that other forms of the word (for 'waiter' we have 'wait', while for 'wader' we have 'wade') are pronounced differently. Clearly, /t/ and /d/ are distinct phonemes in English (it is a trivial task to find minimal pairs in all positions *except* the one permitting flapping). Nonetheless, it is an automatic consequence of the phonetic environment that /t/'s and /d/'s are pronounced the same. As we saw earlier, this amounts to a case of contextually-determined neutralization, but it is also an illustration of a morphophonemic process, or an **alternation**. between two phonemes.

## 6.2   An extended example

In Polish there is an automatic process devoicing obstruents in word-final position. The following examples (although not the discussion) are from Kenstowicz (1996). If we collect pairs of forms of words, one with a final vowel, the other without that final vowel, we can see this illustrated:

(1)  SG.   PL.    Gloss
     klup  klubi  'club'
     trut  trudi  'labor'
     wuk   wugi   'lye'

---

frequent words initial /t/'s in unstressed syllables can flap: 'We'll see tomorrow' [wilsiɾəmɔɹoʊ]. One of the exercises below deals with this question.

**2.**   It should be mentioned that these words are not always pronounced identically. This is in part because flapping is an optional (although frequent) process, and also in part because we are aware the words could sound the same, and may want to differentiate them. There is also an extensive, and inconclusive literature on whether they are actually pronounced exactly the same, or whether there are minute differences that phoneticians can measure but speakers perhaps can't perceive. We will leave this issue for a more advanced class to deal with.

How do we know that what is going on here is not voicing of these stops (p, t, k) between vowels? Because there are also similar words in the language that do not exhibit this kind of alternation:

(2)  trup   trupi   'corpse'
     kot    koti    'cat'
     wuk    wuki    'bow'

We can also note that there are no words in the language that end in voiced obstruents. That is, there are no words like *[wug]. The fact that the language has /p,t,k/'s that do not alternate, and sounds that do indicate we are dealing with six sounds here, not three. We are saying that the singular forms of 'club', 'labor', and 'lye' are basically /klub/, /trud/ and /wug/, but a process of final devoicing always and automatically changes them to the version with the final voiceless consonant, unless they are pronounced in the plural, where the final vowel 'protects' the final consonant from final devoicing, and permits it to appear. It takes a little getting used to to accept the idea that the singular form of a word is derived from something that is not actually pronounced, but this is actually not a new idea. After all, we have been arguing since chapter 10 that *allophonic* alternations (English aspiration, nasal assimilation in Spanish, and so on) amount to our pronouncing words differently from how they are stored. What makes morphophonemic alternations different in kind from allophonic ones is that native speakers *can* hear these differences, because the output of the process is a sound that is actually a member of a different phoneme. That is, final devoicing in Polish produces a variant of, say, /d/ that *sounds like* /t/. Such alternation is normally audible, and the orthography may or may not take account of it. Although both German and Turkish have similar processes of final devoicing, German orthography maintains the voiced spelling (thus **Bund** [bʊnt] 'union', **gab** [gap] 'gave', **Weg** [vɛk] 'way'), but Turkish does not:

(3)  Nominative   Accusative   Gloss
     kitap[3]     kitabı       'book'
     (top)        (topu)       'ball'
     Mehmet       Mehmedi      name
     (sepet)      sepeti       'basket'
     armut        armudu       'pear'
     (at)         (atı)        'horse'
     ağaç         ağacı        'tree'
     (saç)        (saçı)       'hair'

As you can see from these data, the Turkish writing system writes final devoiced stops as voiceless, while German writes devoiced stops as voiced. Opinions differ as to whether this

---

3. These words are presented in Turkish orthography. The examples in parentheses illustrate words with underlying final voiceless stops, and hence do not alternate. The symbol ⟨ç⟩ represents [tʃ], while the symbol ⟨c⟩ represents [dʒ]. The symbol ⟨ğ⟩ is problematic, and, since it is not relevant to the discussion, can be ignored. The symbol ⟨ı⟩ represents [ɯ].

difference represents merely cultural convention or whether it indicates the relative degree of accessibility of the results of the devoicing process in the two languages.

The methodology for dealing with alternations is fundamentally different from dealing with allophonic variation, because we are dealing with sounds that *do* contrast with one another under most circumstances. Thus, for example, in German, voiced and voiceless stops contrast and exhibit minimal pairs, in initial and medial position:

(4)  Pein   [pɑin]   'pain'   Bein   [pɑin]   'leg'
     Knappe [knɑpə]  'page'   Knabe  [knɑːbə][4] 'boy'

What corresponds to the idea of 'minimal pair', however, is pairs of words that do and do not alternate. To take a well-known example from German, the word 'colorful' *bunt* occurs in both singular and plural forms

(5)  [bʊnt]   [bʊntə]

and so does the word 'union' *Bund*:

(6)  [bʊnt]   [bʊndə]

so here we see that the plural represents a minimal pair, but when we subtract the suffixes the singulars are homophonous. The **morphophonemic** solution to this set of data is to assume that the words 'colorful' and 'union' have different **underlying representations**[5] (this term was borrowed from syntax, where it reflected the general metaphor of *deep* and *surface* structure). The underlying form for 'colorful' would be /bʊnt/, while that for 'union' would be /bʊnd/, with the alternating noun represented as it appears in the plural form, even though that particular form, without a suffix, is quite literally unpronounceable.[6]

The concept of alternations raises a number of issues that will be dealt with in some detail in Chapter 10. One is the fact, raised by the Polish discussion, that sometimes we will need more than one rule, and it will be crucial which order the rules apply in. This has come to be known as the '*rule ordering* question'. As a kind of preliminary, let us look at some additional Polish data:

(7)  SG.    PL.    Gloss
     ʒwup   ʒwobi  crib
     trut   trudi  labor
     kot    koti   cat
     lut    lodi   ice

---

4. The vowel length difference represents a complicating issue that we will ignore for the time being.

5. Other terms that have been proposed include **systematic phonemic** representation, morphophonemic representation, and simply phonemic representation, using, of course, a slightly different definition of 'phonemic'.

6. I have actually seen native German-speaking linguists struggle to overcome the effects of final devoicing and failing to do so – the constraint against final voicing is very strong.

| | | |
|---|---|---|
| grus | gruzi | rubble |
| nos | nozi | nose |
| vus | vozi | cart |
| koʃ | koʃe | basket |
| nuʃ | noʒe | knife |
| wuk | wugi | lye |
| wuk | wuki | bow |
| sok | soki | juice |
| ʒur | ʒuri | soup |
| dom | domi | house |

How can we make sense of what is happening here? Some words with /u/ in the singular have /u/ in the plural, but other words have /u/ in the singular and /o/ in the plural, and finally, some roots have /o/ in both singular and plural. We can sort them out as follows:

(8)  u vs. u     u vs. o        o vs. o

| trut | trudi | ʒwup | ʒwobi | kot | koti |
|---|---|---|---|---|---|
| grus | gruzi | lut | lodi | nos | nozi |
| wuk | wugi | lut | lodi | koʃ | koʃe |
| wuk | wuki | vus | vozi | sok | soki |
| ʒur | ʒuri | nuʃ | noʒe | dom | domi |

The examples where 'nothing happens' (i.e. where the vowel stays constant) are, of course, uninteresting. Unless there is overwhelming evidence to the contrary, we can conclude that 'an *o* is an *o*, and a *u* is a *u*' (what you see is what you get). But what about the cases where the singular has a *u* and the plural has an *o*? Do those words have anything in common phonologically? If you scan them carefully, looking specifically at the root forms, you should see that the words with a u ~ o alternation have roots with *voiced consonants* on the end. Let me emphasize what we have just found, however: the roots that have a vowel alternation are the roots that end in *underlying* voiced consonants.

Now, we need to figure out what the rule governing the vowel alternation is doing. There are three possibilities: it is basically a /u/ becoming an /o/, basically an /o/ becoming an /u/, or perhaps it is some totally different vowel, becoming /u/ under some circumstances and /o/ under others.

If we assume it is basically a /u/, we would assume that the word for 'nose' is underlyingly /nuʒ/, and the vowel is converted to /o/ in the plural form (perhaps because a vowel follows, or something. But this would be contradicted by words like 'soup', /ʒur, ʒuri/, where the vowel *doesn't* alternate. We would have to find some hidden difference between the two. This would be the route we would take to settle on the third solution mentioned above, namely that the word has some other vowel, neither /u/ nor /o/. The problem with *that* solution is that the vowel we would posit would have to be a vowel that is never actually pronounced in Polish – it always comes out either /u/ or /o/. In the technical vocabulary of **Generative Phonology**, this would be an **abstract** vowel, and we will discuss this issue in Chapter 10.

The other alternative, therefore, is to assume that the vowel is basically /o/, and is raised to /u/ under the opposite circumstance, namely in a final syllable. But, you say, we can't do that because there are words that have /o/'s that don't raise: 'house, juice, basket'. But, in fact, that set of words has a distinctive difference from the words where the vowels *do* alternate: the alternating forms all end in *underlying* **voiced** consonants, while the non-alternating roots all end in underlying **voiceless** consonants.

So, we can say that the rule for dealing with this vowel alternation is a rule raising /o/ to /u/ when a word ends in a voiced consonant:

(9)    o → u / \_\_\_\_ $\begin{bmatrix} C \\ +\text{voice} \end{bmatrix}$ #

But there is a slight problem with this rule: in the cases where it applies (the singular forms) the final consonant is not actually voiced, because we have already established that there is a process of final devoicing. We are forced to conclude that, in some sense, the raising rule applies *before* the final devoicing rule erases its environment.

This requires us to permit rules to operate *sequentially*, pausing as it were between each rule so that the next rule gets a crack at the output of the preceding rule. This is what is known in phonological theory as 'rule ordering', or, for those who disapprove of the idea, as 'serial derivationalism'. But regardless of one's ideological commitments, it would be worthwhile to see how to talk about this kind of alternation. [Generative Phonology] used the following way of expressing how processes line up sequentially:

(10)    Underlying Form:    /noʒ/
        Raising               nuʒ
        Devoicing            nuʃ
        Surface Form:       [nuʃ]

The first line lists the underlying form, the next line(s) list the name of the rule applying, with the result of applying that rule to the form above, and each successive line continues this process. In some analyses of various languages the derivation can be quite long and contain a number of lines.

There are a number of things that are crucial about such a theory of phonology. First, it is extremely important that the rules apply in the order given. If they apply in the opposite order the voiced consonant will disappear before the raising rule 'sees' it, so the whole analysis would fall apart. Presumably anyone acquiring Polish, therefore, must acquire the fact of the ordering, and this idea has had a rocky history in recent years, first coming under attack in the mid seventies. Again, this question will be revisited in Chapter 10.

Another objection to the 'derivational' view is that it is not clear whether sequential rule processing is cognitively plausible. Do people actually go through the steps seen above while pronouncing words in real time? Many have argued against such a view, from Cognitive Linguists like Langacker through the proponents of Optimality Theory who have an alternative way of capturing the same facts that we will see later.

Another question raised by this analysis is just how different from actual surface forms underlying forms can be. In some cases that have been seriously proposed by phonologists, the difference between underlying and surface forms is very great, and sometimes linguists have proposed underlying forms that actually never surface at all, always being changed in some way or another (one thing happens when a suffix is added, something else when a suffix is not added). This leads to what has become known as the *abstractness* problem, and has yet to be settled among practising phonologists. We will discuss it in Chapter 10.

Finally there is the question of whether processes that produce allophones exclusively (allophonic processes) are different in kind from those that have morphophonemic effects (in one sense, changing one phoneme into another). In a famous article published in the early sixties Halle (1959) argued that we cannot distinguish between allophonic and morphophonemic processes – some processes were both, depending on the particular phoneme that they applied to. I would argue that processes themselves are either real or not (i.e. apply automatically, unconsciously, exceptionlessly), but are not distinguishable by what their output turns out to be. However, processes that have morphophonemic effects are not totally unconscious, because their effect is perceptible. For example, we can hear that the /t/ in *butter* 'sounds like' the /d/ in *ladder*, but that does not make flapping any less of a process. And note, for example, that the process is 'one way'. The /t/ sounds like a /d/, but we would never say that the flap in ladder 'sounds like' the /t/ in butter. Again, this issue is discussed in chapter X, but it is important to recognize that it has not been settled definitively.

## 6.3 Exercises on alternations

### 6.3.1 English past tense

There is a well-known alternation in the form of the English past tense. It varies among /d/, /t/, and /t/ and /əd/ as illustrated by these forms (you will need to supply your own transcription):

| laughed | browsed | trotted |
| raced | swerved | raided |
| wrapped | rubbed | |
| wrecked | tagged | |
| wished | garaged | |
| watched | budged | |
| warned | | |
| warmed | | |
| broiled | | |
| cared | | |

Examine first the simple voicing alternation in the first two columns. What is the underlying form of the past tense? What effect does the existence of words such as 'ant', 'cart', 'pint' have on your conclusion?

Next, consider the cases with schwa. Here there is either an epenthesis or a deletion going on. Think of similar, non-past tense words that would lead you to choose one analysis over the other. Then, provide a complete derivation of the word 'trotted'. What can you conclude about rule ordering for these two rules?

# Chapter 7

# Fluent speech

7.1 Introduction
7.2 English
7.3 German casual speech processes
7.4 French reductions
7.5 Exercises

## 7.1 Introduction

So far we have primarily been looking at speech as a sequence of phonemes implemented almost one at a time. Certainly we have treated speech as a concatenation of phonemes in much the same way as a train is a concatenation of railroad cars. Of course, when we look at processes we see that individual sounds are affected by adjacent sounds, and that phonemes are assembled into larger groups such as syllables and feet. However, if you listen to anyone speaking any language at all you will hear that there is an enormous difference between how words are pronounced one at a time with a careful style and how they are pronounced in context at normal speaking rate. Some of these changes are so obvious and striking that they come to the attention of native speakers, and clever writers attempt to write these changes in the limited 'phonetic' transcription allowed by the native orthography. For example, one can often see such things as

(1) Didja          'did you?'
    Wanna         'want to'
    Fugeddaboudit[1]  'forget about it'

---

1. Be careful to distinguish this from spellings such as 'sez', which have a different sociolinguistic status. Everybody always says [sɛz], regardless of formality, speed etc. This is a way of marking that the person is speaking sloppily (or in some stigmatized dialect), but has no *linguistic* reality – there's nothing non-standard about how they pronounced the word. The technical name for this kind of spelling is **eye dialect**.

However, this kind of modification of words in connected speech is not limited to set phrases (although it may occur most often in such situations). In fact, it seems to happen almost all the time, most often in speech that is casual rather than formal, deals with old rather than new information and is deemphasized rather than stressed. In the rest of this chapter I will explore specific processes that occur in a small number of languages to illustrate just how 'distorted' speech can become simply through the application of large numbers of totally natural, and minimal operations on a string of phonemes. It is extremely important to realize, incidentally, that the kinds of reductions that I am discussing are not caused by speaking rate. It is not the case that we speak so fast that we don't have time to make certain sounds, or to make certain gestures with precision. It is possible to have very rapid speech that is very precise, and contrarily, it is possible to have very slow speech that is very 'sloppy'. There is enormous individual variation in these parameters. We all know people who speak quickly and precisely, and, on the other hand, people who speak very slowly but leave out lots of segments.

Similarly, reductions happen frequently when the speech involved is repetitious. One good place to listen for the reductions I am talking about is in speech formulas that are endlessly repeated. If you listen, for example, to the safety instructions read by flight attendants (how to fasten your seatbelt, or to put on a life preserver) you can frequently find a goldmine of reduced speech.

## 7.2 English

The most obvious reductions in English are virtually obligatory, and may not even be classifiable as casual speech. The first is the well-known process of 'flapping'.[2] The prototypical environment for flapping is intervocalic inside a word, following a stressed vowel and preceding an unstressed one:

(2) city  [ˈsɪɾi]
    ladder [ˈlæɾɚ]
    sunny [ˈsʌ̃ɾ̃i]

If this were the only case, the process would be uninteresting, but there are numerous other instances of flapping that occur in environments other than between a stressed and unstressed syllable within a word. Flapping occurs, for example, between words, and under certain circumstances the restriction on syllable stress is relaxed. For example, words like 'but' can have a flapped /t/ even if the next syllable is stressed:

(3) but everyone is doing it   [bəɾɛvɹiwʌnɪzduɪŋɪt]
    I bet all of you want to   [aɪbɛɾɒləvjuwõʔtʰu]

---

[2]. This process is limited to North American English, and Australian. An analagous process occurs in many non-RP dialects in Great Britain, but the replacement sound is a glottal stop rather than a flap. Note that some phoneticians prefer the term **tapping**, and call the sound in question a **tap**. Most American linguists use **flap**, however, and we will continue that tradition.

More interesting, however, are other reductions that take place at a more casual level. For example, the flaps introduced by the preceding process can be omitted entirely. This kind of reduction, however, is by no means obligatory, and many speakers may deny that they speak this way. Similarly, schwa can be deleted under almost all circumstances. The deletion is most common when the schwa is sandwiched between two other syllables (recall from Chapter 5 that this is called **syncope**):

(4) family [fæmli]
desolate [dɛslət]
separate [sɛpɹət]
factory [fæktɹi]

More interesting, however, is the fact that the schwa can be deleted in initial syllables, producing consonant clusters:

(5) banana [bnænə]
petunia [ptjunjə]
salami [slɑmi]

Most interesting, however, is the fact that this process interacts with the process aspirating sonorants following an aspirated voiceless stop. Normally sonorants are devoiced (i.e. the delayed return to normal voicing overlaps the sonorants):

(6) please [pl̥iz]
crew [kɹ̥u]
twin [tw̥ɪn]
cute [kj̥ut]

However, if a voiceless stop comes to be adjacent to a sonorant because a schwa between them has been deleted, the voicelessness does not overlap the sonorant:

(7) police [plis, *pl̥is]
Kareem [krim, *kr̥im]
Tawana [təwɑnə, *tw̥ɑnə]
Cayuga [kəjugə, *kj̥ugə]

The fact that these differences occur ([pl̥iz] vs. [plis]) shows that the constraint we are dealing with here is not just physiology, but is governed by linguistic rules. It is not the case that all aspirated voiceless stops spread their aspiration over following sonorants. Notice that it is not even the difference between stressed and unstressed syllables:

(8) prepare [pɹ̥əpér]
Platonic [pl̥ətɔ́nɪk]

Simply put, there is a constraint against devoicing *derived* stop-sonorant clusters. What controls the devoicing is the underlying target, not simply the configuration of vocal tract gestures.

There are also other constraints against deletion of schwas. Recall from chapter IV that onset clusters in English (and most languages) must exhibit rising sonority. Thus we find clusters like pl-, kr- and so on, but never *rt-, *lm-. This constraint, unlike the one on devoicing covered above *does* apply to derived environments:

(9)    salami    [slámi]
      lasagna    *[lsánjə]
      Toronto    [tr̥ánto]
      retention    *[rténʃən]

This constraint forbids onsets with falling sonority slopes. Intriguingly enough, however, the constraint takes a slightly different form than the one defining the basic form of English words, in that consonants with *equal* sonority may appear in a derived onset:

(10)    petunia    [ptʰúnjə]
       catastrophe    [ktʰǽstrəfi]
       Sephardic    [sfárdɪk]

Additionally, consonants with much closer sonority slopes may come to be adjacent, so, for example we can find nasal+sonorant combinations

(11)    Melissa    [mlísə]
       Milosevic    [mlósevitʃ]
       miraculous    [mrǽkjələs]

The fact that this slightly looser form of the sonority sequencing constraint is operable at the derived level, while the tighter form is operable at the underlying level causes mild problems for theory-builders, but we will not deal with it as an issue at this point.

An even more intriguing reduction (mentioned briefly above) that applies at a relatively casual level is the deletion of flaps. This process produces speech that sounds quite 'sloppy', although you can hear it all the time if you listen closely. One good place to listen for it is in radio announcers and others who recite schedules. The word 'Saturday', for example, is frequently pronounced [sǽədeɪ]. However, it is not only flaps from underlying /t/'s that are deleted – all three sources of flaps are vulnerable:

(12)    as a **matter** of fact    [mæɚ]
       I'm **madder** than Hell    [mæɚ]
       the **winner** and still...    [wɪ̃ɚ]

One kind of reduction that has been extensively studied, and which is somewhat controversial (as mentioned in an earlier chapter, Zsiga has proposed an alternative view), involves combinations of a coronal stop and the /j/ glide found either in the word 'you' or in the /ju/ rising diphthong in words such as 'united' and 'unique'. At least at first blush this combination results in an alveopalatal. Coronal fricatives result in alveolapalatal fricatives, while coronal stops result in alveopalatal affricates:

(13) s/z + j
bless you [blɛ́ʃu]
this year [ðɪʃíɚ]

(14) t/d + j
I've got your mail [gɔ́tʃɚ]
We bid you good night [bídʒu]

These reductions can add up, so that common phrases become very reduced:

(15) What are you doing? [wɑtʃəduɪn³]
Did you eat yet? [dʒitʃɛt]

As a final example of this kind of reduction, consider the following phrase:

(16) Something to eat.

This can be reduced all the way down to [sʌ́pnít]. The process by which it arrives there is an intriguing one. Notice that the primary-stressed syllable remains as is: [it]. However, many things happen to the secondarily stressed word 'something'. Although the procedure that will follow can be described as an ordered series of steps recall that it is rather controversial among linguists whether it is appropriate to describe phonological patterns as serial procedures. Nonetheless it is very convenient to do so, especially when first looking at casual speech phenomena, so we will use the model despite the controversy, at least for the following discussion.

First, a regular process inserts a 'transitional' [p] between the [m] and the [θ]. This is a widespread epenthesis, as we saw above, applying between any nasal and any voiceless fricative:

(17) hamster [hæmpstɚ]
cancer [kæntsɚ]
tenth [tɛntθ]
strength [strɛŋkθ]

The final [ŋ], as mentioned in footnote 3 can be realized as [n]. The infinitive 'to' is reduced to [ə] under most circumstances. This leaves us with an intermediate stage of

(18) [sʌmpθɪnəit]

Further reductions can delete the [θ], reduce the [ɪ] to a syllabic [n̩] and leave us with

(19) [sʌmpn̩əit] n̩

---

3. The replacement of [ŋ] with [n] in the present participle form and a few other words ('nothing', 'something') is a separate issue, and it is probably not a process in the traditional sense, although it does seem to be limited to unstressed syllables – note that the noun 'thing' and 'bring' do not reduce to *[θɪn], *[brɪn].

Schwas preceding full vowels are normally absorbed by the following vowel, and there is a mysterious process whereby nasalized vowels spontaneously denasalize before voiceless stops (examples include 'Clinton' [klɪʔn̩], 'sentence' [sɛʔn̩s]). Finally, the syllabic [n] can desyllabify before a vowel. This leaves us with the result mentioned earlier:

(20)  [sʌpˈnit]

When seen on paper this seems incomprehensible, but spoken aloud we realize that it is said all the time.

## 7.3  German casual speech processes

The fact that casual speech processes are linguistically specified, rather than being simply 'mush-mouthing' can be illustrated by contrasting these processes across languages. German has somewhat different processes of assimilation dealing with unstressed syllables. An extensive discussion of these processes, incidentally can be found in Kohler (2000). Voiceless stops are replaced, as in English, with glottal stops, but, unlike English, syllabic nasals assimilate to the point of articulation of *preceding* stops, even in only moderately casual speech:

(21)  geben    [ɡeːbn̩]    [ɡeːbm̩]
      gucken   [ɡʊkn̩]     [ɡʊkŋ̩]
      offen    [ɔfn̩]      [ɔfm̩]
      suchen   [zuxn̩]     [zuxn̩]

The result of this process is that what are underlying quite similar inputs in English and German come out quite differently in casual speech. In English /t/ is pronounced with a glottal stop before a following alveolar

(22)  cotton  [kɑʔn̩]  vs.  bottom  [bɑɾəm]

but

(23)  fahrten  [fɑɐʔn̩][4]  vs.  stecken  [ʃtɛʔn̩]

As a result of this, some contrasts of presence vs. absence of a consonant end up simply as presence vs. absence of glottalization:

(24)  können    [kœnn̩]
      könnten   [kœnʔn̩] or even [kœn̩n̩]

## 7.4  French reductions

Perhaps the most studied reduction process in French is the deletion of schwas. French has a vowel that is traditionally treated as a schwa, despite the fact that it is pronounced as a

---

4. Note that German syllable-final /r/'s are often vocalized similarly to British English.

lower mid front rounded vowel [œ]. One of the reasons it is treated as a schwa is that it is frequently deleted:

(25)   petit         [pti]
       demain        [dmɛ̃]
       franchement   [fʁɑ̃ʃmɑ̃]

However, if there are schwas in two adjacent syllables, only one of them may be deleted, and, in general, no schwa may be deleted such that the result would be the coming together of three or more consonants. Thus the (somewhat famous) sentence

(26)   Tu ne me le redemande pas.   [tynəmələʁədəmɑ̃dpa]

can be said a number of ways:

(27)   [ty.nəm.ləʁ.də.mɑ̃d.pa]
       [tyn.məl.ʁəd.mɑ̃d.pa]

This fact is well-known in French linguistics, where it is known as the 'law of three consonants' (loi des trois consonnes).

The deletion of these schwas can lead to sounds becoming adjacent, and thus able to influence each other in interesting ways. A well-known example, analogous to one in English is the phrase

(28)   Je ne sais pas.   'I don't know'

This phrase is pronounced

(29)   [ʒənsɛpa]

under fairly careful circumstances, but can be rather reduced in informal settings. The first reduction is one that is probably not phonological at all – the deletion of the negative particle 'ne'. This particle is rarely pronounced in modern French, but there is no general deletion of /n/'s, and the schwa is deleted even when it would otherwise not be permitted, so it is probably analogous to the deletion of similar function words in other languages. However, the result of the deletion of the schwa of the first person pronoun ('je' [ʒə]) leads to the following:

(30)   [ʒəsɛpa]   →   [ʒsɛpa]   →   [ʃɛpa]


## 7.5  Exercises

Here are some extremely reduced American English expressions. See if you can calculate how they got reduced that way. For each step you need to justify the change by finding other cases that are simple illustrations:

           'did you eat yet?'      [dʒitʃɛt]
           'it would be good … .'   [ɪdːbigʊd]

# Chapter 8

# Historical phonology – Processes frozen in time

8.1 Introduction

8.2 Simple phonetic changes

8.3 Phonologization

8.4 Exercises

## 8.1 Introduction

In some senses, it was historical linguistics that was the origin of phonology, because much of what we know about how the phonologies of languages work came out of original research done by the nineteenth century historical linguists, particularly those who first developed what has come to be known as Indo-European. This chapter is not intended to be proper introduction to historical linguistics methodology – good references include Hock (1986), and Janda and Joseph (2004).

We will look at two different aspects of historical phonology in this chapter. One is the fact that we can think of historical change of languages over time as the *permanent* operation of the processes we have been looking at in earlier chapters. In some simple sense, a process happens, then the output is simply learned as the new underlying form. For example, suppose that the month, February, which is 'officially' supposed to be pronounced [fɛbruɛri] came to be pronounced [fɛbjuɛri] under all circumstances by everyone. If that were to happen, English speakers would eventually (certainly by the next generation) forget that the word were ever pronounced differently, and we would have seen a sound change take place.[1] Thus the process of dissimilation (the actual change is probably more complex than that, but that is not important for our purposes) has been transformed from an active process in the language to a **correspondence** between the word at an earlier stage of the language and a later one. The view of correspondences between two stages in a language as being describable with the use of the process labels we developed in earlier

---

1. Of course, the fact that the word is *spelled* with two r's would have an influence, as speakers are normally aware of, and even influenced by the spelling. But not all languages are written, and not all writing systems are as distant from the phonology as English's is, so the general point remains.

chapters is traditionally known as **phonetic change**. The fact that the Yiddish word 'away' is pronounced /avek/, but corresponds to an earlier pronunciation */aveg/ illustrates the concept of phonetic change, specifically **final devoicing**. Note, importantly, that this is not, any longer, a process (no substitution is being made in the head of a native speaker), but is a correspondence between the word as pronounced some time ago, and the word as it is pronounced now.

It is traditional to use a different notation to represent sound changes, or correspondences between earlier and later stages of a sound or word. In place of the arrow with a shaft that we have been using up until now we use an arrow without a shaft (the 'goes to' and 'comes from' angle brackets <, and >). Thus, the change in Yiddish discussed above would be expressed as follows:

1. *aveg > avek

It is easy to slip and use one arrow in place of the other, but it is very important to remember that the arrows express very different concepts. The shafted arrow represents a claim about what a speaker is doing in producing an utterance, while the unshafted arrow represents a description of an event in the history of a language.

The other major area we will discuss in this chapter goes under the traditional name of **phonological change**, sometimes also referred to as **phonologization**.[2] This refers to the fact that we find changes not only in how individual sounds or words are pronounced, but changes in the phonological structure of the language. That is, phoneme *systems* change as well. Specific phonemes can disappear from a language (Old and Middle English had a velar fricative, for example, in words such as 'right' and 'laugh'). Two distinct phonemes can come to be pronounced as the same (Middle English long /ɛː/ and /eː/ were once distinct, but now are both pronounced the same (as /i/ under most circumstances – *wheel, speak*[3]). Such a change is called a **merger**. On the other hand, two sounds that once were allophones of the same phoneme can come to be distinct phonemes, a process known as **split**. In Old English the dental fricatives [θ] and [ð] were allophones. The voiceless one occurred initially and finally, and the voiced one between voiced sounds. This state of affairs is still reflected in the English orthography, which represents both sounds with the same grapheme ⟨th⟩. But for reasons we will explore later in this chapter, the two sounds came to be distinct phonemes, leading to the presence of such minimal pairs as 'thigh:thy', 'ether:either' and 'wreath:wreathe'. Such a change would be called a split, and the allophones can be said to have phonologized.

There is a third possibility for a sound change, namely a sequence of changes in different phonemes within a set such that they appear to be chasing each other around the

---

2. Some theorists distinguish these terms, but I will simplify things here by not worrying about the difference between them.

3. The actual history is somewhat more complex, as the two sounds did not always end up the same – consider words like *bread*, for example. But the general example holds.

phoneme chart without 'catching' each other, so that the number of phonemes remains the same, but they have all changed places. These kinds of change will be discussed later in the chapter.

## 8.2 Simple phonetic changes

I will begin with a number of simple phonetic changes that almost exactly mirror the processes discussed in the chapter on that subject. Remember, however, that each of these is not a mental operation but rather a correspondence between an earlier and a later stage of the language.

Palatalization has occurred in the history of English in various ways. The proto-Germanic word for 'chin' was *kinnuz*,[4] Old English *cinn*, now with a palato-alveolar. Similarly *chill*, Old English *ciele*, related to the Latin word that gives us *jelly, gelato, congeal*.[5] With a different vowel, incidentally the same Indo-European root in Old English gives *cold* and *cool*.

Palatalization of alveolars also occurred in the history of English, where the combination of /t/ with a palatal glide leads to phonemic /tʃ/ and /ʃ/ in words such as *nature* and *nation*.[6]

Nasalization, followed by deletion of the nasal consonant led to the existence of nasalized vowels in French, although the spelling system reflects the original state: *un* /œ̃/ *bon* /bɔ̃/ *vin* /vɛ̃/ *blanc* /blɑ̃/. As we will see, this is also an instance of phonologization, because there are now phonemic nasalized vowels in French, whereas Latin did not have them.

Nasal assimilation is, of course, illustrated in words such as *impossible* vs. *inoperative*, where the fact that the spelling is involved suggests that this change happened a very long time ago (it actually happened in Latin, since these spellings can be found in Latin writing too). Note that this process is still an active one in modern English.

Vowel reduction can be seen throughout modern English where schwas occur in words spelled with all five vowel letters. In many cases we are forced to argue that these are simply contemporary schwas, because we can find no related words that provide alternations. So, although, given *photograph* vs. *photography*, where we can argue (perhaps) that the process producing schwas is a contemporary process, there are other words, such as *banana, honest, pituitary, purpose, bos'un*, where the schwa originates from some other vowel historically but there is no way (other than the spelling) to permit anything other than schwa to be reconstructed.

---

4. Related words in other Indo-European languages have /g/, because Indo-European *g phonemes are reflected as /k/ in Germanic languages such as English. So we have Greek γενυ /genu/ 'chin'.

5. Pay attention to the spelling, not the pronunciation for these words – Latin-based languages also went through palatalization, yielding [dʒ] or [ʒ] depending on the language and the time.

6. These represent two different times where the same sound change occurred, a complication we need not dwell on here.

Deletions, are, of course, easy to find – virtually every silent letter in the English orthography represents a historical deletion of some sound: all 'silent' e's (actually *almost* all of them – some were added because they look good, as in *come*). Similarly final voiced stops in *lamb, climb,* and *sing, long* represent evidence of earlier consonant clusters now forbidden in Modern English.[7]

Since this is not a text in historical linguistics this must suffice, but we could illustrate all of the processes discussed in Chapter V with corresponding historical changes.

## 8.3 Phonologization

The number of phonemes in a language does not remain constant, but changes over time. This normally happens because of one of two possible changes. Either two different phonemes come to be pronounced as the same (which is called **merger**) or the allophones of a single phoneme develop into two distinct phonemes (which is called **split**). I will illustrate each of these in turn, first with a contemporary example, then with a more complex, and older, historical change.

### 8.3.1 Merger

Merger occurs when two phonemes which were distinct at an earlier stage come to be pronounced identically at a later stage. Merger can either be partial (in a specific phonological context) or complete (all instances of the sound). Both of these can be illustrated with contemporary American English dialects.

In most southern dialects, and African American Vernacular English, the vowel /ɛ/ before nasal consonants is pronounced /ɪ/. Thus *pen, then, emphasis, any, benefit* are pronounced, respectively, [pɪn, ðɪn, ímfəsɪs, íni, bínəfɪt]. This change is without exception, and speakers of these dialects have some difficulty learning to spell these words because the speakers have no mental representation other than /ɪ/ for these words. But this change has occurred only before nasals.

On the other hand, there is a total vowel change that has occurred, roughly west of the Mississippi river (and for all of Canadian English, regardless of location). In Eastern American English there is a distinction between /ɑ/ and /ɔ/, illustrated by minimal pairs such as *rot:wrought, cot:caught, bot:bought, Don:dawn*, and so on. In the Western US and all of Canada, these are not minimal pairs, but are rather homonyms, and the vowel contrast is entirely lost. Phonologically we can say that the contrast /ɑ/ vs. /ɔ/ has disappeared, and these two vowels have merged.

---

7. Interestingly, the ⟨b⟩ in *subtle* represents an ahistorical addition – the word was *sutil* in Shakespeare's time, and also *debt*, which was earlier *dette*, with the ⟨b⟩ inserted by purists because the word derives from a Latin root which contains one.

There are many famous cases of mergers with which we could illustrate this phonological change. For example, Indo-European had a contrast between *e, *o and *a, but these three sounds have merged in Sanskrit, so that they are all represented by */a/:

(1)     I-E        Sanskrit    Latin
       *dekm*     daśa        decem    '10'
       *g$^{hw}$os     gav-         bos       'cow'
       *ghans     hansa       anser     'goose'

How do we know that there was a merger here? We can collect large numbers of Latin or Greek words with /e/ in them, and the corresponding Sanskrit words show /a/. Similarly we can find large numbers of Latin and Greek words with /o/, and again there are corresponding Sanskrit words *also* showing /a/. Finally, there are Latin and Greek words with /a/, again with corresponding Sanskrit /a/. Since we can find nothing about the phonetic surroundings of the Latin and Greek words to indicate that the different vowels in those two languages are conditioned by their environments (using exactly the same tools, incidentally, that we used in Chapter 3 on *complementary distribution*) we can conclude that the original language had all three vowels, but that they have *merged* in Sanskrit.

### 8.3.2 Split

Now, as we know, phonemes have allophones. The existence of allophones is itself, technically a historical change, known as **primary split**. That is, the phoneme has split into two different sounds. Of course, the sounds are not, to the native speaker ear, different, but allophonic variation is the first step along one of the paths of development of new phonemes in a language. Recall that when we hear allophones we assign them to the phoneme from which they have been derived because we sympathetically 'undo' the process (which we also share) that produced them in the first place. So we hear English nasalized vowels as oral because we know that we nasalize vowels before nasal consonants. This is not mysterious, nor does it require innate language abilities, merely the fact that we perceive human actions through the filter of our own knowledge of our own bodies and abilities.

Suppose, however, that, for some reason, the *conditioning environment* is no longer available. One possibility, of course, is that the speaker no longer produces the allophone, because the process is no longer triggered. However, the other possibility is that the hearer hears the allophone *as is*, without perceiving it as being caused by the conditioning sound. In that case, the allophone will now be heard as an intended sound, rather than as a modification of some other intended sound. In this case the sound in question has now become a phoneme on its own. The single phoneme has now split into two phonemes, one the original sound, and the other the now non-conditioned 'allophone' of the original. This is what is traditionally called **secondary split** or **phonemicization**.

The most famous example of this is the development of front rounded vowels in German. In very early German there was a process of regressive vowel harmony called

**umlaut**, in which back vowels fronted if there was a high front vowel or glide in the next symbol. Thus /u/ became /y/ and /o/ became /ø/.

At the earliest stages of German this process was allophonic, and the front rounded vowels were simply allophones of the back rounded vowels. However, there must have come a stage where the vowels frontness was no longer perceived as *caused* by the /i/ and /j/. Exactly how this came about is a matter of some controversy. Some linguists believe it happened when the high front vowel /i/ **merged** with other vowels at the end of words, becoming schwa. Since the cause of the fronting had now disappeared, the fronting was without an excuse, and was therefore perceived as a basic target, rather than an adjustment of some other target. Other linguists believe that the change happened earlier than the loss of the fronting environment, and that the front rounded vowels came to be perceived as intended (i.e. as *phonemic*) simply through repetition and habit. The issue depends on how active a role we believe listeners play in perceiving speech, and is not a question that has easy answers, so at this point we will simply note the existence of the debate and move on.

The German umlaut example is interesting not only because it produced new phonemes in German (the front rounded vowels /y/ and /ø/) but because the other back vowel, /ɑ/ was also affected. Since /ɑ/ is not round, it fronted, in some dialects, to /æ/, but in most dialects it shifted to /e/, that is, it merged with a pre-existing vowel. Thus the earlier vowel /ɑ/ underwent a **partial merger**, merging with /e/ under some circumstances (before /i, j/) and remaining the same in others (elsewhere). For example, the word *Gast*, 'guest', had a plural suffix /-i/, and the result was that the root vowel of the word changed to /e/ in the plural: *Gesti*. When the final vowel merged with /ə/, the result was singular /gɑst/, plural /gestə/. This introduced into the language a **morphophonemic alternation**, because the root 'guest' now had two different forms, or **allomorphs**.

### 8.3.3 Alternations

Alternations produced in this way raise all the problems that were discussed in the chapter on processes. Recall that we distinguished between 'processes' and 'rules' – processes operate automatically, below the level of consciousness, while rules may well not 'operate' at all, but rather just represent relationships among related words. Here we can see where 'rules' come from – they arise when we have partial splits, conditioned by morphological operations (usually the addition of suffixes) that have phonological effects, but whose original effects have been covered up by later changes. So, plurals in Old High German that were marked by /i/ caused root changes, but then the plural suffix ceased to be a high front vowel and became a schwa, so that the root appeared to change 'all by itself' when it was pluralized.

These kinds of alternations happen all over languages – English is full of them, in fact many of the same kind as the German example: *mouse:mice, goose:geese, man:men* illustrate the three examples we have discussed already (fronting from earlier /u/, /o/ and /a/), but with the further complication that English lost all its front rounded vowels, so that all the alternations were partial mergers, with earlier /y/ becoming /i/ and /ø/ becoming /e/.

In short, the morphology of a language can be greatly complicated when a succession of processes pile up one on top of another, so that the causes of the earlier changes are obscured by later changes erasing those earlier causes.

Now, the 'erasure' is only from the point of view of a speaker acquiring the language. Historical linguists have ways of getting at the sequence of changes, and they essentially use the methods discussed in the chapter above on 'alternations'. Doing this from a historical linguistics point of view is called **internal reconstruction**, because what is being done is reconstructing an earlier stage of a language on the basis of data internal to that language.[8]

As I mentioned above, whether these 'reconstructions' are accessible to native speakers acquiring their language naturally is highly controversial, and, in fact, many of the hottest issues in phonological theory over the past thirty or so years have dealt with the facts that are due to partial splits. A number of these issues will be dealt with in Chapter 10, including the **abstractness** problem, **rule ordering** and **opacity**.

For now, however, let us just briefly look at two cases on opposite ends of the continuum. Consider the examples mentioned above of English noun plurals. A few English nouns had a plural suffix /-i/, which caused back vowels to front. Thus in Old English we had

(2)    singular /muːs/ plural /myːsi/.[9]

In Middle English the final /i/ was reduced to schwa, then dropped (although it is normally retained in the spelling, where it is written with an ⟨e⟩). Furthermore, in late Old English the front rounded vowel /y/ unrounded to /i/. This left us, by Chaucer's time with an alternation

(3)    singular /muːs/ plural /miːs/

here we have gone from a motivated, phonetically natural relationship to a totally unmotivated one in which the vowel difference itself *expresses* plurality. Of course in Modern English things are further obscured because both root vowels have changed, becoming the diphthongs /aʊ/ and /aɪ/, respectively: *mouse:mice*. But no one would argue that umlaut in its phonetically conditioned form represents a synchronic description of the singular ~ plural alternation in these words.

On the other hand, one aspect of the alternation between the noun *house* and the verb *house* in modern English seems similar, if we look at the data in sufficient phonetic detail, but in fact the psychological facts are quite different. As we know, in contemporary American English vowels in monosyllabic words are much longer when the word ends

---

**8.** The other method is, of course, **comparative reconstruction**, which involves comparing related words in different languages in order to reconstruct some hypothetical ancestor from which the daughter languages are assumed to have sprung.

**9.** This was a stage before the writing system was developed, so the final vowels were not ever written, and the front rounded vowels were, in general, also not written differently.

in a voiced consonant than when it ends in a voiceless consonant. Thus we have pairs like these

(4)     bɪt    biːd    bit : bid
        leɪt    leɪːd    late : laid
        læp    læːb    lap : lab etc.

However, these words are not transcribed exactly, because most speakers of American English devoice final obstruents, which in some sense erases the conditioning of the vowel length. On the surface, then, it would appear as if these words contrast only in vowel length:

(5)     bɪt    bɪːt
        leɪt    leɪːt
        læp    læːp

However, this is clearly not the correct analysis. Native speakers are totally unaware of the vowel length, and, however difficult it is to learn to spell in English, children do not find *these* words hard to learn, nor are they puzzled about why vowels that sound different are spelled the same while consonants that sound the same are spelled different. This is because, of course, the vowel differences are not 'heard', and the consonant differences *are*. But the historical facts are the same as those in the *mouse:mice* case – 'earlier' processes whose causes are obscured by 'later' processes.

How we differentiate cases where the split has happened from cases where it has not remains a long-term issue in phonological theory, and it is not possible to solve this puzzle easily, especially not in an introductory-level textbook, but we can simply note that this is an intriguing problem and move on.

### 8.3.4 Chain shifts

The sound changes we have looked at so far all involve **mergers**, where some sound came to be pronounced the same as a neighbor, leading to the loss of the distinction between the sounds. However, not all sound changes lead to mergers. Sometimes, when one sound begins to approach another, the encroached-upon sound 'runs away', and the distance between the sounds remains the same. Such a development is known as a **push chain**. One of the most significant sound changes in the history of English is an example of just such a chain shift.

In Middle English there were both long and short vowels. The long vowels had four distinctive heights, as follows (orthographic representations are shown in italics):

(6)     iː     *i* 'mice'       uː     *ou* 'mouse'
        eː     *ee* 'feet'       oː     *oo* 'food'
        ɛː     *ea* 'eat'        ɔː     *oa* 'coal'
                       *a* 'late'

Some time between (roughly) 1500 and 1700 all of these vowels moved around in the vowel space, as you can see by pronouncing the sample words. While there is not a consensus on which changes happened first, let us assume that the lower vowels began the movement (an alternative view is that the high vowels moved first, which would amount to a **pull chain**). The front vowels are not exactly parallel to the back ones, so we'll deal with each separately.

The upper mid front vowel /eː/ moved up to become the high front vowel /i/, as in *feet, need, creek*. The lower mid front vowel /ɛː/ merged with this vowel so that ⟨ea⟩ is frequently pronounced the same as ⟨ee⟩, namely /i/ *eat, steal, cream*. There are exceptions to this change, in words such as *steak, bread* (where something else happened too).

The low vowel /aː/ fronted and raised to 'fill in' the gap (or began the process by 'pushing' on the vowels above it), becoming modern English /eɪ/ as in *late, came rage*.

Finally (or perhaps, first) the high vowel /iː/ 'broke', becoming some kind of diphthong (opinions differ on whether the first move was to [eɪ] or [əɪ]). The nucleus of the diphthong then lowered to its present position as a low vowel, /aɪ/, as in *like, mice, file*.[10]

In the back there were no mergers. The high vowel /uː/ broke to [eu] or [əu], then the nucleus lowered to [aʊ]. The upper mid vowel /oː/ raised into the slot left behind (or pushed the higher vowel out of the way), so *food, doom etc.* are pronounced /u/. The lower mid vowel moved into the long-o slot: *coal, boat* are pronounced with /oʊ/. This can be diagrammed as follows:

(7)
Step 1: i and u drop and become aɪ and əu
Step 2: e and o move up, becoming i and u
Step 3: a moves forward to æ
Step 4: ɛ becomes e, ɔ becomes o
Step 5: æ moves up to ɛ
Step 6: e moves up to i
A new e was created in Step 4; now that e moves up to i.
Step 7: ɛ moves up to e
The new ɛ created in Step 5 now moves up.
Step 8: eɪ and əu drop to aɪ and au

Image copied from http://facweb.furman.edu/~mmenzer/gvs/what.htm, Jan. 2, 2008

As you can see, except for the front mid vowels, each vowel moved in lock step, each one 'staying out of the others' way'. This kind of change is called a 'chain shift', and although chain shifts are not common, they do occur every now and then. Later we will briefly examine a similar change that is currently taking place in the lax vowels in the English spoken in the US upper midwest, known as the 'Northern Cities Vowels Shift'.

---

10. There are those who have suggested that the vowels in 'Canadian Raising' represent remnants of this earlier stage. Others have pointed out that the change is occurring again in Australian English, where 'me' is pronounced [məɪ].

Another famous chain shift involves consonants. In proto-Polynesian there were four voiceless stops: labial, alveolar, velar and glottal. In Hawai`ian the proto-Polynesian glottal stop was deleted, and the coronal and dorsal consonants shifted 'rightwards':

(8)   p   *t > [11]k   *k   >   ʔ

Note that this leaves a 'hole' in the consonant inventory, because there is no longer a coronal stop:

(9)   p   k   ʔ
          h
      m   n
      l

An earlier change merged *f and *s as /h/, incidentally.

One final topic that we should consider while looking at phonological change is what could be considered the 'bread and butter' of historical phonology, and served as the basis for all original phonological change research, as well as the very beginnings of phonology per se. This is the technique known as 'comparative reconstruction'. Here we are not talking about a particular kind of change but rather a way of looking at data so as to reconstruct earlier stages of a language.

As you know, the study of Historical Linguistics (and many would say, linguistics itself) began when the systematic similarities between Sanskrit, Latin, Greek and Gothic were noticed, originally by Sir William Jones in the eighteenth century, then more systematically by the Grimm brothers, and later researchers such as Schleicher, Verner, and others. The fundamental activity was to array a set of cognates – words with similar meanings and similar forms, and examine them, looking for **systematic sound correspondences**. As you have undoubtedly seen similar examples in your introductory linguistics texts, a single example should suffice. If we line up horizontally a small number of words in a number of Indo-European languages we can see that there are regularities in the sounds involved:

(10)   Sanskrit   Latin         Greek   Gothic   English
       pitar      pater         pater   fadar    father
       pad-       ped-          pou-    fotus    foot
       panča      (quinque[12]) penta   fimf     five

As you can see, the words for 'father,' 'foot' and 'five' all begin with a /p/ in Sanskrit, Latin and Greek, but with a /f/ in Gothic and English. This is what is known as a 'systematic

---

11. For those who like details, examples of these changes can be seen by comparing, say Hawai`ian and Tahitian or Samoan. For example, there is a channel between the Hawai`ian islands called Ke'ala'ikahiki. This is four words: ke 'the' ala 'road' i 'to' kahiki 'Tahiti' (the placename may not actually refer to present-day Tahiti, but that does not matter here.). The definite article ke/ka is te in, for example, Maori (Kiri te Kanawha). Another placename in Samoa is Savaiki, which, if you do the arithmetic, comes out /hawaiʔi/ in Hawai`ian.

12. Probably originally *pinque, but it acquired a 'qu' because of the word for 'four': quattuor.

sound correspondence', in that the same pattern across several languages recurs in large numbers of words. As you know, this situation leads one to believe that the words with similar meanings and similar sounds must stem from some earlier single form from which the different language forms have developed. Using what we know about natural processes, and several tricks of the trade we could reasonably conjecture that the original words in the first three rows must have begun with a voiceless labial sound, and that, since most of the languages show a stop, only Germanic words having a fricative, the original words probably began with a voiceless labial stop *p. This is further reinforced when we see a similar pattern for the coronal and dorsal sounds – stops everywhere except in Germanic. This correspondence, of course, is known as Grimm's Law (it's only part of Grimm's Law, because there is also the set of voiced stops in all languages except Germanic corresponding to voiceless stops in Germanic, and voiced aspirated stops in Sanskrit corresponding to voiced stops in Germanic.) We don't need to go into the details here (any basic introductory text will cover them) but what we do need to note is that knowledge of what is a plausible sound change will allow us to triangulate back from the daughter languages to what must have been the original sounds. Thus knowledge of phonology is part and parcel of reconstructing protolanguages on the basis of cognate sets.

## 8.4 Exercises

### 8.4.1 Phonetic changes

Identify each of the following phonetic changes, describe the articulatory or other phonetic modifications, and classify it as a fortition or lenition. Write your answer in paragraph form, but use phonetic charts and/or features as appropriate. These exercises are from Crowley (1992: 60–61)

    a.    Paamese (Vanuatu)

| *kail | > | keil |
|---|---|---|
| *kaim | > | eim |
| *haih | > | eih |
| *auh | > | ouh |
| *sautin | > | soutin |
| *haulu | > | houlu |

    b.    Toba Batak (Sumatra)

| *hentak | > | ottak |
|---|---|---|
| *kimpal | > | hippal |
| *cintak | > | sittak |
| *ciŋkəp | > | sikkop |
| *pintu | > | pittu |

    (only consider intervocalic consonants)

c. Banoni

*manuk   >   manuɣa
*kulit    >   ɣuritsi
*nɟalan  >   sanana
*taɲis    >   taɲisi
*pekas   >   beɣasa
*poɣok  >   boroɣo
(only consider word-final position)

d. Tok Pisin (a Creole based on English, spoken in Niugini and elsewhere in the South Pacific) – several different changes in this set.

| English Origin | Tok Pisin | Gloss |
| --- | --- | --- |
| axe | akis | 'axe' |
| outside | ausait | 'outside' |
| down below | tamblo | 'down' |
| cards | kas | 'playing card' |
| empty | emti | 'empty' |
| good day | gude | 'hello' |
| alieve him/them | alivim | 'help' |
| capsize | kasfait | 'tip over' |
| monkey | maŋgi | 'boy' |
| torch lamp | sutlam | 'torch' |
| stand by | sambai | 'be prepared' |

(All these words derive from English sources, but with some semantic shifts. Not all changes are neat and tidy. Do not worry about the ones that seem strange or obscure – just deal with the obvious ones.)

### 8.4.2 Phonemic changes

Motu is a Papua New Guinea language and Hiri Motu is a pidginized variety. Both are spoken in many parts of the southern area of Papua New Guinea. Here are some words in both languages:

| Motu | Hiri Motu | Gloss |
| --- | --- | --- |
| gado | gado | 'language' |
| hui | hui | 'hair' |
| kehoa | keoa | 'open' |
| ŋau | gau | 'thing' |
| hahine | haine | 'woman' |
| haginia | haginia | 'build it!' |
| boga | boga | 'belly' |
| maɣani | magani | 'wallaby' |
| tohu | tou | 'sugarcane' |

| | | |
|---|---|---|
| ɣatoi | gatoi | 'egg' |
| heau | heau | 'run' |
| sinagu | sinagu | 'mother' |

(Assume that the Motu words reflect the original forms, and that the Hiri Motu forms are derived from them. What *phonemic* changes have taken place? Think in terms of inventories, splits, mergers etc.)

# Chapter 9

# First and second language acquisition

9.1 First language acquisition
9.2 Second language acquisition
9.3 Exercises

## 9.1 First language acquisition

### 9.1.1 Introduction

Beginning with a couple of early 'diary' studies (Grégoire (1937), Leopold (1939–49)) linguists have listened carefully to what children say and compared it to what the adults around them were saying. And equally early they noticed systematic relationships that piqued phonologists' interest. Jakobson's classic work on phonological universals, of course, was entitled in part *Kindersprache*, 'Child Language …' (Jakobson 1968). It has been clear since the beginning of the study of child language that a simple model of imitation by children of what they hear around them could not begin to account for the facts that were plainly hearable even by untrained adults. When a three-year-old of my acquaintance refers to the [jaɪthaʊs] in the harbor we are visiting he is not imitating what he hears around him in any simple fashion. First it is clear that he replaces all initial /l/'s with /j/'s. Second the change of [l] to [j] is frequent in the histories of a number of languages – Italian (Romance), Nauruan (Oceanic/Austronesian) to name two. What we are seeing is phonology at work. Apparently this little boy has his own phonology, operating on English underlying forms[1] to produce surface forms that do not coincide with what, in the next section of this chapter we will call the **target language**.

The fact that children make their own substitutions (which couldn't conceivably be due to generalizations they have extracted from the ambient speech), and that those substitutions are reminiscent of the well-known processes of phonetic change discussed in the Historical chapter was first discussed extensively by Jakobson, as mentioned above.

---

1. Evidence that children do not store pure surface forms, but rather slightly abstract, *phonemic* representations will be presented later in the chapter.

Stampe, in his Natural Phonology extended and deepened the analogy by arguing that children are pre-equipped with a set of natural processes which they apply to the input speech they hear around them, and that historical change consisted of one or another of those processes applying unrestrictedly to an entire language, leading to a restructuring of the underlying representation.

It is important to note, however, that Stampe did not intend to say that the processes were 'innate' in the Chomskyan sense. He was not arguing for an innate genetic predisposition encoded in our DNA, but rather that the human vocal tract and perceptual system is uniform across the human race, and that therefore there are a limited number of 'solutions' to the inherent limitations that the speech production/perception system provides. Thus each child discovers for itself the processes that make speech both pronounceable and perceptible, but is required by the contingencies of the target language to overcome those limitations in order to accommodate its speech to the surrounding speech community.

This view is, in many senses, what I have been arguing for in this book, and I will suggest that it can account for much of what is known about the process whereby children acquire the phonologies of their native languages. Later in the chapter we will see that a similar case can be made for the acquisition of a second language, with the proviso that the processes that are active have already been 'sculpted' by the first language to a subset of the total available.

### 9.1.2   What are the basic facts?

There seem to be a number of things that uniquely characterize children's speech. Many children go through a stage in which they almost exactly mimic the target of a subset of words, while simultaneously radically altering most other words, oftentimes beyond recognition, except to the doting parents (and sometimes to older siblings). As time goes by the mimicked words (traditionally known as phonological idioms) fade, and at the same time the intelligibility of the other words increases as the child masters the details of additional phonemes. It should be mentioned, incidentally, that not all children go through the traditional 'one-word' stage in which they produce single-word utterances (although some of the single words can be adult multi-word phrases such as 'all gone'). Some go through a stage in which they produce larger stretches of highly reduced, unintelligible strings that appear to be whole adult utterances, but 'ground down' through application of the same processes that we have been discussing.

There appears to be no uniformity, incidentally, in which processes a particular child will 'choose' to apply, with the result that there is enormous variability in child speech, both within and between children learning the same language. On the other hand, there is uniformity across languages in which processes individual children will choose to apply.

What is known, however is that children systematically distort their speech in ways that often seem to correspond to otherwise attested historical changes and allophonic and morphophonemic processes elsewhere in the world. As children's speech improves they gradually eliminate these processes, and the target pronunciations systematically reappear.

A point that has been repeatedly noted is that children normally do not have to rehear the original word for the formerly distorted pronunciation to be eliminated in favor of something closer to the correct one. Thus the child mentioned above did not need to rehear *light* to replace the [j] with an [l], leading to the conclusion that the child had the /l/ stored in some way and only needed to be able master its production.

## 9.2 Second language acquisition

### 9.2.1 Introductory comments

We all know that speaking one's native language affects our pronunciation of a second language. This, of course, is one of the reasons that we say that someone 'has an accent'. Furthermore, the identity of the first language has an influence on the pronunciation of languages learned later. Again, it is common knowledge that we can identify someone's first language by listening to them speak – we can recognize a French or a Japanese accent in English (and, of course vice versa: Japanese and French speakers can recognize an English accent). One of the goals of phonological theory is to account for this fact.

The basic theory of what happens when languages collide has been called **Contrastive Analysis**, and originated within the American Structuralist school of phonology during the nineteen fifties. The original version assumed the validity of the structuralist phoneme, and suggested that we could predict what would happen when one language 'met' another by superimposing the phoneme chart from the second language over the phoneme chart of the first. Problems would be predicted in those cases where there failed to be an exact overlap. A classic work in this area is Weinreich (1970). Interestingly enough, even though this work is widely considered the basis of the theory of contrastive analysis, very much an American Structuralist theory of second language acquisition, it is itself a European Structuralist work, and is about bilingualism, not necesarily about language learning per se. More recent work can be traced in James and Leather (1987).

### 9.2.2 Conflicting categories

The theory of the phoneme advanced in this book, namely that phonemes are mental categories of groups of sounds which native speakers treat as equivalent has a direct application in second language acquisition. When a language learner hears a sound in a second language (traditionally abbreviated L2) s/he perceives it as belonging to the category it is a member of in the first language (abbreviated L1). Under some circumstances this results in no noticeable difference. For example, there is an /f/ in English and an /f/ in French, and they have virtually identical allophones in both languages. Thus any [f] made by a French speaker and heard by an English speaker will be perceived simply as an instance of the phoneme /f/.

The case of exact overlap, however, is not the most common one. The most obvious problem would be a case where the L2 sound simply doesn't exist at all in the L1.

Thus English /θ/ is not an allophone of any sound at all in French, German or Japanese. We would thus expect that speakers of those languages would be unable to make this sound without extensive practice, and, as we know, this is the case. What we predict will happen instead, however, depends to a certain extent on what kind of sound we are talking about. In some cases (probably the most common ones) the speaker will substitute a sound that is in some way similar to the target sound, but does in fact exist in the L1. So, continuing with our example above of English /θ/, French speakers generally replace it with /s/.[2] In other cases, however, L2 speakers will actually attempt the sound, even if they are somewhat unsuccessful. Speakers of non-click languages attempt to make the clicks, for example. As mentioned in footnote 2, incidentally, there are sometimes alternative renditions available, often by replacing a non-existent feature combination with a more familiar one by changing the value of one feature. Such is the case with the replacement of dental fricatives with either dental stops or alveolar fricatives. There may be more complex replacement behavior going on, however, when the target sound is relatively complex. For example English target /ð/, for example, is often replaced by either /z/ or /d/, but can occasionally be replaced by some kind of /r/ or /l/ depending on what might be available in the first language. And some learners replace the relatively complex dental fricatives with even more complex dental *affricates*, an extremely rare sound among the languages of the world. In this case we are dealing with a behavior that has been called the **excelsior** principle (see (Donegan 1978: 246–51 for extended discussion). Since there are processes lurking to simplify the relatively difficult sound to one that is already in the L1 speakers may set up an even more complex target, so that unsuppressed simplification processes will leave behind something closer to the actual target.

This principle, which is simply a case of fortition, also applies in extremely emphatic speech in monolinguals. When a speaker of American English wishes to emphasize a word beginning with a voiced stop it is not unusual to find it being replaced with an implosive, which is a kind of 'super' voiced stop, even though most speakers of English can't voluntarily produce these as targets when attempting, for example, to acquire Vietnamese or Hausa, which have them contrastively.

If a sound in an L2 is the same as one attributable to the result of an allophonic process in the L1, the speaker will assume that the allophonic process had applied in the L2 as well, and adjust the phonemic representation accordingly.

For example, the [ɛ̃] of *bend* results from vowel nasalization, a context-sensitive lenition process which has no exceptions in English. Since this [ɛ̃] results from a regular lenition process, it is taken by speakers to be the same as the vowel of *bed* (Stampe (1969)

---

**2.** Actually, European French speakers replace [θ] with /s/, but Canadian French speakers replace the same sound with /t/. And other languages (or even other speakers) take other routes, including /f/.

shows that it is indeed the same vowel if anything interferes with the nasalization process, in similar examples.) (Donegan 1978: 249).

Hence we hear a foreign language 'sympathetically', as if the speakers were speaking our own language, and applying our own allophonic processes. If we hear one of 'our' allophones, we assume it comes from one of 'our' phonemes, and adjust the underlying form accordingly.

What happens if there is no way to attribute a sound to the operation of an allophonic process without causing worse problems?

> The English pronunciation of French *maman* [mamã] is [mama]. In French, the nasalized vowel is followed by no nasal to which English speakers can attribute its nasality; neither can they attribute its nasality to a deleted nasal, since there is no lenition process in English which deletes word-final nasal consonants in accented syllables: If we assumed a phonemic representation /maman/, we would have to *say* the /n/: [maman]. So we attempt to say */mamã/ and say /mama/ (Donegan 250).

Just as this 'excelsior' process makes learners reconstruct the causes of features of some L2 phonemes by inserting additional segments, the same process may well cause speakers to reconstruct whole additional syllables. The classic case of this is Japanese second language learners of English. In Japanese syllable structure is limited to CV (with the exception, as we saw above in Chapter 3, of /n/, which may occur in a coda, and the first half of a geminate, as in /nip.pon/ 'Japan'). Thus Japanese-accented pronunciation of words with consonant clusters will be strongly affected by this constraint.

However, there is a casual speech process in Japanese variably deleting the high vowels /i,u/, particularly between voiceless consonants. Thus /watakusi/ 'I' is normally pronounced [watakʃi],[3] and /suki/ 'like, is pleasing' comes out [ski].

Consequently, when English words such as 'strike' are pronounced by Japanese speakers (in the case of this example the word has actually been borrowed into the language), the consonant cluster that Japanese speakers hear is attributed to the operation of the deletion process. We would thus expect something like /suturaiku/ What makes this even more interesting, however, is that there is an additional complication, because there is another allophonic process which affects /t/ before /u/, producing [ts]. Thus speakers do not say */suturaiku/, because that would come out [stsraik].[4] The process of deletion applies also to mid vowels, but more rarely. Consequently a 'safer' vowel to insert would be /o/, and that is indeed what we find: /sutoraiku/ '(baseball) strike'. Note, by the way, that the language would have permitted the insertion of an /i/ in final position instead (but not, incidentally, after the initial /s/, since the obligatory palatalization process would have produced [ʃtoraik]). In fact that word also exists – /sutoraiki/ is a labor dispute kind of 'strike'.

---

3. Palatalization of [s] to [ʃ] is an obligatory allophonic process whose effects will be discussed below.

4. The other vowel which could be inserted is /i/, but a corresponding process produces [tʃ] before /i/, so that would leave (roughly) [stʃraik].

In sum, therefore, the contrastive analysis view (which, to my knowledge has never been seriously challenged) takes exactly the view advocated in this book: phoneme systems are categorizations of incoming and outgoing speech. Speech that does not conform to the categorizations of our native language is perceived as if it does, so that speakers of L1 interpret L2 as if were a string of phonemes in L1. Because this book takes a non-autonomous view of the nature of language, we would expect that people would interpret almost any sound as if it were a string of phonemes in our native language. We can see this not only in the hundreds of articles written on second language phonology, but also in handbooks of bird identification. Note that bird calls are always written in orthography. Not only traditional representations (cluck-cluck, tweet-tweet), but also those found in bird identification books. For example, the 'eared grebe' is described in the Sibley Guide to Birds as saying 'ooEEk or ooEEkah', (27) while the 'western grebe' says 'krDEE drDEE' (29). Clearly the author of these texts expects that readers will be able to interpret these 'phonemic transcriptions' as something that sounds in some respect like bird song, despite the fact that birds lack human vocal equipment entirely (and vice versa, of course). And equally clearly these 'orthographic tricks' work reasonably well or they would not appear in every bird identification book.

Similarly, and perhaps even more wildly, I once read an article about 'underground' newspapers and magazines that were printed on mimeograph machines. These were clumsy mechanical machines that made multiple copies by squeezing ink through a master that one produced by typing with a typewriter with the ribbon removed. They made a remarkable rhythmic sound, and the article about these articles was entitled 'Kapoomcha Kapoomcha'. And that's not a bad representation of the sound they made. Contrastive analysis, as filtered through the cognitive/natural phonology view espoused in this book is not in the least surprised.

## 9.3 Exercises

### 9.3.1 First language phonology

Here are some words said by Amahl, the subject in the classic work by Neil Smith. For each word we see a progression through time – each number represents a roughly two week interval, with 1 being 2 years 60 days.

| 'bath' | [baθ] | b̥ɑːt | (1) |
| | | bɑːt | (11) |
| | | bɑːts | (20) |
| | | bɑːs | (22) |

The ring under the [b] is the IPA diacritic for voiceless, and is intended to represent the fact that the sound is voiceless, unaspirated and perhaps lax.

'cat'  g̊æt      (2)
       kʰæt     (14)
'cheese'  d̥iː    (4)
       tʰiːd    (15)
       tʃiːd    (20)
       siːz     (22)
       siːz/tsiːz (26)
       tsiːz    (27)

While the data are somewhat limited, what generalizations can you draw about how Amahl produces obstruents?

### 9.3.2 Second language phonology (Data from Selinker & Gass 1984)

Native speaker of Spanish

| English | Spanish |
| --- | --- |
| Bob | [bɔp] |
| Bobby | [bɔbi] |
| red | [rɛt] |
| redder | [rɛðər] |
| big | [bik] |
| bigger | [biɣər/bigər] |
| brave | [bref] |
| braver | [brevər] |
| proud | [praʊt] |
| proudest | [praʊdəst] |
| sick | [sik] |
| sickest | [sikəst] |
| zone | [son] |
| fuzzy | [fʌsi] |
| father | [faðər] |
| freeze | [fris] |

What general changes appear to be going on? Note that not all changes are regular.

# Chapter 10

# Theoretical apparatus and formalisms

> 10.1 Introduction to theoretical issues
> 10.2 European structuralism and the Prague School
> 10.3 American structuralism
> 10.4 Generative phonology
> 10.5 Usage-based and Exemplar Theories
> 10.6 Some concluding thoughts on OT and cognitive phonology

## 10.1 Introduction to theoretical issues

The purpose of this chapter is to present the most important ideas of the most influential phonological theories that have had an influence on how phonology is practiced in the early twenty-first century. We will begin with the European structuralist school, followed by the competing and complementary American Structuralist school. After that we will look at **Generative Phonology**, primarily as it is concerned with a number of theoretical issues that have been touched on in this book, and which, in many cases have not been resolved, even today. In some cases the questions have simply ceased to be of interest, and in others the controversy surrounding them goes on, with practicing phonologists taking both sides (or, in some cases, several different variations on possible sides).

## 10.2 European structuralism and the Prague School

As mentioned in the introduction to this book, European structuralism is the source of a number of concepts that are still current in phonological theory, including **features, neutralization,** and **archiphonemes**. European structuralism, particularly its best known version, the Prague School, was strongly anti-psychological, not because the Prague School linguists were opposed to speculations about the mind, but rather for reasons of 'division of labor' – the strong feeling that linguists have their own principles and methods of investigation that are different from, and unrelated to the ways in which psychologists operate. Trubetzkoy said 'Reference to psychology must be avoided in defining a phoneme since the latter is a linguistic and not a psychological concept' (Trubetzkoy 38)' Further, 'The phoneme is, above all, a functional concept that must be defined with respect to its function. Such definition cannot be carried out with psychologistic notions.' (Trubetzkoy 39)

Since phonemes, for the Prague School were defined entirely through 'oppositions', that is, by pairs of contrasting sounds, the inability to find contrasting sounds for certain pairs of phonemes had theoretical significance.[1] For example, in English (and also in German) there are no minimal pairs contrasting /t/ and /d/ in word initial position after /s (ʃ in German)/. In such cases we actually find sounds that are 'midway' between the two – voiceless unaspirated stops. Since there is no contrast between these two sounds, which otherwise share features, the linguist has no right to declare the sounds to be one rather than the other. Instead the linguist is required to propose a special kind of sound which is *neither*, but rather lacks the non-contrasting feature, and is thus an incompletely defined sound. Such a sound is an **archiphoneme**. Traditionally archiphonemes are represented with an upper case letter, so the sound in words like 'stop' and 'stew' would be represented as /T/.

While archiphonemes are a mainstay of a number of current theories, including most varieties of **Generative Phonology**, and have been proposed by some Cognitive Grammar theorists, Stampe (1973) and I (Nathan 2008) have argued that they are psychologically implausible entities. If one believes that phonemes are generalizations extracted from numerous instances of sounds stored in memory then it is quite possible that speakers could propose relatively schematic abstractions such as incompletely specified representations. However, if one takes the traditional psychological view of the phoneme as an image of an idealized sound then it must be totally specified, complete with articulatory instructions and acoustic specifications at a considerable level of detail We know what a 't-sound' sounds like, and can say it to ourselves, even if, as we have seen, we may pronounce it quite differently in some particular circumstance. Ask someone to say the word '*cotton*' out loud and you will get (from the average American) the pronunciation [kɑʔn̩], but if you ask them to say the word sound by sound you will get a pronunciation [tʰi] or perhaps [tʰə], and they will happily match the third sound in the word to the first sound in the word '*tea*'. This kind of behavior is quite different from that found when we see a dachshund or a St. Bernard and say it's a 'dog'. We notice the distinction between kinds of dogs, even if we have formed a category of 'dogs' by abstracting from individual instances. Of course, except to an expert, all St. Bernards look alike.

A second enduring concept from the Prague school is **neutralization.** The situation wherein two phonemes, under certain circumstances, share an allophone is called neutralization, because the *contrast* between the two distinct phonemes is said to be **neutralized**. (See Mompéan-González (2001) for a Cognitive Grammar discussion of this concept.) Thus we

---

1. We're not talking here about the accidental inability to find minimal pairs for sounds such as /h/ vs. /ŋ/, incidentally.

find **archiphonemes** in positions of neutralization. The example discussed above for English, where there is no contrast between /t/ and /d/ after /s/ constitutes a position of neutralization, so words like 'star' and 'spy' must be transcribed phonemically /sTɑr/ and /sPaɪ/. These words will always be transcribed this way, but more interesting cases occur when some word (or morpheme) contains a neutralization only in some cases, while in other cases the 'true' phoneme reappears. Consider, for example, American English cases involving /t/ and /d/. For verbs ending in one of these two sounds, the present participle places these phonemes in a position where the appropriate allophone for either phoneme is the flap [ɾ]:

(1)  'get'    [gɛt]    'getting'    [gɛɾɪŋ]
     'bread'  [bɹɛd]   'breading'   [bɹɛɾɪŋ]

This is a case of conditioned neutralization, which leads to variation in the *phonemic* spelling of the morpheme involved, according to the Prague School. A morpheme such as 'get' will need to be represented as /gɛT/ in the suffixed form, and as /gɛt/ in the root form. Such an alternation is referred to as **morphophonemic**. A much more famous case is that of German, where final obstruents may only be voiceless. Thus there are words in the language which have a voiced consonant at the end when a suffix is added, but exhibit a voiceless correspondent when the suffix does not occur:

(2)  Bund   'union'   [bʊnt]
     Bunde  'unions'  [bʊndə]

In final position the Prague school linguist would posit an archiphoneme /T/, then need to specify that the word 'union' exhibited two forms, one, with a /T/ in final position, the other with a /d/ when in non-final position. As we saw in an earlier chapter, this situation is referred to as an instance of **alternation**, and raises all the issues of rule ordering and abstractness that we will discuss below.

## 10.3  American structuralism

The American Structuralist school was generally characterized by a much more concrete view of phonological structure. This was in part because most American Structuralists were heavily influenced by the prevailing philosophical trend in America in the thirties and forties, namely positivism, and the prevailing psychological school at the same time, namely behaviorism. Both views put a strong premium on the purely observable and operationally definable aspects of reality.

American structuralism accepted the idea of the phoneme, but viewed it as primarily a way of classifying the sounds that linguists could find in their narrow phonetic transcriptions.[2] For the American Structuralists, phonemes were classes of phonetically similar

---

2. There was a certain amount of dissent from the views I am about to describe. Edward Sapir accepted the psychological view of the phoneme that I have presented above, and Kenneth Pike had

sounds in complementary distribution, and nothing more. This led them to reject some of the basic concepts found in Prague School phonology. Thus, for American Structuralists there were no archiphonemes, and no neutralization. If a contrast between two phonemes was neutralized in some context, we classify the sound as being a member of the phoneme it is closest to. Thus, for German, where there is final devoicing, the sound in final position *is* a member of the voiceless phoneme, not an abstract entity unspecified for voicing.

This strong preference for concreteness had some interesting consequences. One was that phonemes could not overlap. That is, a single sound could not be an allophone of two different phonemes. This view was often expressed in the aphorism 'once a phoneme, always a phoneme'. Taking a classic example, the English flap [ɾ] was argued to be always and only a member of the /d/ phoneme, since, by being voiced, it is most similar to the other allophones of /d/. If there is an alternation such as those discussed above: *late ~ later*, this is a fact about the *morphology* of the language, not the phonology: the morpheme *late* has two different phonemic 'spellings' (i.e. two allomorphs): /leɪt/ and / leɪd/, conditioned by the presence vs. absence of a vowel-initial suffix. This view, which has largely been superseded within linguistic theory as a whole is still found in the view that, for example, the English plural suffix has three phonologically conditioned allomorphs /z ~ s ~ əz/.[3] The alternative view, which has been taken in this book, is that these are not facts about morphology, but about automatic consequences of habits of pronunciation, and hence are part of the phonology, thus contrasting strongly with what are clearly morphological facts such as the vowel alternations in plurals like *teeth*, *lice* and so on.

Another important principle in American Structuralism is a strong desire for symmetrical 'solutions' to phonemic problems. This view has had a strong influence on how linguists view the vowel system of English.

### 10.3.1   The Trager-Smith analysis of English

It is well-known that American English vowels come in pairs: [i ~ ɪ][eɪ ~ ɛ][u ~ ʊ][oʊ ~ ɔ]. The first member of each pair is systematically longer than the second, but also has a 'colored' off-glide, in the direction of /i/ for the front vowels, and /u/ for the back ones. It is further the case that American English has two glides, /j/ (traditionally written /y/ in North America, and for this section that transcription will be used) and /w/. These glides at first glance only appear at the beginning of syllables: 'you, yet, yellow; we, wall, watermelon'. They are thus in complementary distribution with the off-glides found in the tense vowels in 'be' and 'bay', 'boo' and 'bow (and arrow)'. Since they are phonetically similar, and

---

a similar, speaker-oriented view. The views presented in this section are primarily those of Leonard Bloomfield, Bernard Bloch and George Trager, among others, and can be found in the Joos reader.

3.   You probably encountered this view in your introductory Linguistics text, since certain basic ways of looking at things get 'stuck', so that they appear in introductory texts even though they have been abandoned by most current theorists.

in complementary distribution, American Structuralist theory states that we must assign them to the same phoneme. Thus, we will transcribe the following words:

(3)   bee   /biy/   bit   /bit/
     bay   /bey/   bet   /bet/
     boo   /buw/   put   /put/
     beau   /bow/   bought   /bɔt/[4]

Again, notice the identification of the diphthongal nuclei with the lax versions (even though the official 'tense' IPA symbols are used). Thus, it is readily agreed that the center of the diphthong in 'bee' is not the same as the vowel in 'bit', but it *is* phonetically similar, and because the two sounds are in complementary distribution, they can be assigned to the same phoneme. The same goes, therefore for the /o/ (although it turns out to be difficult to find examples of the non-diphthongal case.)

Continuing on, we can note that there are at least three more diphthongs in English, in the words 'I', 'now' and 'boy'. Again, in each case we can identify parts of those diphthongs with pre-existing phonemes – for example the [a] in 'I' is phonetically similar to, and in complementary distribution with the [ɑ] in 'father', and the [y] corresponds to the [y] in 'yacht'. Thus we are justified in transcribing these three words as:

(4)   I   /ay/
     now   /naw/
     boy   /bɔy/

Transcriptions such as these have had a very long history, and current textbooks in many fields (ESL, communications disorders, speech synthesis) still use them, even though the theoretical assumptions on which they are based seem to be incorrect, and even though (as was pointed out by Kenneth Pike as early as 1947) they are not in accord with the intuitions of native speakers. For example, if you ask someone to say the word 'lie' backwards, the answer you will get will most likely be something like [ayl], but the Trager-Smith theory will predict an answer like [yal]. The fact is that English speakers do not perceive the diphthongs of English as consisting of two phonemes, and do not classify the upglides in 'buy' and 'cow' as the same as the onset glides in words like 'yes' and 'wall'. No native speaker of American English would accept 'wok' (or 'walk') as an example of 'cow' said backwards. If phonemes are basic-level categories then the traditional American analysis is getting it wrong. Pike (1947) raised this issue almost immediately after the original proposal.

There is an additional complication in the Trager-Smith analysis of American English that still has traces in the twenty-first century. Trager and Smith proposed an additional off-glide to account for the minimal set of contrasts found in words such as 'merry~Mary',

---

4. The fact that the vowel nucleus of the 'lax' version differs from that of the tense version is an added complication that we need not go into. You can consult the original articles, found in the bibliography (Bloch and Trager, Trager and Smith) or find an old introductory linguistics text, such as Gleason for the arguments.

'bomb~balm'[5] and 'pod~*Pa*'d'.[6] This sound, which, in some instances was realized as mere length, and, in others as a schwa-like off-glide, occurred only as the second half of ing-liding diphthongs. Hence, it was in *complementary distribution* with initial /h/, and, since phonetically similar (this caused howls from some critics, such as Pike), they could be assigned to the same phoneme, often written /h/, although some rejected the connection with the sound in 'hat/he/etc.' and preferred /H/. I mention this because there is a tradition in American dialectology to refer to the variants of the vowel in words such as 'coffee, caught' as /oh/, or /OH/. This can be found even in contemporary transcriptions such as those found on William Labov's excellent website on phonological variation in American English (http://www.ling.upenn.edu/phono_atlas/home.html).

## 10.4 Generative phonology

The dominant phonological paradigm in the early twenty-first century is some version of what could (etymologically) be called Generative Phonology. It arose out of what was once called Transformational Generative grammar, although virtually all of what was subsumed under that rubric has been revised, in many cases so radically that a putative Rip van Chomsky would not recognize any of it. In addition, the field has fragmented ideologically so that, both in Syntax and in Phonology there are internal schisms wide enough to be considered competing theories. Although the founders of Cognitive Grammar (Lakoff and Langacker) would now deny that they practice anything remotely connected with 'generative' grammar, they were both practitioners of generative semantics, an early branch of generative syntax. Within phonology almost all contemporary theorists, and in particular those who are developing and extending Optimality Theory were students of Morris Halle, and thus in a direct 'genealogical' line to the origins of generative phonology. As long as the term is understood purely in a historical sense, then, we are all 'generative phonologists'.

### 10.4.1 Classic generative phonology

Throughout most of the last quarter of a century, the dominant theoretical orientation of phonologists, at least in North America, Europe, and, to a certain extent, in Japan, has been one variety or another, or a descendant of the theory known generically as **Generative Phonology**. It is only in the past ten or so years that the theory has been supplanted by a new one, Optimality Theory (OT). Since there is an enormous literature written within the framework of **Generative Phonology**, it is important to understand its assumptions,

---

5. The preceding two only for those dialects (such as mine, incidentally) that differentiate these words solely by vowel length.

6. As in 'Pa'd like you to leave'. Remember that colloquial English constitutes perfectly acceptable data.

and to be able to read the various formalisms. In addition, much research within OT simply assumes the existence of GP analyses and attempts to reanalyze them within the new theory.

**Generative Phonology** originated in the nineteen fifties with an analysis of English stress patterns, but really came into its own in the sixties with the publication of the monumental *Sound Pattern of English* (Chomsky & Halle 1968). This book is actually five books in one. It contains an analysis of the stress patterns of English, of the morphophonemic alternations of much of English derivational phonology, a theory of phonological features, a theory of rule notation, a history of the English vowel system since Middle English and a theory of markedness. Each of these parts has been enormously influential in the development of phonology, although virtually every detail in it has been supplanted in the forty years since it was published.

Perhaps the most influential aspect of the **Generative Phonology** model was its claim that the distinction between phonemic processes and *morpho*phonemic processes was an error. Remember from our discussion of American Structuralism above that cases such as German final devoicing constituted morphological, rather than phonological behavior. Given the principle (often cited as 'Once a phoneme, always a phoneme') that alternations between sounds at the phonemic level were properly described in the morphological chapter of the grammar, this had as a result that some totally automatic, phonologically motivated patterns were removed from the phonology chapter. In a very famous paper (Halle 1959) argued that this led to conclusions that could not be correct.

The case involves standard Russian. In Russian there is a series of 5 obstruent stop and affricate phonemes:

(5) p t ts tʃ k
 b d g

Note particularly the voiceless/voiced asymmetry – there are more voiceless than voiced stops. Now, there is a (totally automatic) assimilation process between words in Russian, whereby words beginning with voiced consonants spread their voicing leftwards to the end of the preceding word if that word ends with an obstruent. Thus, if a word ends in a voiceless obstruent, and is followed by a voiced obstruent beginning the next word, the final obstruent is voiced. That this is an living process in the language is attested to by the fact that it even occurs in the English of native speakers of Russian, as I mentioned above.

Within the American Structuralist model this process must receive a somewhat odd interpretation. For the cases involving the voicing of /p t k/ the process is *morphophonemic*, because there is an independent set of /b d g/ within the language. However, for the cases of /ts tʃ/ the result is [dz dʒ]. These sounds, since they are not distinct phonemes, are *allophones* of the voiceless sounds, and the process is allophonic for these two cases. Not only does the theory require two different processes, but they would be (at least metaphorically) in different chapters of a grammar (and presumably learned in two different ways by native speakers). But our intuitions as linguists is that this is a totally automatic, physiologically-motivated assimilation process regardless of what the output of the rule is. In neither case are speakers aware that this is happening. This led Halle to conclude that there should be no distinction between allophonic and morphophonemic processes – all phonological processes are the same.

For a long time **Generative Phonology** accepted this argument as is, and consequently there was only one phonological component in the grammar, and it was responsible both for the distribution of such allophonic features as aspiration and vowel length in American English as well as the relatively more complex (and almost certainly less *phonological*) alternations illustrated in such pairs of words as 'divine' ~ 'divinity' (the vowel alternation known as the Vowel Shift) and 'electric ~ electricity' (the consonant alternation known as Velar Softening.)

The model presented in the *Sound Pattern of English* (normally abbreviated **SPE**) assumes that every morpheme in a language is entered in the lexicon in an underlying form consisting of a string of sounds, each sound being simply an unordered list of features. Throughout most of the book it is assumed that every sound is specified for every feature, but in the famous Chapter Nine Chomsky and Halle suggest that many of the features can be omitted and inserted by a set of markedness rules.

The lexical items are basically underived forms of morphemes, and, as a result of the items being placed in positions in a syntactic tree, some of the morphemes are attached to each other, leading to a syntactic tree with a series of strings of phonemes as 'leaves'. This structure, a tree with sounds, constitutes the underlying form, or input to the phonological rules of the language. At this point, a series of phonological rules apply to the string of morphemes. The rules change the values of features, and in some cases, delete, insert, or even change the order of specified sounds. Just as a trivial illustration before we look at some real, and complex examples, the regular noun plural suffix in English is assumed to be /z/, that is a sound specified as

(6) $\begin{bmatrix} \text{CORONAL} \\ \text{+continuant} \\ \text{+voiced} \end{bmatrix}$

This underlying form is attached by the 'syntax' (in some current theories this would be a morphological, rather than a syntactic operation) to a noun. If the noun to which the suffix was attached ended in a voiceless stop, a phonological rule would come into play, changing the value of the feature *voiced* from + to –. After the application of all the phonological rules, we have, as a result, a 'surface' form, using the now defunct metaphor of grammatical structure as having a deep and a surface structure.

It is assumed that all the features in the underlying form remain the same unless some phonological rule changes them. Thus the rule making plural suffixes agree in voicing has no effect on the point of articulation, continuancy and so on of the underlying form, and consequently whatever is left at the end of the **derivation** (the sum of changes produced by the rules) is what is pronounced.

In its simplest form, the underlying form was subject to an application from each rule in the ordered list of rules, and the result was the surface pronunciation. However, even at the beginning there were tricky issues about exactly how often, and when, the rules got to apply. Since some words with layers of suffixes acted as if rules had applied when one suffix was added, then acted as if the rules had *reapplied* after the addition of more suffixes, it was suggested that rules applied **cyclically**, applying to the innermost form of a word, then reapplying as a suffix was added, then reapplying if additional suffixes were added. This was particularly true with stress rules, where English often behaves as if some syllable was assigned primary stress, then has the stress move off that syllable, leaving a secondary stress behind while primary stress goes elsewhere. A classic case is a word set like *théater, theátrical, thèâtricálity*. Here the primary stress falls on the first syllable in the basic word, but that syllable seems to have been reduced to a secondary status in the second word (with the addition of *-al*), and, with the addition of *-ity* stress again shifts, to the preceding suffix, leaving lower degrees of stress on both formerly primarily stressed syllables.

Cyclic rule application was invoked in a number of areas to account for complex morphological operations, but in recent years the number of cases to which it seems to apply has diminished and many writers are no longer sure that this is the appropriate model to account for morphological operations.

During the time after SPE was published a number of questions arose that were intensely debated, up till about 1978, when the model began to fall apart. We will address two of the issues here: abstractness and rule ordering.

### 10.4.2 The abstractness question

As we have seen, if we use morphological alternations as evidence, we can construct underlying forms that are somewhat different from the surface forms which we use to establish them. For example, in some dialects of German the alternation generated by the process of final devoicing, connected with a process spirantizing intervocalic voiced stops would lead to alternations such as the following:

(7) [tak] 'day'
    [taɣə] 'days'

A sensible analysis of this alternation would follow the lines hinted at above: the underlying form would contain a final /g/ which devoices in final position and spirantizes intervocalically. What might be considered problematic in such a solution is the fact that the /g/ occurs in *neither* of the surface forms, and, therefore, is, in some sense, an abstraction. In cases such as this one it is not much of an abstraction, since there is, after all, a /g/ in the language, say in other words such as /gut/ 'good', just not in any given instance of that particular word.

Where things became a little trickier is in cases where the analysis posits an entire *phoneme* that never occurs as such in the language, but in every case merges with some other phoneme. There are a number of famous examples that we could examine. Let us look at perhaps the best known, and most convincing case. In the Yawelmani dialect of Yokuts, spoken in California, there are processes of vowel harmony, and shortening in closed syllables. The following description is based on the extensive discussion in Kenstowicz & Kisseberth (77–99).

Suffixes in Yawelmani agree in roundness and backness with the root vowel if the root and suffix vowel are of the same height. Thus, there is a suffix /-hin ~ -hun/, with the /u/ variety occurring after roots with a /u/:

(8)     xat-hin    bok'-hin
       xil-hin     k'oʔ-hin
       **dub-hun**   **hud-hun**

Other suffixes that behave similarly are /-mi ~ -mu/ and /-nit ~ nut/.

On the other hand, there are also suffixes that alternate between /a/ and /o/: /-al ~ -ol/, /-xa ~ -xo/ and /-taw ~ -tow/. These choose their value depending on the vowel of the root also, but we get the back rounded variety if the root vowel is /o/:

(9)     xat-al     max-al
       dub-al     hud-al
       **k'oʔ-ol**    **bok'-ol**

We can sum up this vowel harmony situation as follows:

(10)    A vowel is pronounced round (and back) if immediately preceded by a round vowel of the same height.

In addition, the language has a general rule that shortens vowels in closed syllables, so that there are vowel length alternations caused when different suffixes, with and without an initial consonant are added to roots with underlying long vowels:

(11)    ṣap-hin    ṣaːp-al
        dos-hin    doːs-ol
        mek'-hin   meːk-al[7]

The interesting set of data are roots that appear to violate vowel harmony, which they do in two different ways. First, there are roots that take high back rounded suffixes even though they have mid vowels, and at the same time, *don't* take back rounded mid vowel suffixes:

(12)    c'om-hun   c'oːm-al
        ṣog-hun    ṣoːg-al

---

7. I am assuming that a shortening analysis is the correct one here. Simply, there are other roots that don't exhibit this shortening behavior, and it is not possible to predict which ones have the alternation and which ones don't. The most straightforward way to deal with this is to assume that there is a length contrast underlyingly, but that it (the contrast) disappears in closed syllables.

In short, these forms behave as if they had high vowels (they take the suffix forms appropriate to high vowels, and don't cause the vowel harmony expected with mid vowels). They also behave as if they have long vowels, since they exhibit the vowel length alternation we mentioned in (7). The language lacks long high vowels[8] on the surface. Suppose, however, that we propose that the forms in (8) have /uː/ in their roots. In such a case, the correct vowel harmony behavior would follow automatically, but we would need to 'clean up' the forms, lowering the vowels to /oː/. We could do this with a rule lowering all long high vowels to mid, but ordering the lowering rule *after* the vowel harmony rule had a chance to apply, and before the shortening rule, since we don't want the /uː/ merged with /u/. Thus, a derivation would look like this:

(13)  Underlying      /cʼuːm-al/   /cuːm-hin/
      Vowel Harm.     ----         -hun
      Lowering        oː           oː
      Shortening      oː           o
      Surface         cʼoːm-al     com-hun

We haven't formally stated the lowering rule, and when we do, we find that it has an odd form:

(14) $\begin{bmatrix} V \\ +high \\ +long \end{bmatrix} \rightarrow [-high]$

What is odd about this rule is that it has no environment – the rule applies to every instance of /uː/ that it finds. That is, it totally neutralizes the contrast between /uː/ and /oː/. The only way that we know that a word ever contained an /uː/ is the irregular vowel harmony behavior. However, there are other hints that this is the right analysis. For example, all verbs in the language that consist of two syllables have the same vowel quality in both syllables, *except for roots that show this odd [vowel harmony] behavior*. Thus, there are bisyllabic roots like this

(15)  CaCaː(C)
      CiCeː(C)
      CoCoː(C)
      CuCoː(C)

These basic forms would look much more regular, and would have rule-governed vowel harmony if the second and fourth forms were underlying

(16)  CiCiː(C)
      CuCuː(C)

Then we could call these 'echo' roots (or something), and the irregularity would appear much less irregular.

---

**8.** There are exceptions to this statement, but they can be ignored for expositional purposes.

So far, this analysis is 'clever', and generates the correct surface forms. Why have I spent several pages discussing it? The point is, the analysis relies on the existence of an underlying /uː/ (and also an underlying /iː/, although the evidence for it is less strong) that never occurs on the surface in the language. That is, we have posited a phoneme that is never pronounced anywhere in the language, but always comes out identical to some other phoneme, either an /o/ or an /oː/. This is a case of **absolute neutralization**, and it made theoreticians in the nineteen seventies uncomfortable. While the Yawelmani case was somewhat persuasive, there were other cases proposed that were less so. Often the phoneme that was proposed was supported by only a few forms that alternated (there are approximately as many /oː/'s in Yawelmani as there are proposed /uː/'s). The question was raised as to whether a child learning the language could ever have discovered the identity of the proposed abstract phoneme. For example, in SPE Chomsky and Halle proposed the existence of a velar fricative /x/ in contemporary English to account for the alternation between *right* and *righteous*. Without going into the fine details, they noted that the tense diphthong /aɪ/ in the suffixed form ought not to be there. In general, English words with two syllable suffixes have lax vowels in their root: *sanity, serenity, trinity*. Since there are two vowels in *-eous* (compare *religiosity*), we need to explain why *righteous* has a tense vowel. If we set up an underlying /x/ in the root: /rixt/, and propose a rule tensing vowels before /x/ ordered after trisyllabic laxing, we can account for the correct vowel. This hypothetical /x/ would also account for the tense first syllable in *nightingale*. Again, since (at least standard) English lacks a /x/ (except marginally in some pronunciations of *yuch* [jʊx] and proper names such as *Bach* and *Loch Ness* [lɔx nɛs]) this is an abstract segment. In addition, the reasons for choosing /x/ (rather than, say, [ɸ] or [ɮ]) are arbitrary). The fact that earlier stages of English showed [x] in these words cannot have been coincidental,[9] but this was never explicitly alluded to in the discussion. However, the methodology of setting up underlying representations to account for morphophonemic alternations is essentially the same as the methodology for internal reconstruction (as discussed in Chapter VIII), so it is not surprising that underlying forms come to resemble earlier stages of a language. This does not, per se argue against abstract solutions to complex morphological alternations, but as early as 1968 Paul Kiparsky, one of Chomsky and Halle's early students and still a major figure in phonological and morphological theory, argued cogently that abstract underlying forms do not behave in historical change the way other, more concrete phonemes do, and there is evidence that speakers simply memorize alternations in many cases, rather than setting up abstract underlying forms. His original article appeared in mimeographed form but was finally published as Kiparsky (1982).

Various ways of constraining the kinds of abstractions that could be posited were proposed, but by the late nineteen seventies the issue had become uninteresting, and people simply stopped worrying about it. It is not clear that there is yet a principled solution, at least within generative phonology.

---

9. Note that the spelling system reflects this earlier stage.

## 10.4.3 Rule ordering

Another hot issue during the nineteen seventies was the question of the appropriate sequence of rule applications. At the beginning of **Generative Phonology** it was simply assumed that rules needed to apply in a specified order, which was, in effect, part of the grammar of the language. It was clearly the case that, in long derivations, the results of one rule had an influence on the operation of a subsequent rule. For example, consider the pair of processes discussed in Chapter VI: the coronal stops /t,d,n/ become flaps under certain stress-defined conditions. Subsequently flaps can be deleted in relatively casual speech. Self-evidently, the flap deletion process must follow the flap creation process – otherwise there would be nothing to delete, since flaps are allophones of other sounds. When **Generative Phonology** was first developing, such cases were used to argue for the importance of sequential rule ordering, because it was believed that earlier, structuralist theories of phonemes and allophones required that all rules applied simultaneously, thus not allowing for the intermediate stage that ordered rules permit.

Almost immediately, however, people began to question the idea that all rules needed to be ordered. In the first case, most rules do not interact – that is, do not have any effect on each other. The process nasalizing vowels before nasal consonants in the same foot has no interaction with the rule aspirating voiceless stops in syllable-initial position. If every rule needed to have an explicit number associated with it, it would be difficult to assign numbers to rules that ignored each other's output. But once the concept of **unordered rules** was admitted, people began to ask whether *any* rules needed to be ordered at all. A famous paper by Paul Kiparsky (Kiparsky 1968) added to this debate when he looked at how languages change their rule orderings over time. In order to study this he developed a typology of rule ordering which has become a standard way of talking about rule interaction.

Kiparsky first looked at cases where the application of a rule created a situation where a subsequent rule could then apply. For example, a rule might create some sound, which a later rule would then apply to. Alternatively, a rule might create a sound, which would then constitute the environment for a later rule. Such a situation Kiparsky called **feeding order**, and the earlier rule was said to **feed** the later one. A simple example would be the flapping and flap deletion processes discussed above. Or consider a language in which stress was assigned by rule, but later some allophone is determined by the placement of a sound with respect to the stress. Here stress-assignment feeds the allophonic rule. For example, the word 'velar' has, for many speakers a dark l, as it is (depending on one's theoretical predispositions) either foot-internal or syllable-final. However, if the '-ity' suffix is added, stress shifts to the syllable following the /l/, with the result that the /l/ becomes syllable-initial, and is clear. Clearly the stress shift has affected the allophonic process controlling l-coloring. In this case, however, if we assume that the process is a rule of 'l-darkening', what has happened is that the stress shift has *prevented* the process from applying. In that case, Kiparsky said, the first rule **bled** the second, and the rules were said to be in a **bleeding** order.

It is often difficult to find sequences of purely allophonic rules, but there are many cases of more abstract morphologically based rules preceding allophonic ones. However, we can find some cases, if we make appropriate assumptions. For example, in a casual pronunciation of the word 'quality', several casual speech processes may interact. There is a /t/, which in that environment would normally be flapped: [ˈkwɒɾəɾi]. However, the word contains a schwa, and, as we have seen, schwas can be deleted under most circumstances, including these. However, if we pronounce this word without a schwa, we cannot have a flapped /t/, as this is unpronounceable: *[kwɒɾɾi], and instead we must say [kwɒɫti]. Hence, schwa deletion bleeds flapping.

Sometimes a rule that could potentially feed a later rule fails to do so. In such a case the rules are said to be in a 'counterfeeding' order. For example, as we saw in the chapter on casual speech, in English sonorant consonants that follow initial voiceless stops are devoiced: 'please', 'clean' [pl̥iz, kl̥in]. This occurs even if the initial syllable is unstressed: 'Pretoria', 'Platonic' [pr̥ətɔriə, pl̥ətɑnɪk]. However, a sonorant that comes to be next to an initial voiceless stop through schwa-deletion does not get devoiced, so 'parade', 'police' are pronounced [preɪd, plis], and devoiced sonorants are ungrammatical: [*pr̥eɪd, *pl̥is]. When the rule-ordering controversy was an active concern examples like these were commonly discussed (although rarely with examples from casual speech). What is going on is that a general pattern (sonorants are normally devoiced after syllable-initial voiceless stops) is *contradicted* in these words, because we have sonorants that are not devoiced following voiceless stops. The devoicing process, in this case, is said to be **opaque**, because we have a voiced sonorant that ought to be voiceless.[10] This situation, where an otherwise well-motivated process does not apply because there 'used to be' an intervening segment that is blocking the operation of the process continues to worry phonologists. The theory we will be discussing next, Optimality Theory, has spent some considerable effort accounting for what have come to be known as *opacity effects*. Within rule ordering the 'solution' was to have *extrinsic* rule ordering, where it was an explicit 'rule' of the grammar that, say, the deletion rule *follows* the devoicing rule. Since, under the theory that included explicit rule-ordering statements, rules got to apply only once per derivation, once a rule had a chance to apply and failed to do so, it lost out forever. The result, for example, in the case being discussed here, is that although the schwa has been deleted, it still leaves a 'trace' in the voiced rather than voiceless /l̥/ that we would otherwise expect.

A famous example concerns Sundanese, an Austronesian language spoken in Indonesia. (Robins 1957). In Sundanese vowels are nasalized after nasal consonants. The nasalization extends from the nasal consonant to the end of the word, unless interrupted by a consonant other than /h/ or /ʔ/. Thus there are words like [mã] and [mãʔã] but [mãta]. However, there is another, optional, process that deletes voiced stops after homorganic

---

10. There is another kind of opacity – cases where a sound that is not supposed to be there is there nonetheless. An example, again from casual speech, would be nasalized vowels in English before voiceless consonants. *Aunt* can be pronounced [æ̃t], because a nasal deletion process removes nasals before tautosyllabic voiceless stops.

nasals. Clusters such as /naŋga/ occur, and are subject to this optional cluster simplification process. However, the process potentially interacts with the aforementioned vowel nasalization process, in that if the deletion process operates a vowel comes to stand after a nasal consonant. In this case, *the vowel is not nasalized*. Hence the generalization that vowels are nasalized after nasal consonants is not true, just in case there was 'once' a consonant blocking the nasalization, even though the consonant is no longer there. In this sense, the oral vowel 'marks' the presence of the deleted consonant. Again, when phonologists talked in terms of the order that rules applied, this was said to be a 'counterfeeding' order, because *if the rules were in the* other *order*, the deletion of the /g/ would have fed the vowel nasalization rule. But it doesn't. Consequently, vowel nasalization is said to be opaque, because its effects are obscured by the presence of a consonant that is no longer there.

I have spent some time explaining these cases because they have caused considerable difficulty in the development of phonological theory. In particular, they have posed a problem for the theory we will in section 5, Optimality Theory, and the solutions that have been proposed are so complex that they have satisfied nobody.

### 10.4.4 Autosegmental phonology – innovations in representation

One thing that remained constant in phonological theory from the introduction of features until the eighties was that features were features of sounds. In classic Generative Phonology each sound was represented, as we have seen from Chapter IV, by a matrix of features, nominally all binary. The features were stacked within extended square brackets. There were various views of how many features were required to specify each sound, but what was not in doubt was that each sound was represented by a stack of features, and each stack represented one and only one sound.

This view was challenged in various ways in the late seventies, with the new views taking full effect by the eighties, where they remain today (even with the revolution of Optimality Theory, to be discussed below).

The simplest way to understand what changed was to think about a kind of phonological entity we haven't spent much time talking about – tone. As we have seen, tones have traditionally been understood either as a series of even levels (called terraced tones) or of trajectories (rising, falling, fall-rise etc.). In a seminal work, John Goldsmith (1979, 1990) pointed out that strange things happen when segments with tones attached interact with each other. For example, in a number of West African languages, final vowels are deleted when words are followed by vowel-initial words:

(17)     V C V́ + V́ C V → V C + V́ C V

However, in some tone languages, while the first vowel in a two-vowel sequence is deleted, the first tone shows up on the remaining vowel. Now, given a view of phonology in which rules can change features, insert or delete segments and nothing else, it is virtually impossible to represent this change – we'd have to assimilate the (to-be-deleted) tone to the following one, then delete the vowel.

Suppose, however, that the segmental features (anterior, continuant etc.) were represented on one line, while the tone features were represented on a line immediately under the segmental features that they were attached to ('associated with'), and connected with a line:

(18)   V
       |
       H

where H was the feature representation for high tone. Let us imagine that the 'association lines' can be deleted. You can think of them as attaching the things below them by suspending them with a piece of string (like a mobile), so if we cut the string they will drop off (or, in the case of something being cut off from the thing below, it will float away like a helium balloon).

Consider then, the representation in (19).

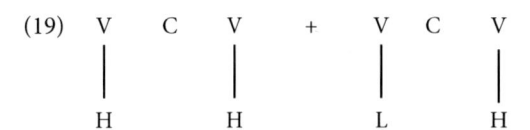

(19)   V   C   V   +   V   C   V
       |       |       |       |
       H       H       L       H

On the first line we have a row of C's and V's (representing, of course, consonants and vowels). Connected to each vowel is a tone. Under normal circumstances consonants don't have tones, but there are cases where we are forced to treat at least voiced consonants as if they have tones too – this is a matter for a more advanced course on tonal phonology). Diagram (20) shows what happens – the word-final vowel is deleted, but the tone attached to it remains (like the smile on the Cheshire Cat in Alice).

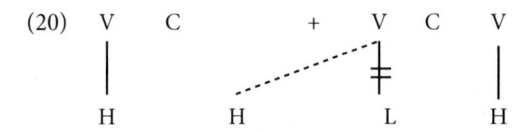

(20)   V   C       +   V   C   V
       |                   ǂ   |
       H       H       L       H

The tone that is leftover reassociates to the vowel to its left (there is still debate within phonological theory as to whether this is an automatic, universal reassociation or language-specific). The reassociation is represented by a dotted line (meaning, essentially, 'draw a line like this') Simultaneously, the tone originally attached to the surviving vowel is also cut off (this is definitely language specific, as we will see). The result is a secquence that began

(21)   V́ C V́ + V̀ C V́

changed to a sequence

(22)   V́ C + V̀ C V́

As mentioned in the preceding paragraph, in other languages it has been found that the tone on the surviving vowel survives too. This results in a vowel with two tones, first a High, then a Low. What would this mean? (see Diagram (23) for an example)

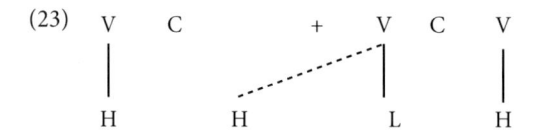

(23)   V     C         +     V    C    V
       |                          |    |
       H     H               L    H

It would mean, of course, a falling tone, and numerous examples of such cases were discovered by Goldsmith and those following him. It certainly makes it look as if tones have an independent existence parallel to the segments they are attached to, and can stay or go independently of the segments they are attached to. This is the origin of the name of this theory – autosegmental phonology, because each line is autonomous.

The image to keep in mind here is one of a musical score – we have, for example, words represented along with musical notes. Sometimes the syllables line up exactly with the notes, but sometimes a single syllable can be sung on more than one note. Bar lines in musical notation keep the various lines of the music in synchrony, but for this, phonological, notation we need a line for each segment to be aligned. Each separate horizontal line of features is called a tier.

What happened next was that people immediately saw other ways in which features behaved indsependently (actually, Goldsmith explored this in his original publication). For example, we know that nasal assimilation is a very common phonological process. A nasal consonant (often [n]) takes on the point of assimilation of the following stop. Suppose we put point of articulation on one tier and the manner of articulation on another. Then, if a consonant lost its point of articulation, it could, by reattaching an association line, get the point of articulation from the following segment. This is diagrammed in Diagram (24).

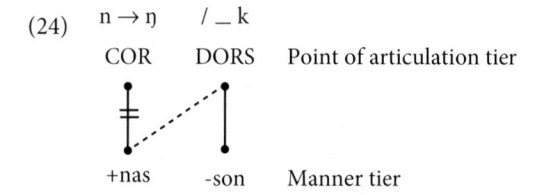

(24)   n → ŋ      / _ k
       COR     DORS    Point of articulation tier

       +nas    -son    Manner tier

Now feature representations are more like orchestral scores, with numerous instruments (and, if it's a score for an opera or oratorio numerous voices) all playing and singing at once, but not necessarily singing the same notes at the same time.

Furthermore, it became clear that features were not simply an unorganized list, independent of each other. Rather than having all features sprout off a single root node (akin to a shower head) they are grouped into divisions that have existed all along in phonology (and phonetics) but without having any official status. So, there is now a 'Point of Articulation' node, off which the major point features attach (LABIAL, CORONAL, VELAR, and RADICAL). All the 'Supralaryngeal' features are a higher level group, independent of the glottal features (voicing, aspiration, constricted glottis). Each of these subgroups were established based on the fact that they assimilated as a group in some language. A typical example would be the nasal assimilation in (24). The full feature tree is seen in Diagram (25). A basic introduction to this way of viewing things can be found in McCarthy (1988), and Kenstowicz (1993) is also a good reference.

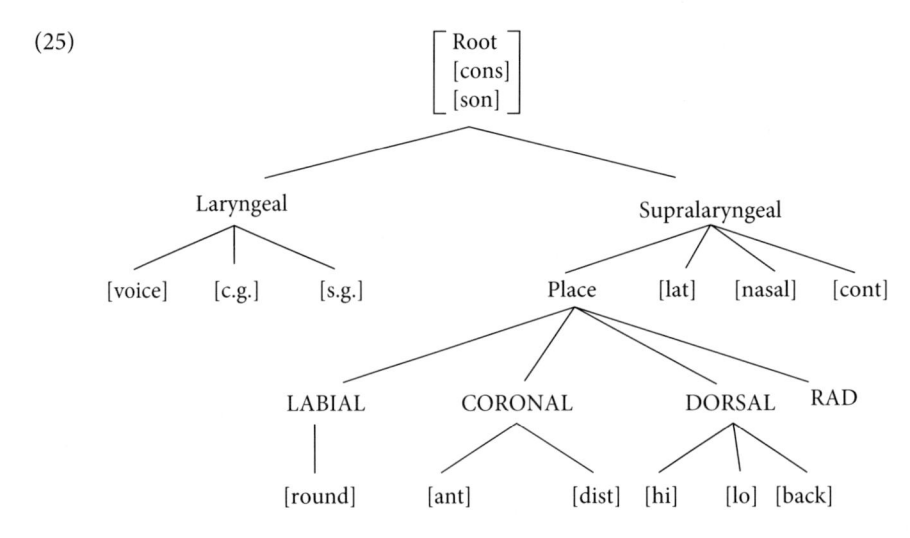

(25)

```
                    ⎡ Root  ⎤
                    ⎢ [cons]⎥
                    ⎣ [son] ⎦
                   /          \
           Laryngeal         Supralaryngeal
          /    |   \         /    |    |    \
     [voice][c.g.][s.g.]  Place [lat][nasal][cont]
                         /   |    |    \
                     LABIAL CORONAL DORSAL RAD
                        |    / \    / | \
                    [round][ant][dist][hi][lo][back]
```

Again, once feature matrices were decomposed in this way, other possibilities opened up. Currently there is a node a the 'top' of the feature tree called the root node, to which all other features attach. This represented the fact that there is a segment, without any information about what it is (all of that is, of course, underneath). But sometimes it's useful to be able to refer simply to the presence of a segment without any specifications. This has led to the root node being dominated by a timing tier – a tier simply representing the duration of a segment. For example, as we have seen, many languages have long segments, both consonants and vowels. Instead of treating them as two identical segments, we could treat them as two timing segments (often referred to as X tier segments) with a single root node below them.

Once we recognize long segments as successive timing segments with co-attached articulatory information, we can easily represent a relatively common phonological process which is almost impossible to represent with the traditional X > Y / ___ Z notation. In many languages there has been a historical change whereby a coda consonant is lost, with simultaneous lengthening of the vowel. It's as if the syllable wants to remain heavy, and when the coda consonant is lost, the nucleus vowel lengthens to compensate – hence the traditional name compensatory lengthening. For example, in the history of English nasal consonants in codas were sometimes lost, with concomitant lengthening of the vowel. The English word 'five' for example, had a long vowel in Old English [fīf] but the corresponding vowels in the other Germanic languages are short and contain a nasal (German fünf, Danish fem etc.).[11] Apparently the nasal was lost with compensatory lengthening of the vowel.

While expressing this change within the original **Generative Phonology** framework would require two rules, crucially ordered (first lengthen the vowel in the requisite environment, then delete the nasal in a very similar environment) we can represent this simply as deletion of an association line with reattachment:

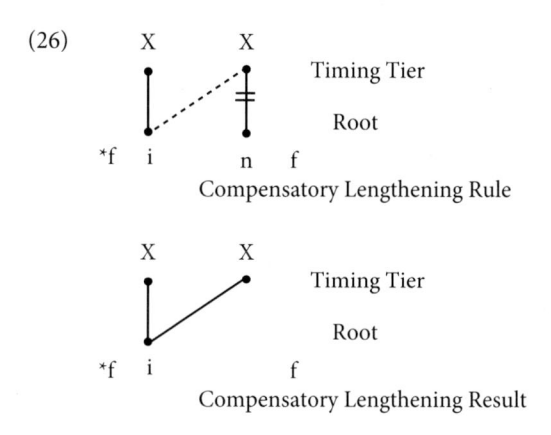

(26)         X       X
             •·······•              Timing Tier
             |    ╪
             |  ╪
             •       •              Root
            *f  i    n   f
             Compensatory Lengthening Rule

             X       X
             •       •              Timing Tier
             |      ╱
             •                      Root
            *f  i           f
             Compensatory Lengthening Result

Numerous other clever things can be done with autosegmental notation, which in some ways is just an additional notational device, and in other ways has revolutionalized the way we think about phonology.[12] Recall that we introduced the idea in chapter IV that segments are assembled into syllables (via the superstructure of onset, rhyme and so on). This view is integrated into autosegmental phonology by having the X-tier link upwards to the syllable structure. The syllable structure, in addition, links, in a different direction, to the principles governing stress (recall that stress is often sensitive to syllable weight, which corresponds to whether the rhyme branches). Visualizing this gets quite complex, incidentally. One image that has been used is to suggest that syllable structure, stress, and segmental information are all linked via a central tier that has the function of a metal spiral in a spiral notebook. I sometimes use Tinkertoys to represent the segmental structure, but

---

11. Similar examples include English 'goose', German *gans*, and English 'tooth', Danish *tand*.

12. In the interests of historical accuracy it should be mentioned that there was a school of British phonology founded by J.R. Firth that considered much of phonology to be trans-segmental (he called it 'prosodic'). His work was most popular in the nineteen fifties and early sixties, but some of his students are still working within a similar framework. Goldsmith acknowledges this influence in his work, incidentally.

it is very difficult to picture the whole thing in a two-dimensional representation such as the page you are reading. For much more information on how autosegmental representations can be used, consult one of the more advanced **Generative Phonology** texts, such as (Ewen & van der Hulst 2000) or (Goldsmith 1990).

### 10.4.5  Optimality theory

In recent years a new theory dealing with the implementation of phonological structures has arisen that takes a totally different tack from the process-oriented view that we have been considering so far. Essentially, the view we have assumed so far could be called the 'factory' metaphor. The input to the phonological system is an underlying form or string of phonemes. These phonemes are then subjected to a **series** of processes, which successively deform the input, adjusting it to fit the phonological constraints that are expressed in rule format – change a vowel to make it nasalized when followed by a nasal consonant,[13] or make a voiceless stop aspirated at the beginning of a stressed syllable.

As we have seen, these processes are normally thought of as following one another, in much the same way as a car being manufactured in an assembly-line style of factory. The car moves along the conveyor belt, with each successive station adding features (seats, wheels.) or changing the appearance (painting, rustproofing.). At the far end, a car emerges. While never explicitly embraced, most phonological theories since the late nineteen fifties have used this metaphor. However, beginning in the seventies there has been some dissent from this view. In the early seventies a number of phonologists began to ask what would happen if rules were not explicitly ordered. Note that the idea that rules apply serially carries the strong implication that the ordering needs to be acquired. At that time most linguists believed that rules needed to be acquired as well, so that left children with a double task – learning both rules and the correct order in which to apply them. This task was necessitated by the fact that most linguists agreed that one way in which closely related dialects could differ was in different orderings of the same rules. In addition, there appeared to be cases where historical change appeared to be best described as change in the ordering of rules.

In the seventies some phonologists noticed that a grammar with rules applying in feeding order gave exactly the same output as a grammar with rules applying without any restrictions at all, over and over again until they had nothing left to apply to. In this case, then, feeding order was equivalent to no ordering *restrictions* at all. Consider, for example, the two rules in American English, one creating flaps, the second deleting them. Clearly, permitting both rules to apply freely at any time has the same effect as serially ordering them Flapping > Flap Deletion.

In addition, counterbleeding order was equivalent to permitting the rules to apply simultaneously. Take, for example, what happens in a number of South American Spanish

---

13. I am grossly simplifying the actual nature of the vowel nasalization rule in, say, English. Nasalization is sensitive to syllable and foot structure, as we have seen.

dialects. Here there is a (very common) rule laxing /e/ to [ɛ] when in a closed syllable. In addition, there is a well-known rule deleting syllable-final /s/ (in other dialects the process is less drastic, removing the supraglottal articulation, leaving an [h] – for that reason the process is known as s-aspiration). In some dialects these processes apply in the order given, a counterbleeding order (if s-deletion applied first there would be no syllables closed by /s/ and the e-laxing rule would not get to apply). So we have a derivation that looks like this:

(27)  Underlying Form   /ombre-s/   'men'
      Laxing            ombrɛs
      Aspiration        ombrɛ
      Surface Form      ombrɛ

But notice that, if we were to apply the rules *simultaneously*, we would get exactly the same result – both rules would look at the underlying form, see their relevant structural descriptions, and apply.

So by permitting rules to apply all at once and over and over again we can get the same results as if we had both feeding and counterbleeding orders. The problematic orders that remain are counterfeeding and bleeding. The linguists that attempted to defend this 'no rule ordering' theory dealt with the leftover cases by reanalyzing known cases of counterfeeding in other ways. Natural phonology, on the other hand took a different tack. Accepting the ideas of free reapplication and simultaneous application the natural phonologists argued that all cases of bleeding order had independent explanations in terms of kinds of rules/processes. First, it appeared that all rules (in the technical NP sense) precede all processes. So rules could bleed processes, without speakers independently needing to learn that particular ordering (and the claim was also that rules and processes could never apply simultaneously). Just as an obvious example, the word '*contrite*' ends in an alveolar stop. When the adjectival suffix *-ion* is added we might expect a flap, but there is a *rule* in English changing /t/ to /ʃ/ before this suffix, which bleeds the *process* of flapping. This ordering has a natural cognitive explanation, incidentally – rules always apply to relate phonemes to one another (or to change one phoneme into another), that is, to intentions. Processes realize intentions, so of course rules will always apply 'before' processes, since rules change the targets that processes then aim at.

Second, fortitions always took precedence over lenitions, so again, no learning was necessary (and it was claimed that fortitions never applied simultaneously with lenitions[14]).

Consequently, any cases of bleeding seemed to have independently motivated explanations. On the other hand, there do seem to be irreducible cases of counterfeeding orders.

---

14. Note that example (27) above involves two lenitions, which can apply simultaneously.

The interactions between schwa deletion and sonorant devoicing discussed in the previous section would constitute examples.

A similar example is cited in Donegan & Stampe (148); where in some southern American dialects, the back diphthong /aʊ/ is monophthongized to [aː] (*house, town*). However, another breaking-type process diphthongizes /ɔ/ to [aʊ] (*saw, dog*). The two processes, however, appear to be restricted so that the 'new' diphthong (from underlying /ɔ/) never monophthongizes (no one in this dialect says *[daːg, saː] for *dog, saw*). Again, we appear to need a counterfeeding constraint. Donegan and Stampe argue that the way to capture this constraint is to say that we simply mark the non-recurring process as being restricted to underlying forms. The function of this constraint, as they argue, is to preserve the underlying contrast /aʊ/ vs. /ɔ/ (say in 'bowed' vs. 'baud'). Permitting the monophthongization process to apply to derived forms would merge the two vowels.

The upshot of this is that there is some evidence that rule *ordering*, that is, the learned serial application of rules and processes is virtually dispensible, with perhaps the exception of a limitation of some processes to apply only to underlying forms.

However, many phonologists have been unhappy with the notion of *any* kind of serial derivation at all. For example Lakoff (1993), argued that the idea of serial derivations has no cognitive reality at all, and a Cognitive Phonology should not countenance them. In that paper he attempted to provide a theory with three separate **levels**, each of which was related to the 'previous' one by a simple statement. This reduced a theoretically infinite series of levels produced by successive applications of serially ordered rules to exactly three. However, Lakoff provided no independent argumentation for the existence of the levels that he posited, and, although he named them 'morphophonemic, phonemic and allophonic' they had no status analogous to the way other linguists used the terms.

Since that time, however, a new proposal has gained ascendance in phonological theory, one that permits no serial derivations at all. This theory, known as **Optimality Theory** (OT), proposes that all derivation take place simultaneously (Prince & Smolensky 1994 was the original source, but now there are hundreds of papers, dozens of books and several websites, including the official one, roa.rutgers.edu). There is simply the input (essentially equivalent to the phonemic form) and the output. A completely different way of looking at what processes do and how they work permits the rules to apply simultaneously.

It is precisely in the area of rule interaction that OT acts differently. Think about what a standard process does: It replaces a specific configuration of sounds with another, differing only in not having that configuration. In principle, then, we could think of this activity as having two parts – a prohibition against a particular configuration (or a requirement for a particular configuration) and a preference for the underlying form to be the same as the surface form. OT replaces the factory notion of process: 'take this combination, and replace some aspect of it with something better', with two notions: 'don't have this combination' and 'don't make the surface form different'.

The crucial difference between the two theories is that OT 'rules' are all statements about what is good and bad, not statements about what to do about it. In some sense, what to do about it is left up to the speaker, but the combination of constraints about what is good and bad is so tight that only the correct output can be produced, even without the process statements of the serial derivation model.

Every 'rule' in OT is known as a **constraint**, and constraints are always expressed declaratively: 'syllables must have onsets', 'vowels are not nasalized', 'stress should fall at the end of the word' and so on. What is crucial about the constraints in OT is that they are **defeasible**. This is a technical term from logic meaning that they do not hold absolutely but can be overridden by a higher-ranking constraint. There are a large number of constraints, and, within the **Generative Phonology** tradition where OT originated, it is believed that the constraints are part of Universal Grammar. This means that they do not have to be learned. Instead, they are all part of the innate knowledge of language that all human beings have. Cognitive Grammar does not, of course, accept the concept of UG, but does accept the view that human beings share aspects of cognition that determine the shape that grammars take. Many OT theorists believe that the constraints of OT are in UG because they reflect aspects of the speech production and perception apparatus (although some have argued that these aspects are only indirectly represented – see the papers in Hayes et al. 2004, for example).

If constraints are numerous and universal it is *necessary* that they also be 'defeasible', because they conflict with each other. Defeasible within OT means that they state facts about how the language works, but they don't all have to be true at the same time. They conflict with one another, and some are more 'powerful' within a particular language at a particular time (power, expressed as ranking, is language-specific) than others, so in a conflict the more powerful one wins. The 'trick' of OT is to say that all the constraints are universal, but the **ranking** of the constraints *is* the grammar. Constraints that are irrelevant in a language are simply **dominated** by all other constraints, so that their effect is hidden by stronger constraints.

The image of power or domination (or precedence, another way of looking at this ranking of constraints) is expressed in the OT formalism by a left to right ordering, with the highest-ranked constraints being on the left. The notation for expressing in prose that a constraint outranks another is the use of double arrowheads: X ››Y.

In order to make this discussion less abstract, let us look at a fairly simple example. Vowels in English are nasalized before nasal consonants in the same syllable. In addition, nasal consonants are elided before a following voiceless consonant. Both of these facts are expressed by constraints about what is and is not permitted. The first could be expressed by stating the existence of a link between the nasality feature of a nasal consonant and a preceding tautosyllabic vowel:

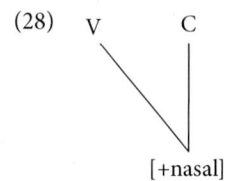

(28)  V     C
       \    |
        \   |
         \  |
          \ |
        [+nasal]

The second could be expressed by a simple prohibition against the forbidden sequence

(29)   *[C, +nas] [-voi]

These particular constraints, which we could call NASALIZE and NO-NASAL respectively are actually not ranked with respect to each other – both 'win', in the sense that both are respected in the output. Thus, given an underlying form /kænt/ 'can't', the pronunciation [kʰæ̃t] violates neither constraint, but forms such as *[kʰæ̃nt] and *[kʰænt] each violate one of the constraints. Thus the permitted form violates the fewest number of constraints, and is the best output form.

The other way in which OT is different from other 'generative' theories of phonology is the issue of levels. OT has only two levels – the underlying form and the surface form. Where do the surface forms come from? The theory assumes that the underlying forms are stored, and an abstract mechanism called **GEN** spews out a theoretically infinite number of alternative pronunciations for the underlying target. Each of the alternatives is then (simultaneously) evaluated (by a mechanism called **EVAL**) to see how many constraints it violates. The alternatives are called **candidates**, and the candidate that violates the fewest constraints is the correct output. The one additional factor is that higher ranking constraints beat out lower ones, so that violating one higher ranking constraint is more fatal[15] than violating fifty lower ranking ones. Thus the ranking is absolute, but the constraints themselves are not.

Given this way of 'generating' surface forms, how do we ensure that all kinds of garbage isn't a candidate? For example, to return to our /kænt/ example above, how do we prevent [glɔrk] from being an output? After all, it violates neither constraint.

The answer is that constraints that function as the equivalent of phonological rules are not the only constraints that exist. The constraints that we have seen so far are called in the OT literature **markedness**[16] constraints, but there are also a number of **faithfulness** constraints. These are essentially constraints that forbid the surface form from differing from the underlying form. They are of three fundamental kinds – feature faithfulness constraints forbid segments from acquiring feature values they don't originate with. MAX constraints forbid surface forms with fewer segments than the underlying form – essentially discouraging unrestricted deletions, while DEP constraints forbid surface forms with more segments than the underlying form, discouraging unrestricted epenthesis. Together these constraints keep the surface form as much like the underlying form as possible. In more recent versions of the theory the three classes of constraint have been replaced with a single kind: IDENT.

How, then, do the markedness constraints interact with the faithfulness constraints? The relationship between individual markedness constraints and the faithfulness constraints determines which markedness constraints get a chance to be expressed. If a markedness constraint is ranked higher than a faithfulness constraint, candidates which obey the markedness

---

15. Note that OT has us saying things that seem a little bizarre from an absolutist point of view. Within OT there are no perfect outputs, only a single one that survives all other challenges.

16. Another term that is often used is to refer to **structural** constraints – the phonetically motivated constraints that correspond to most phonological rules in other theories.

constraint are preferable to those which are closer to the underlying form. Thus, rather than saying that a language does or does not have a particular 'rule', OT says a language either ranks a markedness constraint higher or lower than a corresponding faithfulness constraint. Let's take a concrete example. The NASALIZE constraint adds the feature specification [+nasal] to the /æ/ vowel in 'can't'. This violates the faithfulness constraint IDENT(NAS), which states that the surface feature value for [nasal] should remain identical to its underlying value. As long as the markedness constraint NASALIZE outranks the faithfulness constraint IDENT(NAS), the candidates which have a nasalized vowel will be better than those without that nasalized vowel. If, on the other hand, the ranking of constraints is reversed: IDENT(NAS) ›› NASALIZE, the candidates with oral vowels will be judged as better.

In sum, this is the mechanism by which OT achieves the same effects as the combination of rules and rule ordering in other, competing theories. To return to the example we have been using, we should now look at the actual formalism used by the theory. A particular set of constraint interactions with respect to a particular underlying form are displayed in a **tableau**. A tableau is a two-dimensional table in which the constraints are listed across the top line, and the candidates along the side. Here is a trivial example:

(30)

| Input: /kænt/ | NASALIZE | IDENT(NAS) |
|---|---|---|
| a.   kænt | * | |
| b. ☞ kæ̃nt | | * |

The winning candidate is marked with a little hand. An asterisk in a column marks a violation of the constraint listed at the top of that column. Every horizontal row represents a candidate, and an asterisk in the leftmost column eliminates the candidate on that line if there are candidates without an asterisk in that column. To work through the tableau, go through the first column and eliminate any candidate that has an asterisk. Then go to the next column and eliminate any candidate that has an asterisk. In this trivial example, of course, the second candidate, b. is the winner.

Just to be sure that the mechanisms in this model are clear, let us take a look at a real analysis, one which convinced a lot of phonologists that this model was on the right track. Imdlawn Tashlhiyt Berber has the remarkable ability to make any consonant the nucleus of a syllable, given the appropriate configuration of other consonants in the word. Under the right conditions, even voiceless stops and fricatives can be syllabic. Sample words include [rA.tK.tI] (capitalization is used here to indicate syllabicity), [tF.tKt] along with the more expected [tR.gLt], [Il.dI].

There are two basic principles of syllable construction in this dialect of Berber. One is that syllables must have onsets – (ON). The other is that, given that syllables have onsets, the syllable nucleus must be more sonorous than any other segment in the same syllable, or, to put it another way, syllables with higher sonority nuclei are preferable to syllables with lower sonority – HNUC.

Given that, we can construct a tableau for the underlying form /txznt/ which selects the only possible candidate. This tableau is taken from the original text on OT, Prince and Smolensky (2004: 15).

(31)

| Candidates | Ons | Hnuc | Comments |
|---|---|---|---|
| ☞ a. tX.zNt |  | n x | optimal |
| b. Tx.zNt |  | n !t | t < x |
| c. txZ.nT |  | x! t | x < n, t irrelevant |
| d. txZ.Nt | *T | z n | Hnuc irrelevant |
| e. T.X.Z.N.T. | *!*** | n z x t t |  |

The ranking we need is that Ons ›› Hnuc. Given simply these two candidates, the only possible output is [tX.zNt]. The first candidate (a) has onsets for both syllables, and has nuclei consisting of [n] and [x]. The second candidate has a less sonorous nucleus [t], but is otherwise comparable, so given the choice we still select (a). For the next (c), [z] is a nucleus, which is a poorer choice than the [n] in the first candidate (a). The fourth and fifth candidates (d) and (e) are ruled out because at least some of their syllables lack onsets, and that constraint rules the forms out when compared to *any* candidates that don't violate it.

Next let us consider a much more complex set of constraint interactions, based on unpublished work by Davis and Shin (1997). In Korean there is a set of assimilations that take place in syllable final position when one consonant is followed by another in the next syllable: stops nasalize before nasals /napnita/ → [nam.ni.da], n becomes l before l /nonli/→ [nol.li], l becomes n after a nasal /kamli/→ [kamni], obstruent-liquid sequences become nasals /puupli/ → [pumni], and everything left remains the same /kalpi/→ [kal.bi].[17] Getting all of these changes to come out right in a sequential rule application analysis turns out to be very difficult, but Davis and Shin are able to account for all of them with a set of well-motivated constraints:

(32) Syllcon: avoid rising sonority over a syllable boundary (this is the 'syllable contact law' discussed in (Vennemann) and elsewhere, where the end of a syllable should have higher sonority than the beginning of the next syllable.)
*Complex: avoid complex onsets and codas
Ident[place]: the faithfulness constraint for point of articulation
Ident-son Onset: keep the sonority value of the onset
Ident-son Coda: keep the sonority value of the coda
Max[lateral]: keep the value for lateral[18]
Max[nasal]: keep the value for nasal

The crucial constraint rankings are Max[lateral] » Max[nasal], which accounts for the fact that the underlying lateral remains in [nolli] rather than the underlying nasal (*[nonni]). Ident[place] » Max[lateral] accounts for the fact that the lateral becomes

---

17. The voicing of /p/ to /b/ is allophonic intervocalic voicing.

18. The fact that both Ident and Max are used is based on a difference between binary and unary features. In Davis and Shin's analysis, [lateral] is a unary feature which can therefore be inserted or deleted, but [sonorant] is a binary feature which has either a plus or minus value but can neither be inserted or deleted. The details are not crucial to the analysis.

a nasal, rather than an obstruent becoming a lateral by changing point of articulation). Finally, Ident-son Onset » Ident-son Coda accounts for the fact that only coda consonants change their original [sonorant] value.

Consider, then, the tableau for underlying /kakmok/, which surfaces as [kaŋmok]. Line (a) is ruled out because it violates the syllable contact constraint. Line (b), with the same segments but different syllabification is ruled out because it has an onset cluster. Line (c) involves a change of point of articulation (and also a change in sonority, but that is irrelevant since Ident-son Coda is ranked so low). Line (d), which involves a change in sonority in an onset (but is otherwise ok) is worse than line (e), which violates only the Coda sonority faithfulness constraint.

(33)   'Derivation' of /kaŋmok/ from underlying /kakmok/

| /kak.mok/ | SyllCon | *Complex | Ident-son Onset | Ident [Place] | Max [Lateral] | Max [Nasal] | Ident-son Coda |
|---|---|---|---|---|---|---|---|
| a. kak.mok | *! | | | | | | |
| b. ka.kmok | | *! | | | | | |
| c. kam.mok | | | | *! | | | |
| d. kak.pok | | | *! | | | | |
| ☞ e. kaŋmok | | | | | | | * |

This tableau gives an idea of the flavor of a relatively involved OT analysis, in which phonetically motivated tendencies and faithfulness to underlying forms are seen to interact in complex ways which require that there be a compromise between sets of conflicting 'desires'. The compromises are worked out by decomposing pieces of each constraint so that phonetic markedness and faithfulness to underlying forms are interspersed in a language-specific way. Some constraints are absolute (nothing in Korean will result in a complex onset or coda, for example), whereas others are relatively permeable (the sonority of codas is relatively flexible).

If we return, for a moment, to the framework of this book, we can ask whether this approach to phonological patterning has anything to offer us in Cognitive Grammar. I believe that it does. We can begin with the question of the status of the individual constraints. Within the generative grammar paradigm constraints are said to be part of UG – Universal Grammar. That means that they are a given, a part of the human linguistic genetic endowment. CG doesn't recognize the existence of a purely linguistic genetic endowment, but does indeed have a place for universals. The universals, however, stem from what might be called 'the human condition'. That is, they stem from facts about human beings that are shared across all cultures. These facts include a perceptual system, a set of mechanisms for forming and enlarging categories (prototype structure, metaphor, metonymy, image schema transformations), and, particularly important for our purposes, an articulatory system.

The constraints in OT are of two fundamental types, as we have seen. Within OT they are called Faithfulness and Markedness constraints. The first essentially preserve the underlying form, while the second set respond to the phonetic constraints imposed by our articulatory system, which is relatively complex, requires considerable effort to coordinate multiple gestures to arrive at a single point in time, and prefers to make fewer gestures in the first place.[19]

In recent work it has been suggested (Tesar & Smolensky 2000) that there is an 'initial state' of ranking of constraints, namely that the Structural constraints initially outrank the Faithfulness constraints. It is assumed, then, that the child's task in acquiring a language is to *rerank* some subset of the Faithfulness constraints above some subset of the structural constraints, the task being to learn which particular constraints are placed in particular rankings.

While it is not explicitly claimed in the OT literature, we need to recognize two distinct types of markedness constraints. One set, which answer to the fortitions of NP, establish ideal sets of underlying segments. Thus there are constraints forbidding combinations of features (such as a preference for voiced sonorants, alveolar/dental coronals over retroflex or palatals) and all the other constraints that account for the fact that phoneme systems follow the markedness constraints originally set down in Jakobson.[20] The other set, which correspond to the lenitions in NP, forbid *sequences* of segments which are phonetically difficult. For example, the fact that alveolar stops in English are replaced with alveolar flaps, the fact that vowels are nasalized before tautosyllabic nasals and virtually all other allophonic 'processes' are examples of lenitive structural constraints.

## 10.5  Usage-based and Exemplar Theories

Recently some researchers working within the Cognitive Grammar framework have argued against almost all current views of phonology of any flavor, structural, generative or natural. Beginning with the Content Constraint, which is that linguistic structures are based solely on meaning and sound, Langacker (1987), and others in Kemmer and Barlow (2000) argued that language was acquired solely through exposure to linguistic input and general cognitive principles of categorization and abstraction. Consequently there was no need for independent linguistic principles. Since Langacker argued that lexical items were stored with all morphology intact, and might or might not even have the morphology analyzed, at least at first, language acquisition was simply a case of storing large numbers of individual instances, then extracting generalizations from the stored instances, while not discarding the instances stored. Thus, we might hear *dogs*, store it as heard, and perhaps later generate a separate stored item *dog*. Or perhaps not.

---

**19.** We will see shortly that articulatory simplicity is not the only class of constraints operative in phonology. A separate set of constraints builds the phonological system of the language by selecting prototypical segments as preferable to less prototypical ones.

**20.** For extensive discussion of this point see (Nathan 1995), where I argue that fortitions are sets of prototypicality statements about segment types. Some of the present discussion comes from Nathan (2006, 2007, 2008).

This view, which came to be called a 'usage-based' theory (Langacker 1988; Barlow & Kemmer 2000) spread naturally to phonology as well. Bybee (1999, 2000, 2002) has argued that words (and probably larger units too) are stored exactly as heard (and as produced). This would indicate massive storage needs, but there is evidence that the brain is indeed able to store enormous numbers of incidences. Thus when children acquire their language they simply store everything they hear, in great phonetic detail. Usage-based theorists have argued that abstract schemas can be extracted from these stored units, and that phonemes, syllables and other higher order units are simply generalizations over stored individual instances.

Bybee has also argued that words are actually stored as individual instances, and that speakers evolve generalizations from similarities among pieces of the words, but without ever recoding the existing words in all their phonetic detail. That is, according to Bybee, phonemes are generalizations built upon existing stored entities, but do not, in any sense, change the way that words are stored. Bybee goes so far as to suggest that, for example, the allophones of phonemes in syllable-onset position may not be stored as in any sense 'the same' as those for what are traditionally thought of as the same phoneme in syllable-final position, suggesting, for example, that clear and dark [l] in English might not be categorized the same (Bybee 2001: 88).

This highly concrete view of phonological processing is also proposed by a group of researchers with phonetic backgrounds. Pierrehumbert (2002), Beckman and their colleagues (Beckman et al. 2007) have been developing a similar view of phonology, using the recently developed concept of categorization that has come to be known as Exemplar Theory (ET). Within this theory, large numbers of individual instances are all stored, but that similar instances are stored, in some sense, 'on top of' each other, somewhat analagous to tracing a path through a park. As more and more instances in the same place are stored a visible path emerges where the grass is worn away, but all the other paths that do not coincide exactly with the bare earth are still there also, and available to be perceived and produced. However, the more frequent instances are 'stronger' and hence more likely to be produced, and instances that are heard and are similar to the 'beaten path' are likely to be assimilated to it.

The problem with the usage-based model is that it cannot account for behaviors that children exhibit while acquiring language and that adults exhibit while producing it.

For example, there are numerous reports of children systematically substituting one phoneme for another in every word containing that phoneme. Smith (1973) is a classic study, for example, but a bilingual child that my colleagues and I have been studying systematically replaced all mid vowels (/e/, /o/) in his Spanish with high vowels for several months. Similarly, a child of my acquaintance currently learning English regularly replaces words containing voiceless dental fricatives (/θ/)with labiodentals (/f/). This kind of replacement, virtually universally reported, poses two problems for any usage-based theory. First, where do children learn to replace what are almost always *more marked* segments with *less marked* segments? They certainly are not learning it from their surroundings, because these are not only non-standard replacements, they are non-existent in the ambient language.

And secondly, unless children are storing the words they attempt *with the phonemes as separate representations*, how else can they know which words contain the relevant sounds. If we assume that phonemes are, in some sense, 'calls to motor routines', rather than simply linguists' classification schemes, we can explain why children alter the routines, leading to replacements in every relevant word.

A second argument comes from systematic ongoing sound changes, specifically the kind discussed in Chapter 8 as chain shifts. The Northern Cities shift, currently ongoing in the US, includes a shift of /ɑ/ forward towards /æ/, while /æ/ shifts upwards (and breaks) into [ɛə]. What this means is that in some sense the /ɑ/ vowel is interacting with the /æ/ vowel, which is interacting with the /ɛ/ vowel (I use the neutral term 'interacting' to avoid a commitment to 'push' versus 'drag' chains, a point that is unimportant to my argument).

If words are simply stored as individual items, perhaps with some cross-classifying 'index', then it would make no sense to say that the /æ/ vowel is 'pushing on' the /ɛ/ vowel, since there is no category of /æ/ vowels to do any pushing. It is certainly meaningless to say that the word 'bag' is pushing on the word 'ready'. We need to have some sense of active cognitive processing, involving categorization and production in real time, not 'recollected in tranquility' if we are to understand how phonemes could move in a coordinated manner, as we know they have done numerous times in the past, and continue to do as we study ongoing living speech. It is only a within a model in which phonemes have some independent, real existence, but are also instantiated in each word that contains that we can understand how real regular sound change, either historical or ongoing could take place.[21] That is, we need the notion of an inventory of actual phonemes and a lexicon of words 'spelled' in those phonemes – that is, a traditional view that words are stored as strings of independently existing sound units, that speech production is a process of implementing those units in context, and that perception is the act of perceiving the units the speaker *intended* to say.

## 10.6  Some concluding thoughts on OT and cognitive phonology

Let us return briefly to the concepts of structural and faithfulness constraints proposed by Optimality Theory to see how they might fit into this 'traditional,' but Cognitive view of phonology I have ultimately argued for.

It is clear that the structural constraints correspond to the phonetic motivation that any theory of phonology in Cognitive Grammar would need in order to account for the fact that languages have similar phonetic constraints. Less immediately obvious, however,

---

21.  Not only does Labov assume (1996, 1997, 2007) mentioned above, that there are real, categorically regular sound changes, but he is convinced that they exist, and that they serve as a counterexample to at least some part of the totally usage-based models that Cognitive Grammar has recently taken to heart (Labov p.c.).

is the function of the faithfulness constraints. Why should languages prefer to maintain the identity of surface forms to underlying forms?

The reason appears to be the general principle, first suggested by Humboldt, and in recent research in a number of frameworks, referred to as Humboldt's Universal. This is the principle often summarized as 'one form – one meaning'. Language appears to disprefer synonymy, whether at the lexical or phonological level. At the lexical level this dispreference leads to the fact (generally taken as an overall research strategy in CG) that there are no synonymous forms~ – that a difference in form is normally associated with a difference in meaning. This is most striking in syntax, where Cognitive Linguists have argued that active vs. passive pairs, dative movement, and perhaps even particle movement paraphrases are not semantically identical, differing in focus, path explicitness and other parameters.

There does, however, seem to be a lower limit to the point at which different forms are actually perceived as different. This limit is the *phonemic* level. Below the difference between phonemes differences in form are either not consciously perceived, or are perceived only as accommodations to the exigencies of speaking, rather than as conscious choices to send a different message.[22] And for the same reason, from the speaker's point of view, the choice whether to flap an alveolar consonant is not made in order to change the message being sent, but rather to accommodate other, more message-oriented choices made at a higher level. Consider, for example, the alternative pronunciations.

(34)  ['dær.i] ~ ['dæːˌdi]

The latter pronunciation constitutes a choice to whine, or to be exasperated, and the phonetic details (vowel length, full stop articulation of the /d/) are automatic *structural* consequences of the choice to accent both syllables of the name. The speaker is not selecting phonetic details but rather contrastive *phonemic* details (what is or is not stressed), and the phonetic details flow automatically from the choice of phonemes.

Thus the faithfulness constraints have as their primary motivation the pressure to keep the amount of variability in speech to a manageable level. In general the faithfulness constraints normally apply to keep variation within the domain of allophones. They attempt to keep Humboldt's Universal by ensuring that for each *meaning* there is only *one* form, at least to the limit of perceptibility of variation within the linguistic system. However, structural constraints occasionally outweigh faithfulness constraints at particular phonetic weakpoints. This leads to a violation of Humboldt's universal in the other direction – *one* form may reflect *several* meanings. For example, in many languages the structural constraint against final voiced obstruents outranks faithfulness to the underlying form, even if the output would be a form that is homophonous to another, contrasting unit. Thus, in German, final /d/ and final /t/ are pronounced identically even though the result would be pairs of forms that violate Humboldt's universal.

---

**22.** They may also be perceived as some kind of deviation – disability, foreign accent, food in the mouth ... But they are not perceived as a different semantic *intention*.

The bidirectionality of Humboldt's Universal then, accounts for a resistance to morphophonemic alternations (I am speaking here only of automatic, phonetically motivated alternations, such as are produced by final devoicing, flapping and so on) as well as the relatively low ranking of faithfulness constraints when compared to the allophonic type of structural constraints. Violations of faithfulness are most tolerable when they are not perceived, which is to say, when they induce variations that remain within phoneme boundaries. Violations of faithfulness that cross phoneme boundaries are tolerated when either phonetic (structural) constraints are strongest (say in weak syllable positions, or in unstressed syllables) or when the communication situation doesn't demand careful maintenance of identity. Thus commonly repeated phrases, phatic communion, and old information foster violations of faithfulness.

I want to emphasize here that I am speaking of variations induced by true, automatic phonological processes, not of *rules* sensu strictu. Rules (in the strict technical sense introduced by Natural Phonology) induce variations that *are* perceptible, and as a result come to signal morphological variations – in short, they *become* the morphemes (or at least the expression thereof). The most extreme cases, thus, would be variations such as *eat ~ ate*, where it is precisely the change in vowel that is the very expression of the semantic effect.

It is important to recognize, as has been repeated often throughout this book, that the construction of speech is an ongoing, on-line task, analogous to any other kind of problem-solving. Speakers do not simply store all conceivable variants for every word, any more than they store all conceivable steps from the front door to the mailbox. Rather, each trip to the mailbox is constructed as we walk, taking account of climatic conditions (is it raining?), ground surface condition (how deep is the mud?), and how much of a hurry we are in. Similarly, we do not store every way of saying 'hello', but rather construct alternative ways of saying it each time, depending on the degree of care we choose to put into the task.

Similarly, we do not need to store all possible pronunciations in order to recognize an instance of 'hello',[23] but rather we hear sympathetically, recognizing some sound as an instance of the word if we could conceive of it as a result of the same intentions *we* would have had. This is not in the least surprising, nor is it limited to the perception of phonetic intentions. When someone waves at us we recognize an instance of 'waving' even if the ceiling is low enough to interfere with the hand movement, or a cup of coffee in the hand requires only finger movement. There is no need to posit storage of multiple instances of 'waving', only the need to be a human being of the same physical type with the same constraints on limb movement. Thus we come back to the original insight of Baudouin over 120 years ago, that speech is an ongoing creation involving the accommodation of stored routines to the exigencies of the speech situation, both for individual phonemes and for their combination into connected speech.

---

**23.** Nor could we, since we frequently encounter people we have never met, who, by virtue of having slightly different-sized and shaped vocal apparatus, different geographic and social backgrounds, and so on, will pronounce every word we hear somewhat differently from however it may have been stored based on all previous hearings.

# Glossary

**Affricate** – A sound consisting of a complete closure followed by a relatively slow release, resulting in the impression of a stop immediately followed by a fricative. Phoneticians and phonologists differ on whether these should be represented by one symbol or two.

**Allophone** – A variant of a phoneme, usually determined by some phonetic factor.

**Alternation** – A variant in the pronunciation of a morpheme, sometimes determined by a phonetic factor (such as an adjacent sound) and other times by nonphonetic factors such as a place in a paradigm.

**Antepenult** – The second last syllable of a word.

**Appendix** – Segments at the end of a word that cannot be assigned to the last syllable.

**Approximant** – A sound made with sufficient obstruction in the airflow to affect it, but not enough to produce turbulence. Could be a liquid or a rhotic.

**Archiphoneme** – A schematic unit standing for more than one phoneme in a structural place where only one of two or more possible phonemes could otherwise occur.

**Assimilation** – A process whereby a sound becomes similar to another, neighboring sound, along some dimension.

**Association line** – Line in an autosegmental representation connecting features associated with each other, often but not exclusively clustered around a single segment.

**Binary** – A feature having two values, plus and minus

**Coarticulation** – The influence of a sound on another. Sometimes conflated with assimilation, but other linguists distinguish them.

**Coda** – The segment or segments of a syllable after the peak or nucleus.

**Cognate** – Words in two different languages that descend from single a common form in an earlier, protolanguage. Display systematic sound correspondences.

**Compensatory lengthening** – Vowel (or sometimes consonant) lengthening caused by the elimination of the articulatory details of a segment with the timing of the entire unit unchanged. The vowel takes up the space of the deleted segment.

**Complementary distribution** – The occurrence of linguistic units in *mutually exclusive* environments, such that where one occurs the other never does.

**Continuant** – Sound characterized by the lack of interruption in airflow. Ordinarily refers to consonants.

**Coronal** – Sound produced with the tongue tip or blade as an articulator. Includes dentals, alveolars, post-alveolars and retroflexes. Some phonologists would add front vowels.

**Counterbleeding** – An ordering situation in which a process which would otherwise interfere with the operation of another process is ordered after is, so that the interference does not occur.

**Counterfeeding** – An ordering situation in which a process would otherwise create instances for another process to apply to, but which is ordered after that process, so that the instances remain unchanged.

**Dactyl** – A metric unit consisting of a strong and two weak syllables. *pálaces*

**Diphthong** – A vowel with a moving location in articulatory space. Usually defined by the beginning and endpoints.

**Dissimilation** – A process in which a sound becomes different from a neighboring sound by the change of one or more features.

**Epenthesis** – A process in which a segment is inserted into a string.

**Faithfulness** – The tendency for surface representations (however understood) to be identical to their underlying counterparts.

**Feeding** – A process which changes a string of sounds with the result that another process applies which would not ordinarily have done so.

**Foot** – A grouping of a stressed and some number of unstressed syllables (including none) that is felt to be a metric unit. In some languages, including English, the smallest pronounceable unit.

**Fortition** – A process that increases the salience of a sound through a change in feature value or the addition of a segment.

**Geminate** – A sound that is felt as significantly longer than the corresponding non-geminate. Often felt as two successive instances of the same sound.

**Harmony** – A process in which non-adjacent sounds become more similar. Most commonly applies to vowels and involves features such as backness or rounding.

**Homorganic** – Having the same point of articulation. Two successive alveolar sounds are homorganic.

**Humboldt's Universal/Law** – The tendency for morphemes to have a single meaning and a single form. Thus, a drive *against* polysemy and allomorphs.

**Iamb** – A foot consisting of an unstressed followed by a stressed syllable. *agáin*

**Infixation** – A morphological process whereby a morpheme is inserted inside another, otherwise unbreakable morpheme.

**Intervocalic** – Between two vowels

**Intonation** – A pitch pattern extending over an utterance (in many languages, a 'breath group') marking semantic and pragmatic, or emotional intent.

**Lax** – A relative term for vowels referring to those that are relatively lower, more central and often shorter than their counterparts.

**Lenition** – A process that decreases the salience of a sound through a change in feature value, shortening or even deletion.

**Marked** – Originally the presence of an additional feature when two similar sounds are compared. Currently meaning linguistically more complex, less expected, rarer, more difficult for first (or second) language learners to acquire. See **unmarked**.

**Maximum Onset Principle** – The tendency for a consonant to affiliate with the following, rather than the preceding vowel in syllabification.

**Merger** – A historical change whereby one phoneme is elminated from the inventory of a language after all words with that sound come to be pronounced with a different sound. The two sounds are said to have merged.

**Mora** – A unit of phonological time. Every syllable contains one or more moras – the first vowel in the nucleus is one, a glide in a diphthong or a consonant in a coda would constitute a second.

**Morphophonemic** – A process that has the result of merging the contrast between two phonemes, thus causing two morphemes to be pronounced identically.

**Neutralization** – The loss of a contrast between two (or more) otherwise different phonemes differing along a common dimension in a particular structural position.

**Node** – The point in a structural tree (syllable, word, phrase etc.) connecting a higher point to a lower one. It may or may not branch

**Nucleus** – The center of a syllable, Most often, but not exclusively a vowel.

**Obstruent** – A sound made with a significant obstruction in the airflow such that there is either complete closure or obstruction sufficient to cause turbulence in the airflow.

**Onset** – The consonant(s) preceding the nucleus in a syllable.

**Opacity** – A situation in the phonology of a language in which some otherwise general process appears not to have applied for some systematic phonological reason. Traditionally 'explained' through rule-ordering.

**Opposition** – Two phonemes (whose existence has been proved through minimal pairs) that differ in a single feature.

**Penultimate** – The second last syllable in a word.

**Phonologization** – The historical change whereby a sound that was formerly allophonic (and thus whose existence was due to the operation of process) becomes phonemic (and thus unpredictable).

**Physiophonetic** – Baudouin's description of processes that have natural, phonetic explanations.

**Progressive** – Direction of the effect of a process as after, or continuing the effects of the causative sound.

**Prototype effects** – Tendency of categories to have internal structure with better and worse examples. Often the examples are related to each other by systematic mental transformations.

**Ranking** – OT method of assigning precedence to constraints over one another.

**Reassociation** – Separation of an association from one segment (or tier) and attachment to an adjacent one.

**Regressive** – Direction of the effect of a process as before, or anticipating the causative sound.

**Schema** – An abstract category formed through consideration of several similar instances.

**Sonority** – A ranking of speech sounds by either their relative openness (an articulatory definition) or by the presence and strength of formant structures (acoustically). Occasionally considered to be solely an abstract measure governing the permitted shape of syllables.

**Syncope** – Deletion of a vowel within a word.

**Tautosyllabic** – Belonging to the same syllable.

**Tone** – A pitch pattern associated with a particular word or morpheme as part of its lexical specification. Tone can be either lexical or grammatical in nature.

**Trochee** – A foot characterized by a stressed syllable followed by an unstressed one. *cátty*

**Ultima** – The last syllable in a word.

**Umlaut** – A historical process most well-known from the history of the Germanic languages whereby a vowel in a root is fronted under the influence of a high front vowel in a suffix.

**Unary** – A feature which is either present or not. The absence of the feature is not a 'value' that can be called upon.

**Underspecification** – A feature categorization of a sound or group of sounds which does not include all the features necessary to uniquely define it.

**Unmarked** – In a pair of similar sounds the one with one fewer feature. More generally (and in contemporary terminology) a structure which is more expected, simpler to acquire and more frequent. See **marked**.

**Vowel Reduction** – Replacement of one or more distinct vowels with one (or occasionally more than one) less distinctive vowel. English schwa is often the result of vowel reduction.

# References

Barlow, Michael. & Susanne Kemmer, (Eds). (2000). *Usage-based models of language*. Cambridge: Cambridge University Press.

Baudouin de Courtenay, J. 1972. An attempt at a theory of phonetic alternations. In Edward Stankiewicz (Ed. & Trans.), *A Baudouin de Courtenay Anthology: The beginnings of structural linguistics* (pp. 144–213). Bloomington/London: Indiana University Press.

Beckman, Mary E., Munson, B. & Edwards, J. (2007). Vocabulary growth and the developmental expansion of types of phonological knowledge. In *Laboratory Phonology* 9, Ed. by Jennifer Cole & José Ignacio Hualde, 241–264.

Bloomfield, Leonard. 1933. *Language*. New York: Holt.

Broselow, Ellen. 1992. Transfer and Universals in Second Language Epenthesis. In *Language Transfer in Language Learning*. Amsterdam: Benjamins.

Boersma, Paul & David Weenink. 2007. *Praat 4.6.09: Doing Phonetics by Computer*. www.praat.org

Broselow, Ellen. 1983. Non-obvious transfer: on predicting epenthesis errors. In: S. Gass & L. Selinker (Eds), *Language transfer in language learning*. Rowley, MA: Newbury House, pp. 269–280.

Bybee, Joan L. 1999. The phonology of the lexicon: evidence from lexical diffusion. In *Usage-based models of language*. Stanford: CSLI.

Bybee, Joan L. 2002. *Phonology and Language Use*. Cambridge and New York: Cambridge University Press.

Chomsky, Noam & Morris Halle, 1968. *The Sound Pattern of English*. New York: Harper and Row.

Cohn, Abigail. 1993. Nasalization in English: Phonology or Phonetics, *Phonology*, Vol. 10, No. 1: 43–82.

Colarusso, John. 1992. *A grammar of the Kabardian language*. Calgary: University of Calgary Press.

Crowley, Terry. 1992. *An introduction to historical linguistics*. Oxford: Oxford University Press.

Davis, Stuart & Seung Hoon Shin. 1997. "Is There a Syllable Contact Constraint?" Ms. Hopkins Optimality Theory Workshop.

Donegan, Patricia J. 1986. *On the Natural Phonology of Vowels*. New York: Garland.

Donegan, Patricia J. & David Stampe. 1979. "The Study of Natural Phonology," In *Current Approaches to Phonological Theory*, Ed. by Dan Dinnsen. Bloomington: Indiana University Press.

Donegan, Patricia J. & David Stampe, 1983. "Rhythm and the Holistic Organization of Language Structure," in *Papers from the Parasession on the Interplay of Phonology, Morphology, and Syntax*, Eds. John Richardson & et al. Chicago: Chicago Linguistic Society, pp. 337–353.

Dressler, Wolfgang U. 1985. *Morphonology, the Dynamics of Derivation*. Ann Arbor: Karoma.

Everett, Daniel L. & Keren Everett. 1984. 'On the relevance of Syllable Onsets to Stress Placement,' *Linguistic Inquiry* 15, pp. 705–711.

Ewen, Colin & Harry van der Hulst. 2000. *The Phonological Structure of Words*. Cambridge: Cambridge University Press.

Gleason, Henry A. 1961. *Introduction to Descriptive Linguistics*. New York: Holt Rinehart.

Goldsmith, John. 1990. *Autosegmental and Metrical Phonology*. Oxford: Blackwell.

Goldsmith, John. 1979. "The Aims of Autosegmental Phonology," in *Current Approaches to Phonological Theory*, Ed. by D. Dinnsen. Bloomington: Indiana University Press, pp. 202–222.

Grégoire, Antoine. 1937. *L'Apprentissage du language*. Paris and Liège: Droz.

Halle, Morris. 1959. *The Sound Pattern of Russian*. The Hague: Mouton.
Halle, Morris. 1964. "On the Bases of Phonology," In *The Structure of Language*, Eds J.A. Fodor & J. Katz. New York: Prentice Hall, pp. 324–333.
Hayes, Bruce. 1995. *Metrical Stress Theory*. Chicago: University of Chicago Press.
Hayes, Bruce & Robert Kirschner, Steriade 2004. *Phonetically Based Phonology*. Cambridge: Cambridge University Press.
Hock, Hans H. 1986. *Principles of Historical Linguistics*. The Hague: Mouton-de Gruyter.
Jakobson, Roman. 1968 [1941]. *Child Language, Aphasia and Phonological Universals*. The Hague: Mouton. Original work published 1941.
Jakobson, Roman, Gunnar Fant & Morris Halle. 1956. *Preliminaries to Speech Analysis*. 2nd Ed. Cambridge, MA: MIT Press.
James A. & Leather J. 1987. Sound Patterns in Second Language Acquisition. Dordrecht, Princeton: Foris.
Janda, Richard D. & Brian D. Joseph (Eds), 2004. *The Handbook of Historical Linguistics*, New York: Blackwell.
Keller R. 1994. *On language change: The invisible hand in language*. Routledge, London.
Jones D. 1967. *The Phoneme: Its nature and use*. Cambridge: Heffer.
Joos, Martin (Ed.) 1966 [1957]. *Readings in Linguistics I*. Chicago: University of Chicago Press. Original work published 1957.
Keller, Rudi. 1985. "Towards a Theory of Linguistic Change," In *Linguistic Dynamics: Discourses, Procedures and Evolution*, Ed. by Thomas T. Ballmer. de Gruyter, pp. 211–237.
Kenstowicz, Michael & Charles Kisseberth. 1979. *Generative Phonology*. San Diego: Academic Press.
Kenstowicz, Michael. 1993. *Phonology in Generative Grammar*. Cambridge, MA: Blackwell.
Kent, Ray D. & Charles Read. 1992. *The Acoustic Analysis of Speech*. San Diego: Singular Publishing Group.
Kiparsky, Paul. 1968. "Linguistic Universals and Linguistic Change," Eds Emmon Bach & Robert Harms, in *Universals in Linguistic Theory*. New York: Holt Rinehart and Winston, pp. 171–202.
Kiparsky, Paul. 1982. How abstract is phonology? In *Explanation in Phonology*. Dordrecht: Foris.
Kohler, Klaus J. 2000. Investigating unscripted speech: implications for phonetics and phonology. *Phonetica* 57, pp. 85–94.
Labov, William. 1994. *Principles of Linguistic Change (Vol. 1: Internal Factors)*. Cambridge, MA: Blackwell.
Labov, William, Sharon Ash & Charles Boberg. 1997. A national map of the regional dialects of American English. http://www.ling.upenn.edu/phono_atl\hich\af0\dbch\af11\loch\f0as/NationalMap/NationalMap.html20 (accessed on March 17, 2008).
Labov, William. 1996. The Organization of Dialect Diversity in North America http://www.ling.upenn.edu/phono_atlas/ICSLP4.html
Labov, William. 2007. Transmission and Diffusion. *Language* 83: 344–387, 2007.
Ladefoged, Peter. 1993. *A Course in Phonetics. Third Edition*. New York: Harcourt Brace.
Ladefoged, P. 2005. *Vowels and Consonants*. Malden, MA and Oxford: Blackwell.
Ladefoged, Peter & Ian Maddieson. 1996. *The Sounds of the World's Languages*. Oxford and Cambridge MA: Blackwell.
Lakoff, George. 1987. *Women, Fire and Dangerous Things. What Categories Reveal About the Mind*. Chicago: University of Chicago Press.

Lakoff, George. 1993. "Cognitive Phonology," In *The Last Phonological Rule*, ed. by John Goldsmith. Chicago: University of Chicago Press, pp. 117–145.

Langacker, Ronald W. 1987. *Foundations of Cognitive Grammar*. Stanford: Stanford University Press.

Langacker, Ronald W. 1988. A usage-based model. In B. Rudzka-Ostyn (Ed.), *Topics in Cognitive Linguistics*. Amsterdam: Benjamins, pp. 127–161.

Laver, John. 1994. *Principles of Phonetics*. Cambridge: Cambridge University Press.

Leopold, Werner F. 1939–1949. *Speech development of a bilingual child*. 4 vols. Evanston: Northwestern University Press.

McCarthy J. 1988. Feature geometry and dependency: a review. *Phonetica* 45, 84–108.

McCarthy, John J. 1982. "Prosodic Structure and Expletive Infixation," *Language*, Vol. 58, No. 3: 574–590.

McCarthy, John J. 2004. *Optimality Theory in Phonology*. London: Blackwell.

Mompean-González, José A. 2004. Category overlap and neutralization: The importance of speakers' classifications in phonology. *Cognitive Linguistics*, Volume 15.4, pp. 429–469

Nathan, Geoffrey S. 1986. "Phonemes as Mental Categories," in *Proceedings of the 12th Annual Meeting of the Berkeley Linguistics Society*, Vol. 12, pp. 212–224.

Nathan, Geoffrey S. 1989. "Preliminaries to a Theory of Phonological Substance: The Substance of Sonority," in *Linguistic Categorization*, Ed. by Roberta Corrigan, Fred Eckman & Michael Noonan, Amsterdam Studies in the Theory and History of Linguistic Science. Series IV – Current Issues in Linguistic Theory. Vol. 61. Amsterdam/Philadelphia: John Benjamins, pp. 55–68.

Nathan, Geoffrey S. 1995. "How the Phoneme Inventory Gets Its Shape–Cognitive Grammar's View of Phonological Systems," *Rivista di Linguistica*, Vol. 6, No. 2: 275–288.

Nathan, Geoffrey S. 1996. "Towards a Cognitive Phonology," in *Natural Phonology: The State of the Art*, Eds Bernhard Hurch & Richard Rhodes. Berlin: Mouton/de Gruyter, pp. 107–120.

Nathan, Geoffrey S. 1999. What functionalists can learn from formalists in phonology. in *Functionalism and Formalism in Linguistics*, edited by Michael Darnell, Edith Moravcsik, Michael Noonan, Frederick Newmeyer & Kathleen Wheatley. Vol 1: Case Studies. Amsterdam: Benjamins.

Nathan, Geoffrey S. 2006. "Is the Phoneme Usage-Based? – Some Issues," *International Journal of English Studies*, Vol. 6, No. 2: 173–195. Murcia: Universidad de Murcia.

Nathan, Geoffrey S. 2008. Phonology. in *The Oxford Handbook of Cognitive Linguistics*, Geeraerts, Dirk & Cuyckens, Hubert, Eds. New York: Oxford University Press, pp. 611–631.

Olive, Joseph P., Alice Greenwood, & John Coleman. 1993. *Acoustics of American English Speech: A Dynamic Approach*. New York and Berlin: Springer-Verlag.

Pierrehumbert, Janet. 2002. Word specific phonetics. In C. Gussenhoven & N. Warner, *Laboratory Phonology 7*. The Hague: Mouton de Gruyter, pp. 101–139.

Pike, Kenneth. 1947. On the phonemic status of English diphthongs. In *Phonological Theory: Evolution and Current Practice*. New York: Holt Rinehart and Winston.

Prince, Alan, & Paul Smolensky. 1993. *Optimality Theory: Constraint Interaction in Generative Grammar*, Technical Report Number 2 of the Rutgers Center for Cognitive Science. RUCCS, excerpt in McCarthy (2004: 3–71).

Prince, Alan, & Paul Smolensky. 2004. *Constraint Interaction in Generative Grammar*. London: Blackwell.

Robins, R.H. 1957. "Vowel Nasality in Sundanese: A Phonological and Grammatical Study," in *Studies in Linguistics*. London: Blackwell, pp. 257–285.

Robins, R.H. 1957. Vowel nasality in Sundanese: a phonological and grammatical study. In *Studies in linguistics*. London: Blackwell.

Rogers, Henry. 2001. *The Sounds of Language: An Introduction to Phonetics*. Harlow: Pearson.

Rosch, Eleanor. 1975. "Cognitive Representations of Semantic Categories," *Journal of Experimental Psychology: General*, Vol. 104: 192–233.

Rosch, Eleanor. 1978. "Principles of Categorization," in *Cognition and Categorization*, Ed. by Eleanor Rosch & B.B. Lloyd. Hillsdale, NJ: Lawrence Erlbaum, pp. 27–48.

Sapir, Edward. 1925. Sound Patterns in Language. Language 1, 37–51.

Sapir, Edward. 1972. "The psychological reality of phonemes [La réalité pschologique des phonèmes]," translated and reprinted from: Journal de psychologie normale et pathologique 30.247–265, in *Phonological Theory: Evolution and Current Practice*, Valerie Becker Makkai. New York: Holt Rinehart and Winston.

Saussure, Ferdinand de. 1974. Course de Linguistique Générale. Edition Critique Préparée par Tullio de Mauro. Paris: Payot.

Sibley, David Allen. 2000. *The Sibley Guide to the Birds*. New York: Alfred Knopf.

Skidmore College. 2008. Introduction to dactylic hexameter. http://www.skidmore.edu/classics/courses/1998fall/cl202/resource/meter/metintro.html, retrieved June 16, 2008.

Smith, N.V. 1973. *The Acquisition of Phonology: A Case Study*. Cambridge: Cambridge University Press.

Stampe, David. 1969. "The Acquisition of Phonetic Representation," in *Papers from the Fifth Regional Meeting of the Chicago Linguistic Society*. Chicago: Chicago Linguistic Society, pp. 443–454.

Stampe, David. 1973. "On Chapter Nine," in *Issues in Phonological Theory*, Eds Michael Kenstowicz & Charles Kisseberth. The Hague: Mouton, pp. 44–52.

Stampe, David. 1979. *A Dissertation on Natural Phonology*. New York: Garland Press.

Stampe, David. 1987. "On Phonological Representation," in *Phonologica 1984*, Eds Wolfgang U. Dressler, Hans C. Luschützky, Oskar Pfeiffer & John R. Rennison. London: Cambridge University Press, pp. 287–300.

Stevens, Kenneth. 1989. "On the Quantal Nature of Speech," *Journal of Phonetics*, Vol. 17, No. 1–2: 3–46.

Stevens, Kenneth & Samuel Jay Keyser. 1989. "Primary Features and Their Enhancement in Consonants," *Language*, Vol. 65: 81–106.

Tesar, Bruce & Paul. Smolensky. 2000. *Learnability in Optimality Theory*. Cambridge, MA: MIT Press.

Trubetzkoy N.S. 1939 [1969]. *Grüncgdzüge der Phonologie [Principles of Phonology]*, trans & Ed. C. Baltaxe. Prague [Los Angeles]: *Travaux du cercle linguistique de Prague* [University of California Press].

Tsujimura, Natsuko. 1996. *An Introduction to Japanese Linguistics*. Oxford: Blackwell.

Vennemann, Theo. 1988. *Preference Laws for Syllable Structure*. Berlin: Mouton de Gruyter.

Weinreich, Uriel. 1970. *Languages in Contact*. The Hague: Mouton.

Whitley, M. Stanley. 1978. *Generative Phonology Workbook*, Madison: University of Wisconsin Press.

Winters, Margaret E. 1988. "Innovations in French Negation: A Cognitive Grammar Account," *Diachronica*, Vol. 4: 27–51.

Zsiga, Elizabeth C. 1995. "An acoustic and electropalatographic study of lexical and post-lexical palatalization in American English," in B. Connell & A. Arvaniti (Eds), *Phonology and Phonetic Evidence: Papers in Laboratory Phonology IV*, Cambridge: Cambridge University Press, pp. 282–302.

# Index of languages

**A**
American English, 8, 11, 19, 21, 27, 34, 82, 96, 101, 106, 109, 110, 120, 127, 128–30, 132, 144
Arabic, 17, 47, 50, 57, 69, 70
Austronesian, 38, 51, 117, 138

**B**
Brahmi, 43
British English, 19, 21, 100

**C**
Canadian English, 106
Caucasian, 18, 38, 39
Chinese, 9
Czech, 46

**D**
Danish, 143

**E**
English, 1, 3–5, 7–11, 14, 15–17, 19–21, 23–25, 27, 28–30, 34, 38, 44, 45–53, 55–59, 61, 63, 65, 66, 68–72, 74, 76, 78, 79–83, 87–89, 93, 95, 96, 98, 100, 101, 103, 104–112, 114, 117, 119–21, 123, 126, 127–33, 136, 138, 143–45, 147, 152, 153
Eskimo, 80
Estonian, 20

**F**
Finnish, 57, 68
French, 3, 4, 16, 19, 20, 34, 39, 40, 47–49, 57, 66, 68, 74, 79, 95, 100, 101, 105, 119–21

**G**
German, 3, 5, 7, 16, 20, 45, 47–49, 65, 66, 89, 90, 95, 100, 107, 108, 120, 126–28, 131, 133, 143, 155
Greenlandic, 80

**H**
Hausa, 18, 120
Hindi, 20
Hungarian, 16, 57, 68

**I**
Igbo, 18, 66
Imdlawn, 46, 149
Inuit, 80
Israeli Hebrew, 17
Italian, 16, 40, 41, 51, 80, 117

**J**
Japanese, 9, 10, 15, 20, 43, 45, 50, 51, 55, 79, 82, 119–21

**K**
Kabardian, 38, 39
Korean, 16, 31, 32, 150, 151

**L**
Latin, 23, 24, 50, 55, 57, 69–71, 80, 81, 105–07, 112

**M**
Malay, 16, 51
Mandarin, 45
Maori, 112

**N**
Nauruan, 38, 117
Navajo, 18
Ntlakapmxw, 39

**P**
Papuan, 38
Polish, 3, 88–92
Polynesian, 112
Portuguese, 20

**Q**
Quechua, 80

**R**
Russian, 42, 56, 78, 80, 131

**S**
Salish, 39
Samoan, 112
Sanskrit, 2, 15, 28, 43, 82, 107, 112, 113
Semitic, 64
Serbian, 10
Slavic, 42, 80
Spanish, 15, 16, 49–51, 77, 81, 89, 123, 144, 153
Sundanese, 138
Swedish, 65

**T**
Tahiti, 112
Tashlhiyt, 46, 149
Turkish, 89

**V**
Vietnamese, 120

**Y**
Yawelmani, 134, 136
Yokuts, 134

# Index of names

**A**
Aristotle, 8

**B**
Baudouin de Courtenay, 3, 4–6, 29, 32, 33, 72, 156
Bloch, 128, 129
Bloomfield, 5, 128
Broselow, 50
Brugmann, 73

**C**
Chomsky, 6, 43, 60, 65, 72, 130–32, 136
Cohn, 79
Coleman, 11, 18

**D**
Dinnsen, 163,
Donegan, 74–76, 120, 121, 146
Dressler, 74, 75

**E**
Eckman, 163
Everett, 71

**G**
Gleason, 4, 5, 32, 129
Goldsmith, 139, 141, 143, 144
Greenwood, 11, 18
Grimm, 112, 113

**H**
Halle, 6, 43, 60, 65, 72, 93, 130–32, 136

Hayes, 55, 147
Higgins, 2
Hulst, 144
Humboldt, 155, 156

**J**
Jakobson, 4–6, 34, 35, 60, 117, 152
Johnson, 9
Jones, 5, 33, 112
Joos, 5, 128
Joseph, 103

**K**
Keller, 40
Kenstowicz, 6, 88, 134, 142
Kent, 11, 32
Keyser, 37
Kiparsky, 136, 137
Kirschner
Kisseberth, 6, 134
Kruszewski, 3

**L**
Labov, 31, 130, 154
Ladefoged, 11, 15, 24, 34, 38, 66
Lakoff, 7, 8, 73, 130, 146
Langacker, 7, 92, 130, 152, 153
Laver, 11
Leopold, 117

**M**
Maddieson, 11, 15, 34, 38, 66
Makkai, 166

**N**
Nathan, 75, 126, 152

**P**
Passy, 2
Paul, 2, 136, 137
Prince, 46, 146, 149

**R**
Rhodes, 165
Robins, 138
Rogers, 11

**S**
Sapir, 4–6, 72, 127
Saussure, 4
Schleicher, 112
Shaw, 2, 25
Sievers, 2
Smolensky, 46, 146, 149, 152
Stampe, 29, 72, 74, 75, 118, 120, 126, 146
Steriade, 164
Stevens, 37

**T**
Tesar, 152
Trubetzkoy, 4, 34, 126
Tsujimura, 20

**V**
Vennemann, 150

**W**
Whitney, 2
Winters, 9

# Index of subjects

## A
absolute neutralization, 136
abstraction, 5, 133, 152
abstractness, 6, 93, 109, 127, 133
accent, 24, 119, 155
acoustic, 10–12, 15, 18, 37, 39, 40, 126
acoustic phonetics, 11
acquisition, 117–19, 152
advanced tongue root, 20, 66
affricates, 12, 14–16, 40, 61, 62, 75, 79, 80, 98, 120, 131
airflow, 12, 17, 62
airstream, 12, 14, 62
alliteration, 46
alliterative, 7
allomorphs, 108, 128
allophones, 4, 5, 6, 10, 27, 28, 31–33, 40, 41, 50, 54, 58, 71, 72, 93, 104, 106–08, 119, 120, 121, 126–28, 131, 137, 153, 155
alphabet, 4, 43, 69
alternation, 6, 74, 80, 87, 88, 89, 90, 91–93, 105, 108, 109, 127, 128, 131–36, 156
American structuralism, 125, 127, 128, 131
American Structuralist, 5, 72, 88, 119, 125, 127, 129, 131
amphibrach, 58
analogy, 2, 4, 12, 32, 118
antepenult(imate), 57, 69, 70
anterior, 63, 64, 67, 140
anticipatory, 77, 78
apheresis, 80
aphesis, 80
apical, 63
apocope, 81
appendix, 52, 53, 57
approximant, 12, 15, 31, 60, 61
archiphoneme, 5, 125–28
aspirated, 7, 17, 28, 37, 47, 54, 58, 67, 74, 83, 97, 113, 144
aspiration, 10, 17, 47, 52, 54, 59, 67, 72, 84, 89, 97, 132, 142, 145
assimilation, 42, 51, 77, 78–80, 84, 89, 100, 105, 131, 132, 141, 142, 150
assonance, 29
autosegmental, 6, 46, 139, 141, 143, 144

## B
backness, 18, 20, 134
basic level, 6, 7, 59
Behaviorism, 5, 127
Behaviorists, 5
bilabial, 15, 16, 37, 63, 67
bleeding order, 137, 145
borrowing, 50, 79, 81
breaking, 146
breathy-voiced, 20

## C
categorization, 5, 7, 8, 152–54
categorizations, 122
CG, 9, 67, 68, 151, 155
click, 16, 33, 120
cluster, 38, 78, 81, 121, 139, 151
clusters, 48, 49–51, 53, 80–82, 97, 98, 106, 121, 139
coarticulation, 77
coda, 45, 46–48, 49–51, 54, 57, 69, 71, 78, 82, 121, 142, 143, 150, 151
cognate, 113
cognitive, 3–7, 33, 39, 44, 59, 60, 73, 74, 92, 122, 125, 126, 130, 145–47, 151, 152, 154, 155
comparative reconstruction, 109, 112
complementary, 30, 31–33, 107, 125, 128–30, 143
complementary distribution, 30, 31–33, 107, 128–30
compound, 24, 52
concreteness, 128
conditioned, 5, 107–09, 127, 128
conditioning, 107, 110,
conditioning environment, 107,
consonantal, 51, 60, 61, 64
constraint, 37, 39, 46, 49, 50, 54, 73, 81, 82, 90, 97, 98, 121, 144, 146–52, 155, 156
Constricted Glottis, 67, 142
continuancy, 132
continuant, 62, 140
contoids, 11
contrast, 4, 5, 14, 20, 21, 37, 50, 58, 72, 90, 106, 107, 110, 126–28, 134, 135, 146
Contrastive Analysis, 119, 122
contrasts, 27, 65, 100, 129
coronal, 14, 31, 34, 37, 39, 51, 52, 63, 64, 67, 77–79, 82, 87, 98, 112, 113, 137, 142
counterbleeding, 144, 145
counterfeeding, 138, 139, 145, 146
creaky, 20
cyclic(ally), 133

## D
dactyl, 23, 24, 55
dactylic, 23, 55
deletion, 80, 81, 84, 93, 97, 98, 100, 101, 105, 106, 121, 137–39, 143, 144–46, 148
dental, 14, 16, 34, 37, 39, 62, 63, 67, 104, 120, 152, 153
derivation, 72, 92, 93, 132, 135, 137, 138, 145–47, 151
derivational, 73, 92, 131
Devanagari, 28
devoicing, 83, 88–90, 92, 97, 98, 104, 128, 131, 133, 138, 146, 156
diphthong, 21, 45, 48, 55, 69, 72, 98, 111, 129, 130, 136, 146
diphthongization, 20
dissimilation, 103
dissimilative, 76
distinctive features, 10, 59, 83
divergences, 3, 33, 72
dorsal, 14, 64, 66, 67, 112, 113

## E

ejective, 17, 18, 33, 38, 34, 37, 68
elsewhere, 40, 41, 108, 114, 118, 133, 150
emphatic, 16, 68, 74, 120
English-speaking 9, 34,
epenthesis, 81, 82, 93, 99, 148
epenthetic, 50
epiglottal, 17
ESL, 129
excelsior, 120, 121

## F

faithfulness, 148-152, 154-56
features, 6, 7, 10, 11, 17, 18-20, 22, 27, 33, 59-61, 63-67, 75, 83, 84-86, 113, 121, 125, 126, 131, 132, 139, 140-42, 144, 150, 152
feeding order, 137, 144, 145
final devoicing, 83, 89, 90, 92, 104, 128, 131, 133, 156
flap, 12, 15, 29, 44, 74, 88, 93, 96-98, 127, 128, 137, 144, 145, 155
flapping, 87, 88, 93, 96, 137, 138, 144, 145, 156
foot, 3, 23, 36, 42, 52, 54-58, 70, 71, 112, 137, 144
foot-based, 55
foot-internal, 137
foregrounding, 74
formant, 18, 37, 38, 60
fortition, 75, 76, 86, 113, 120, 145, 152
free variation, 30-32
fricatives, 7, 14, 15-17, 34, 38-40, 48, 60, 61-63, 67, 75, 76, 78, 79, 80, 98, 104, 113, 120, 136, 149, 153

## G

geminate, 53, 80, 121
Generative, 5, 6, 33, 57, 72, 83, 87, 91, 92, 125, 126, 130-32, 136, 137, 139, 143, 144, 147, 148, 151, 152
Generative Phonologists, 72, 87
Generative Phonology, 6, 57, 72, 83, 91, 92, 125, 126, 130-32, 136, 137, 139, 143, 144, 147
glide, 15, 16, 21, 48, 60-62, 76, 79, 85, 98, 105, 108, 128-30
glottis, 67, 142

Great English Vowel, Shift 76
grid, 79
grooved, 14
guttural, 14, 64, 67

## H

harmony, 66, 107, 134, 135
heavy, 7, 12, 45, 69-71, 142
height, 18, 20, 21, 64-66, 134
high, 18-22, 34, 37, 42, 64, 67, 75, 79, 80, 85, 108, 111, 121, 134, 135, 140, 141, 153
hiragana, 43
HNUC, 149, 150
homorganic, 51, 138

## I

iamb, 23, 24, 55
iambic, 23, 54-56
implosive, 18, 37-38, 68, 120
innate, 107, 118, 147
insertion, 55, 56, 81, 82-84, 121
intervocalic, 96, 113, 133, 150
IPA, 13, 14-16, 19, 20, 39, 45, 62, 67, 87, 122, 129

## J

Jakobsonian, 76

## K

katakana, 43
Kindersprache, 117

## L

labiodental, 15, 16, 34, 67
laryngeal, 11, 17, 20, 67
larynx, 17, 18
lax, 20, 34, 57, 58, 65, 66, 74, 76, 84, 111, 122, 129, 136
laxing, 136, 145
laxness, 66
length, 6, 20, 22-24, 37, 55, 66, 68, 69, 71, 90, 110, 130, 132, 134, 135, 155
lengthening, 142, 143
lenition, 74, 75, 77, 86, 113, 120, 121, 145, 152
London school, 5

## M

mark, 9, 23, 24, 35, 81, 146
marked, 24, 35, 45, 64, 69, 75, 108, 149, 153
markedness, 35, 59, 131, 132, 148, 149, 151, 152
Maximal Onset Principle, 53, 54

merger, 79, 104, 107, 108, 110, 111, 115
metaphor, 33, 60, 72, 74, 90, 132, 144, 151
metonymy, 9, 10,151
metrical, 6
minimal, 20, 30, 31, 86, 88, 90, 96, 104, 106, 126, 129
monophthongization, 146
mora, 71, 72
moraic, 55
morpheme, 6, 52, 87, 127, 128, 132, 156
morphology, 44, 74, 109, 128, 152
morphophonemic, 74, 80, 87, 88-90, 93, 108, 118, 127, 131, 132, 136, 146, 156
motivated, 7, 34, 35, 72-74, 87, 109, 131, 132, 138, 145, 148, 150, 151, 156
motivation, 50, 154, 155

## N

nasal assimilation, 77, 78, 89, 105, 141, 142
nasalization, 78, 79, 105, 120, 121, 138, 139, 144
Natural Phonology, 72, 118, 122, 145, 156
neutralization, 88, 125, 126-28, 136
neutralized, 126, 128
node, 52, 142
nucleus, 12, 45, 46, 48, 69, 111, 129, 143, 149, 150

## O

obstruents, 17, 47, 52, 56, 60, 61, 78, 79, 88, 89, 110, 123, 127, 155
onset, 15, 17, 36, 44, 45-49, 51, 52-54, 71, 81, 98, 129, 131, 143, 1, 147, 149, 50, 151, 153
opacity, 10, 109, 138
opaque, 10, 138, 139
opposition, 5, 65, 126
optimality, 73, 92, 130, 138, 139, 144, 146, 154
ordered, 99, 133, 136, 137, 143, 144, 146
ordering, 90, 92, 93, 109, 127, 133, 135, 137, 138, 144, 145-47, 149
orthography, 26, 53, 89, 95, 104, 106, 122

## P

paleophonetic, 72
parentheses, 83, 89
penultimate, 57, 69–71
peripheral, 20, 65
periphery, 75
perseveratory, 77
pharynx, 17
phoneme, 3, 4–6, 10, 16, 22, 27, 28–34, 38, 39–41, 49, 50, 58, 60, 85–89, 93, 104, 105–07, 119, 122, 126, 127–131, 133, 136, 145, 152, 153, 156
phonetics, 1, 2, 7, 11, 17, 18, 21, 22, 25, 28, 59, 62, 65, 68, 142
phonological change, 104, 107, 112
phonological rules, 6, 33, 59, 132, 148
phonological theory, 2, 4–6, 92, 109, 110, 119, 125, 139, 140, 146
phonologization, 103, 104–06
physiophonetic, 72
pitch, 22, 23, 25, 68
Prague School, 4–6, 33, 35, 59, 125, 126–28
process, 9, 27, 51, 72, 73–83, 86–90, 92, 93, 96–100, 103–05, 107, 108, 111, 118, 120, 121, 131–33, 137–39, 141, 142, 144, 145–47, 154
processing, 5, 7, 74, 92, 153, 154
process-oriented, 72, 144
progressive, 77
pronounceable, 21, 40, 118
proprioceptive, 18
prototype, 8, 10, 40, 151
prototypicality, 7, 35, 39, 75, 76, 152

## Q

quantitative, 71
quantity sensitivity, 71

## R

radial prototype, 8
ranking, 48, 147, 148–50, 152, 156
reassociation, 140
reattaching, 141
reconstructing, 109, 113
reconstruction, 109, 112, 136
reduction, 97–101, 105
reductions, 74, 95–97, 99, 100
regressive, 77, 78, 107
repair, 50, 51
rhotics, 15, 60, 61
rhyme, 6, 25, 29, 44–46, 59, 71, 143
rhythm, 22–24, 36
robin, 8
rounded, 19, 20, 34, 35, 37, 63, 65, 75, 80, 101, 107–09, 134
rule ordering, 90, 92, 93, 109, 127, 133, 137, 138, 145, 146, 149

## S

schema, 73, 151
schemas, 33, 153
serial derivationalism, 92
shortening, 74, 134, 135
sonorant, 60, 61, 76, 83, 97, 98, 138, 146, 150, 151
sonority, 43, 47–49, 51, 75, 98, 149–51
sonorous, 21, 149, 150
spectrogram, 11, 18, 19, 44
spelling, 25, 44, 81, 88, 89, 95, 103, 105, 109, 127, 136
spirant, 12
spirantizing, 133
spondees, 55

Spoonerism, 28
Structuralism, 4, 125, 127, 128, 131
structuralist, 4, 5, 10, 27, 44, 72, 88, 119, 125, 127–29, 131, 137,
syllabary, 79
syllabic, 45, 55, 74, 99, 100, 149
syllabicity, 149
syllabification, 53, 54, 151
syllabified, 46, 53
symmetry, 34
syncope, 80

## T

taps, 12, 15
subphonemic, 28
tautosyllabic, 74, 138, 147, 152
tense, 20, 46, 52, 65, 66, 76, 78, 81, 93, 128, 129, 136
tone, 22, 28, 42, 139–41
tonic, 25, 70
Trager-Smith, 128, 129
transformational, 130
trills, 12, 15
trisyllabic laxing, 136
trochaic, 23, 55, 56, 58
trochee, 23, 55
trochees, 24, 55, 70, 71

## U

ultima, 69
umlaut, 108, 109
unary, 63, 150
underived, 132
underspecification, 33
universals, 117, 151
unmarked, 35
unmotivated, 109
unnatural, 44

## V

vocoids, 11
voice onset time, 17
vowel harmony, 66, 107, 134, 135